D1046313

Love Never Fails

My Tale of Cancer, Loss, and Life –
And The Tail Who Wagged Me Through It

Liane N. Rowe

May these words bless your heart –
Love,
Liane

© Copyright 2014 by Liane N. Rowe

Love Never Fails
Published by Yawn's Publishing
198 North Street
Canton, GA 30114
www.yawnsbooks.com

All rights reserved. No part of this book may be reproduced or transmitted in any form, electronic or mechanical, including photocopying, recording, or data storage systems without the express written permission of the publisher, except for brief quotations in reviews and articles.

The information in this book has been taken from various sources, and is presented with no guarantee of its accuracy. All photographs used were submitted for this publication. We assume no liability for the accuracy of the information presented or any photos used without permission.

Library of Congress Control Number: 2014955754

ISBN13:978-1-940395-53-1   paperback
        978-1-940395-54-8   eBook

Printed in the United States

To Jesus and Ginger.
The Dynamic Duo who saved me from myself.

Love is patient and kind;
love is not jealous or boastful;
it is not arrogant or rude.
Love does not insist on its own way;
it is not irritable or resentful;
it does not rejoice at wrong,
but rejoices in the right.
Love bears all things,
believes all things,
hopes all things,
endures all things.
Love never fails.

1 Corinthians 13:4-8

CONTENTS

CHAPTER 1

LOVE IS KIND

And [God] said to me, "Write, for these words are true and faithful."
- Revelation 21:5 -

Most folks spell love as a four-letter word. I add two more letters, factor in four fur-covered paws and call her Ginger. This beloved dog, with the same name as a delicious apple pie spice, spent fourteen years trying to teach me the finer points of love and life, claiming success despite the hefty handicap of my human flaws. Our unbreakable bond outlasted the life of most cars, small appliances, and sadly, an alarming number of today's marriages. We spent more time together than I've ever managed to accomplish with any human being. Call me crazy; I preferred it that way.

Fourteen years is a long time to share with anyone, especially when those years comprise moment-to-moment memories on a daily basis. Let's face it; even the period of time a baby spends bonding with its mother from birth until learning how to turn over and crawl is a blink of an eye in the scheme of things. A spouse might work half the day or more for two-thirds of each week while children spend eight-hour days five days a week in the company of other children and a handful of substitute caregivers. Ginger and I breathed the same air from the same space in all of our days, but for a handful, when I dared venture out alone to forage for grocery store food or one-week vacations.

I've always thought that leaving a legacy is one of the most rewarding gifts a person can give another. The legacy Ginger

1

left me is rich with wisdom and brimming with whispers of worthy notation. Time and experience suggest that some tales are better left untold, but amidst the pages of her well-worn life there thankfully emerges a story that meanders through several chapters of my own and leaves me breathless with adoring admiration for her attention to detail…and me.

What we play is life.
- Louis Armstrong -

Long before the day on which I connected with this paragon of virtue, I roamed the boundaries of my childhood in a parkland half the size of our tiny town that one of America's industrial giants of the 1800's had seen fit to leave his fellow citizens. Harvey S. Firestone (of automobile tire fame) was born and raised in our humble burg and apparently held enough fond memories of his own childhood to remember us long after acquiring fame and fortune. Together with friends Henry Ford and Thomas Edison, they worked and played themselves into "The Millionaires Club" and managed to revolutionize the world.

Hailing from a small town, his big ideas never forgot where he came from, and Harvey S. Firestone Recreational Park still stands in the middle of Columbiana, Ohio to this day. I'm one of many who had the privilege of growing up within walking distance of childhood heaven. Sixty-eight acres of green space loaded with now-towering trees overlook the grounds that my grandfather actually surveyed and helped to create. More legacy – awesome, I know. It was incredible having a state-of-the-art swimming pool, football stadium, track and field, tennis courts, baseball fields, ice-skating pond, and old stone picnic pavilions with swings and seesaws right in our own backyards. And to think that all of this was ours to enjoy free of charge in a town with no fast food, one bank, and two gas stations with as many police.

I never had a dog of my own before Ginger, and with a playground the size of the one I grew up in, I've thought a lot about why. My limited experience with animals included a family cat who only came when my brother whistled a halting version of "Bridge over The River Kwai," his pet chameleon who changed colors daily in a worn out aquarium on the porch, a few goldfish, and a playmate's crazy Dalmatian. Aside from occasionally feeding the fish or running the electric can opener to get the cat's attention, I was clueless in the ways of complicated animal husbandry until many years later when I acquired sole ownership of a cat in lieu of a boyfriend. Unfortunately, this experience didn't shed anything more than hairballs onto my quest for knowledge, and I found myself accepting defeat in even that brief encounter with pet ownership, eventually surrendering her to an overwhelming preference for Grandma's lap.

Friends are God's way of taking care of us.
- Anonymous -

Perhaps my lack of skill in the pet department was just as well. It gave me more time to focus on the finer points of kindergarten, allowing me to meet my first best friend with whom I shared everything. At the age of five, "everything," unfortunately, included bites of peanut butter and jelly sandwiches and a piece of infamous half-chewed gum – just days before my new best bud contracted a prolific case of chicken pox. We roamed the woods that day, selecting a huge rock on which to devour our picnic. I recall with tender mirth when my friend decided to launch into a boisterous solo of "Shenandoah," reluctantly relinquishing her gooey glob for my enjoyment – accompanied by a fervent wish not to choke on her refrain.

The memory of what might've been still sends shivers down my mother's back, but the unlikely blessing of already having been exposed to the dreaded disease as a baby saved us both from weeks of sleepless nights. Unfortunately, my fearless friend and I would cause much more stress than that on future pranks and reckless abandon, but we somehow grew and matured through pimples, boyfriends, and break-ups without killing each other or turning Mom's hair completely gray.

As my friend blossomed into a blonde, beautiful, and buxom social creature with a smile that melted many a man's heart, I waited in the wings with my flat chest and corkscrew hair, passing notes and setting up dates for her would-be suitors in a good-natured attempt at retrieving her cast-offs. We couldn't have been more different in our appearance and approach, but opposites attract, and our unlikely friendship formed a bond that I thought would last forever.

Unfortunately, forever doesn't recognize unemployment realities, and necessities require more monetary compensation than barter and trade. My Dad had poured a lifetime into the business of building bridges with his father and the other two brothers who made up "and sons," but the dwindling demand for engineering marvels made from concrete and steel no longer supported a dynasty with four families' mouths to feed.

Mom and Dad would leave the only house they'd lived in for a total of their 22 years together, and my brothers in college would always feel like gypsies on spring break. The rest of my extended family didn't fare any better, but I was tempted as a teenager with one year of high school and social drama under my belt to think that my world was the only one in ruins. After years of playing the game of who's who, I finally scored a place on the JV cheering squad with an order in the mail for that coveted letter sweater and matching pleated skirt. I already knew the lay of the lockers and who and what hallways to avoid… all simple, albeit painful pleasures in the rite of high school passage.

Ready or not, dubiously willing and able, I found myself moved across the state and into a foreign world of flat farmland and unfamiliar traditions that took me out of anything resembling my comfort zone. Faithful friendship was no longer a quick walk next door, and I floundered in my feeble attempts to make new ones. It just wasn't the same. Instead of embracing a new collection of confidants, I chose instead to plant myself firmly in the role of loner, hoping to erect a shield powerful enough to ward off the possibility of letting anyone enter my heart who could ever break it again.

Believing I in any way would have a shield of steel that rivaled the one on Superman's chest was perhaps extremely unwise, but that, and the fact I had no history from which to pull that would endear me to the joy of dogs (or any pet that required daily maintenance) merely amplifies the significance of my beloved Ginger. Her ability to pierce my rigid defenses and silently herd me through the crazy maze of my chaotic life had her worming her way into my heart without even trying. How very like me not to notice God's will until long after stumbling through my own devices and ending up with the blessing in spite of myself. One of my favorite song lyrics proclaims that, "If I'd never met you, think of all the things I'd missed." Ginger was my warm-up to understanding Jesus. I wonder if she knew how precious she really was…probably so.

5

**In every walk with nature
one receives far more than he seeks.
- John Muir -**

A wonderful surprise lies right in the middle of The Great Smoky Mountains known as Cade's Cove. A trip along the steep winding roads of this peaceful forest suddenly gives way to gently rolling pastures, drenching the fertile ground with all the bright sunshine that barely manages to filter through the dense foliage from which you've just emerged. When I first saw this little piece of heaven on earth years ago, the acreage of carefully farmed soil was still passing from father to son through generations of hearty settlers determined to succeed in the middle of nowhere. It was a working farm with grazing cattle, endless rows of corn, and wild turkeys that crossed the roads on a whim whether gawking tourists were driving by or not.

Amidst the awe of discovering the simple life just miles from hotel row and Dollywood, I suddenly found myself within the path of nature's fury as the baby blue sky turned deep navy and filled with the most beautiful angry clouds I've ever seen. The storm spent itself as quickly as it had come, leaving the fields drenched with stalks of corn bowing to the ground under the weight of their watered burden as if bestowing honor and glory to God's magnificent visit.

Unfortunately running out of daylight and feeling the pangs of hunger in a land devoid of creature comforts, I reluctantly turned the car toward what we like to think is civilization and left idyllic paradise to visit another day. I also left my desirous yearning for peace and quiet on the last post of fence bordering the crooked lane and took an odd mixture of humble pie and expectation with me. The sheets of rain had washed me as clean as it had the sky, turning my outlook on life as colorful as the purple twilight twinkling overhead.

I can't help to compare the rush of that storm with the arrival of Ginger into my life. Storms are disruptive and unpredictable at best, never leaving the scene the same way they found it. Ginger was no less likely to change – well...everything.

When what you want is a relationship, and not a person, get a dog.
- Deb Caletti -

Ginger came into our lives as a puppy rescued from the local shelter after considerable misgivings on my part. I admit it; I was desperate. Our oldest son had been out of school for months with a mysterious fever and pain that no amount of medication or testing could solve. The doctor was tired of hearing my diagnosis of "his eyes look funny" – which, by the way, was 100% effective in spotting ear infections, so we bought into the possibility of traditional medicine's theory that it was all in his head and decided to try the companionship of a pet.

A dog had been on his wish list for years, but the saner part of my brain suspected that an ailing ten-year-old lying on the couch with imploring eyes was *not* going to be able to follow through with his promises to care for this new bundle of joy. My disjointed and sadly lacking skills in the animal department kept echoing a refrain of "no, no, no." I already had four mouths to feed (not counting my own), and I was justifiably skeptical that a dog was going to get its own meals or take a turn at emptying the dishwasher. After fourteen years, I've finally conceded that sanity was right and that I would've been able to save myself countless hours of contradiction if I'd just admitted from the start that Ginger was *my* dog.

We arrived at the shelter on a dreary Saturday morning with

all three kids in tow. A reconnaissance mission was probably a more prudent plan, but we were already out of the car and bunching up at the front door. The smell of diluted urine and an overabundance of disinfectant had already smacked us in the face, and so far no one had sounded retreat.

Our first stop brought us to the older dogs. I began to sweat and hyperventilate when a huge attack dog jumped at the wire kennel with his overly enthusiastic marketing strategy, causing me to make a quick exit and ask to see the restroom. They gave directions to the puppy room instead where I was able to catch the breath I'd been holding and soon begin to enjoy the sight of little balls of fur in a wide variety of makes and models. They corralled the most obvious candidates into a makeshift playpen of chicken wire, but my curiosity was piqued when I spied a wee ball of fluff huddled outside the fence in the back corner of the room.

Perhaps she touched the kindred spirit within me in her desire to be apart from the popular crowd. Her independence and vulnerability were irresistible as I walked my way over. She took that as a sign to flee even further away, and with the assistance of two helpers and all three kids, she was finally extracted from behind a stash of file boxes. We had more in common than I thought. I also spent an excessive amount of time huddled in the corner instead of opening up to what might be waiting on the other side of the room.

My son was the one who'd plucked her from hiding and instinctively gotten down on her level to provide a warm cocoon with his crossed legs and arms. She nestled into his lap and nearly fell asleep with his gentle touch. I would've thought that all those years of begging and countless dog training manuals procured from the library would've prepared me for the look of pleading and desire in his eyes. I finally understood his request for having a pet was more than just adding an inconvenience to our lives.

This animal was more than a page in a book. She was alive…and adorable. Her fur was silky-soft, and there was just something about the effect her little bark, gigantic ears, and trembling body had on my nervous system. The warning of mothering instincts aside, I couldn't imagine leaving without her. Fate sealed me as an official owned-by-my-dog kind of person, which was virgin territory for this former cat woman. I shook my head at the irony and fell into step behind the caravan to the car.

To be fair, my son bought the crate, leash, bowls, and *first* bag of dog food, as well as paying the requisite fee and signing on the dotted line to eventually have her spayed. He also spent the first night of Ginger's homecoming in *his* bedroom listening to her pathetic barking from inside her crate – which no doubt she began even then to think of as "the cage." I always thought it suspicious when things got quiet in the middle of the night, but we were all so grateful for the silence that any doggie hair I might've found on the bed covers the next morning were quickly disposed of (and never mentioned again).

She was supposed to be his responsibility – and was, for about a week. Then reality settled in as it occurred to me how easily I'd been delegated to the one making all the predawn and midnight potty runs, the unanimously designated clean-up crew of one, and the crazy fool who'd lost her heart to a licking, quivering canine being small enough to fit in the palm of my hand. I could now relate to the humorous kick God must get out of dealing with me.

Brothers and Sisters are as close as hands and feet.
- Vietnamese Proverb -

When each of my children was born, the pain of their natural births was never as hard to endure as getting through the process of deciding on their names. Their father always had firm ideas in mind, and even though he always listened politely to my own list of favorites, it came as no surprise that birth certificates were destined to reveal his original choices.

God's sense of humor and balance blessed us with a lovely little girl the first time around, who unfortunately came into the world with only a name suited for a boy. I had suggested the possibility of this outcome several times, but naming our firstborn for his own sire took for granted the impossibility of my prediction. It wasn't surprising to learn that her name was already picked out and in place by the time we signed her birth certificate, nixing any of *my* ideas for even her middle name.

Our second child was a 9 pound 10 ounce full-grown baby boy, arriving three years and several attempts at achieving my middle name ideas later. I thought naming him for both fathers was a grand idea but eventually settled for ousting the improper use of "junior." We deemed him a royal-sounding "II" as proud mama claimed small victory number one.

Rounding out our family trio was another nine pounder-plus, with a full head of fair hair that spiked in downy peaks until he began to toddle. Again, my husband declared the intention to choose a girl's name only, and if not for several nights of fierce persuasion, our son would reap the improbable benefits of a stubborn papa to this day.

With a history like this, deciding on a name for our new little puppy wasn't a task we chose lightly – especially with the acute sensitivity I have concerning my own. I enjoy the dubious distinction (to me) of sharing the name of a Russian ballerina on tour in the States during my mother's pregnancy, unusual spelling and all. I've endured years of having correspondence returned with "corrected" interpretations as well as countless encounters where people finally gave up and walked away instead of taking a stab at its pronunciation. With the advent of computers, I was also user-*un*friendly and created many an error report with the absence of a middle name. Hence, the unusual sensitivity to something most people take for granted. I'm unique, to say the least, and even though I wanted our dog to shine with individuality, I sure didn't want her to experience unnecessary teasing from any of the other neighborhood dogs.

Several names took a trial run before we made a final call. Sophie was a close runner-up, but she never did answer to that, and I thought we stood a better chance of positive reinforcement if she'd at least respond occasionally to her name and basic commands like "no." That strategy had worked with my kids, so I figured it was worth trying. Therefore, Ginger it was.

As a puppy, Ginger's coat was as brown as the spice, with splashes of black and a little white here and there. It's no exaggeration to say that her ears seemed to take up nearly half her body at that point, and thankfully she'd later grow into her beauty. Perhaps we had more in common than I thought. She always did have better-looking hair, but at least my tongue was short enough to keep inside my mouth…and I only drool at night.

"Australian Shepherd mix" was the breed listed on her veterinarian's records. Ginger lived up to her heritage with herding instincts and speed to rival the purest of pedigrees. Her poor little tail was bobbed by the time we found her, which turned her distinctive wag into a whole body experience guaranteed to produce a smile. The entire back half moved in much the same way as a hummingbird suspends itself in one place while flying near its food source, with Ginger moving just as quickly whenever her own stomach was on the prowl. No wonder I was always getting into trouble with the vet for her weight gain – it was impossible for me to refuse edible rewards for her obvious delight in interpretive dance.

I find it shelter to speak to you.
- Emily Dickinson -

In the beginning, she herded the entire family with nudges and barks until we'd all get the hint and finally settle down in the same room. Unfortunately for her, as the novelty of a new pet began to wear off, she soon learned to conserve energy, ceased trying to rouse the kids from behind closed bedroom doors, and concentrated on me instead. Once she had me located and surrounded, it seemed to be her sole mission in life to keep me within reach at all times. With a nose on my knee or head on my foot, she could predict and detect my movements split seconds before *I* even knew I was moving. She became the shadow of my steps and the protector of my heart.

We communicated in a comfortable blend of talk and listen. Surely, every good relationship requires two to tango, and Ginger listened with undivided attention and silent devotion every time my mouth was open. It wasn't hard to accomplish; we were joined at the hip anyway. The kids began to voice their concerns that I might love her more than them, but the truth was she was just *easier* to love.

As a stay-at-home mom with a husband who worked from home his entire career, my life consisted of requests, suggestions, and chaos. Is it any wonder that I would find solace in the unconditional demands of my new best friend? She became the girlfriend I didn't have, the silent observer, the constant and faithful companion who always met me at the door just because she was ecstatic to see me safely returned. She slept by my side, guarded the bathroom door – from the inside, and made sure that I received the daily-recommended dose of sunshine and exercise. We fell into a pattern of trust that would carry a lifetime of whispered confidences with her to the grave.

When you reach the end of your rope,
Tie a knot and hold on.
- Franklin D. Roosevelt -

It didn't take long to realize that roller coasters and Ginger have a few things in common. They're both full of excitement, careen down steep drop-offs, sail around unexpected corners at speeds that scare, surprise, and delight all at the same time…the perfect description of my childhood fantasy vacation. A week of rides and cotton candy was a notion that hovered somewhere between last and nonexistent on the list of ideas for our usual annual one week family holiday. Dad worked hard and steady the other 51 weeks out of the year, so if anyone else's suggestion didn't include fishing rods, bait, and campfire food, they hit disqualification immediately.

I grew up thinking that every family's vacation consisted of a 12-hour drive (in one day) to remote Canadian waters in a vehicle jammed with four adults, three children, and enough food to feed an army. In the days before seat belts, GPS, and in-flight movies, I, being the youngest, always rated the position of lying across the women in the backseat. Perhaps this explained why bumpy rides and butterflies in my stomach were associated with fun.

The best part about being the baby of the family was reaping the benefit of my Grandma's undivided attention as she lightly stroked my face with her calloused hands in a futile attempt to silence my boredom's whimpers and lull me to sleep. I suppose it must've worked at least part of the time, or she wouldn't have kept doing it. My memory recalls a twinkle in both our eyes as I'd always whisper for more.

As the number of fish to catch began to dwindle and my brothers and I grew older, the idea of a day at the amusement park finally became a reality, and I fell in love with the Jack Rabbit. It was an ancient rollercoaster – even in *my* childhood, built of wood and steel tracks that click-clacked all the way to the top of the first hill. Consisting of only half a dozen two-seater cars, it was intimate enough to hear each person's gulp of fear and subsequent scream as we careened down the Rabbit's running start through a course of jerks and terror. I don't recall safety bars or words of warning to keep all hands inside the car, but I'm here to tell about it fondly just the same.

> **Nothing makes a woman more beautiful**
> **than the belief that she is beautiful.**
> **- Sophia Loren –**

My life is a lot like that memorable ride, and I thank God for sending me four therapists along the way to apply pressure when needed with more than a few Band-Aids in the process. Two of them were trained psychologists; one was my hair stylist; and then there was Ginger.

Dr. Neiner pulled me from the brink of depression at a time when I felt as though the world had moved on without me, leaving me to bear it alone. She convinced me that I wasn't running solo and laughingly proposed one day that each of us design quilt squares of our most embarrassing, frustrating, and harrowing moments. We could then stitch them all together, proving once and for all that every person on earth has enough drama to cover a king size bed. She also suggested that I create a summary of my accomplishments, which got me to wondering "why not" instead of "why bother." It's reassuring to note that I was able to think of enough distinguished merits to fill more than one page.

Ten years later, suffocating from the weight of that king size quilt, I discovered Dr. Pike. She introduced me to the concept of shifting and the profound statement that even though Jesus was a man who was maligned, mistrusted and murdered, the opinions of those who did that to Him do not shape *my* opinion of who He was. Likewise, I'm not the person who others say or think I am. I'm the daughter of the King and am redeemed by the blood of the Lamb. What a powerful statement.

Sukey is my hug of the month. Every thirty days or so over the last twenty years she's been my hair stylist in charge of taming my unruly locks, as well as providing a steady stream of honest advice and unwavering support that is lovingly included with each cut and dry. As time has taken its toll, she now includes several shades of red dye and a standing date with the queen of wax and tweeze. She's a bona fide genius in affairs of the heart as well as hair. One day she offered the insightful notion that the reason for having a good haircut is due to the overwhelming percentage of time people look at the back of my head and not the flawed face that *I* see in the mirror each morning. That comment definitely took the pressure off self-importance. It also highlights the usefulness of wrap-around mirrors.

Then there's Ginger. I've read experts who don't think their research reveals that dogs see color, understand human language, or hold grudges. They've obviously never met Ginger. She certainly wasn't perfect, but she was perfect for me - kind, affectionate, loving, and gentle. Sometimes I think about her loving nature, and the lines between describing the benevolence of Ginger or Jesus begin to blur. I believe He sent her to teach me how to be more like Him.

Imagine, *me* - walking and talking with a handpicked gift from God. She spent every day of her life serving, teaching, caring, protecting, and loving...me. For all those days when I may have doubted my significance, I need look no further than memories of Ginger and the promises of God. Angels are all around me giving good advice and offering bits of wisdom that dangle like carrots just waiting for me to snatch up and tuck away for future use. All I have to do is be willing to look, and then reach out and grab them.

CHAPTER 2

LOVE IS NOT ARROGANT OR RUDE

**Enjoy the little things,
for one day you may look back
and realize they were the big things.**
- Robert Brault -

In this day of instant everything, it's hard to believe that I grew up in a time when manners were actually important enough to be included in my third grade public education. They made their way alongside our daily dose of reading, math, and the art of cursive writing. Each week between Labor and Memorial Day began with the Lord's Prayer, Pledge of Allegiance, and Miss Bycroft. She was a lovely young woman with a brunette beehive hairdo and the kind of lilting voice that put a person to sleep while reading from the latest *Weekly Reader* or next week's lunch menu. In my vast experience of eight-year-old wisdom, I thought she was the most intelligent and glamorous person to ever grace the halls of my elementary school. She was exactly who I wanted to become.

Miss Bycroft taught me the value of a firm handshake and a memorable first impression with regular role model classes with my peers long before self-help seminars thought they invented the concept. We were used to the idea of having thirty to forty students in one room under the supervision of one teacher. It amazes me how the liberal use of discipline and respect for authority enabled one woman to keep so many rambunctious youths in line with nothing more than the raise of her eyebrow.

17

Paired off into girl and boy couplets, we took turns practicing the fine art of introduction with minor glitches encountered during an occasional muddy handshake or bruised forehead from an ill-timed bow and curtsy. Thanks to Miss Bycroft, I graduated the third grade with teaching aspirations, straight A's on my report card, and a well-rounded vocabulary including "please, thank you, and how do you do."

Perhaps this explains the persistent voice in my head that kept whispering to me that something was amiss in our newly acquired dog's manners. In the beginning, she would've tried even the patience of Miss Bycroft with her inability to play well with others. Ginger was a barking jumper with a stubborn streak and a love of leather, curiosity with trash, and an uncontrollable urge to dismantle my son's stuffed animals. Every lion, tiger, and bear had seen needle and thread by the end of her first month's stay, as each one passed through a makeshift hospital for the wounded in action. Apparently, Ginger thought the fake fur menagerie on the bed posed some sort of threat, as she set out to destroy anything with button eyes and a tail.

Ginger's love for leather led her to items in the house that need only smell remotely of cowhide and tanning oil to attract her attention. She left a wake of chaos throughout her domain (including my favorite pair of heels) inevitably bringing what little was left of her treasures to my closet for final destruction. Temporarily hypnotized by her ability to distract me with soft fur and melting eyes, I put aside my desire for her social graces…until she messed with the leather cover of the wrong book. The curiosity that endeared her to my soul was also to be what ended her unbridled lifestyle and would soon prompt massive life changes for all.

The book in question was a pocket-sized Bible that my

18

Father-in-Law protectively carried throughout his four-year Army service in Europe during World War II. It survived three parachute evacuations from his crashing B-17 bombers, a harrowing escape from behind enemy lines through the French Underground, and more missions in his post at the machine gun turret than he cared to discuss. In addition to being the final word on eternal life, this Bible represented the celebration of his opportunity to live longer in *this* life.

Having a dog...*my* dog...rip the corner off the cover of its holy pages seemed almost criminal. No amount of duct tape or glue was going to mend the damage, as all frantic attempts to reposition the shredded bits of leather back into place were futile. My heart sank as I realized what had been lost, and a certain amount of fear seeped into my consciousness when it occurred to me that Ginger's fate was about to be decided by the son of our war hero – my furious husband.

As I placed myself between Ginger and her firing squad, I reminded anyone who would listen that everyone deserves a second chance. All of us have better than we deserve and grace is a gift that we accept and pass on. Ginger was one of *us* now, despite the fact that she was just a dog. I ceased thinking of her as "just a dog" weeks ago, and I was prepared to defend her despite her obvious flaws. I pointed out that she was already on her back in subservience and remorse (or maybe just waiting for another belly rub) and bargained for leniency. In the end, Ginger would remain in our home and soon begin a six-week puppy obedience class at the local pet store in lieu of deportation.

At the time, we were living in a lovely community connected by miles and miles of paved pathways on which to enjoy walking, biking, and golf carting for pleasure. Most folks used their carts as a second car, with many sporting customized paint jobs and a private garage. Through the generosity of a well-deserved bonus from my husband's company, we acted on impulse and for once traded the urge to sock it away in savings for the luxury of our very own cart. It was a four-seated beauty equipped with lights, turn signals, and even a zippered rain cover for twelve months of pleasure. That particular upgrade qualifies only if you happen to enjoy riding outdoors in below freezing temperatures without the benefit of heat – which Ginger did. Who wouldn't, with a fur coat like hers? She never missed an opportunity to ride with the wind in her hair and paw on my steering arm. I guess she thought she was in control, which was probably closer to the truth than I care to admit. Most dogs like to ride in a car with the window rolled halfway down, eyes plastered shut by the wind, and as much of their head sticking out into traffic as possible. Ginger much preferred the freedom and quiet of the electric cart, with its open-air policy and windshield option that allowed for keeping her eyes wide open.

We all adjusted to this luxurious recreation with surprising (and somewhat embarrassing) ease. The whole family enjoyed life on the town while carting the paths to picnics at the lake, grocery shopping, school activities, and countless practices and games. We began to take for granted that life was relatively calm, and that notion alone should have put me on alert to lurking danger. I've learned the hard way that Satan likes to hit me from behind and should know by now the importance of watching my back. Just about the time I was busy calculating how to squeeze Ginger's first obedience lesson into our schedule between three basketball games and a chorus concert, the devil got into my details and turned my "calm" upside down.

What is a home without children? Quiet.

– Henny Youngman –

I've heard it said that most accidents happen within five miles of your home. We didn't even get out of the driveway to test that theory. The kids (and Ginger, of course) were practicing their skills with cart safety in a harmless repetition of driving up and down our suburban stretch of concrete, when Ginger randomly decided to eject on a whim and suddenly found herself beneath the tire of the cart's screeching halt.

Never one to do things in a small way, I guess she wanted to test my theory of life being one breath away from change. The kids began screaming in unison as I heard the beginnings of the keening wail emanating from our little injured puppy. The heart-wrenching sound chilled my soul as I pulled her from the pavement and wrapped her gingerly (no pun intended) in a towel retrieved soft and warm from the dryer.

In between checking on kids in shock and frantically searching the yellow pages for the nearest pet emergency clinic, I made a quick inventory of her wounds. Her left hind leg was bleeding profusely, but it didn't look broken. Her wailing turned into a constant high-pitched whimper, and I thought I even saw tears in her eyes until I realized that my own were splashing onto the phone book instead.

Somehow, I managed to get the kids buckled into the van and Ginger held tightly in her blood-soaked towel as we began an emotional hour's journey to the emergency room. Rush hour was atrocious as we tried to hurry through traffic, but we made it there in one piece and dashed inside…only to meet another mass of congestion as we maneuvered into position with all the other casualties in the waiting room. Several nail-biting hours later, we were finally ushered into their version of pet post-op

21

and had the shocking reality of Ginger's injuries revealed. Extensive surgery had left her unconscious and limp, but she was still breathing and given permission to return home.

I came through the experience with a newfound appreciation for fathers who patiently wait through the labor of their children. In my multiple experiences with natural childbirth, I always believed that *I* was the one who should be comforted since *I* was the one going through the pain. Now that I have the added perspective of being the caregiver who is helpless to act throughout the waiting process, I no longer believe one role is worse than another. Pain has many faces, and none of them resembles a smile.

Ginger left the clinic with stitches too numerous to count, a bottle of antibiotics, and the instructions to keep all shaved areas clean and dry for the next several weeks. These "areas" included the back half of her anatomy where all necessary body functions exit the building, so to speak. All pet owners must surely agree that keeping an animal from checking out that area dozens of times within the span of a day is virtually impossible. With no barrier between Ginger and her stitches, we were in for a long night.

Mother Nature has given animals the instinct to care for their own without the benefit of registered nurses or pharmacies on every corner. In Ginger's case, her self-medication quickly revealed she must truly believe that cleanliness is next to Godliness and seemed to strive that night for a personal interview in heaven at record-breaking speed. Her stitches were like magnets to her tongue, and no amount of that horrid no-lick spray repellent could keep her from washing them clean. We were doomed to a night of frustration in a battle for supremacy. Either we would succeed in keeping the area "clean and dry," or

Ginger would lick until she finally collapsed from exhaustion. She won.

Make your own recovery the first priority in your life.
- Robin Norwood -

Barely lucid after minimal sleep, I was on the phone at daybreak begging the vet's receptionist for the doctor's first opening. Ginger seemed confused from her own lack of sleep, but still filled with enough adrenaline to continue her whining and hygienic marathon, as I saw hundreds of dollars swirling down the drain with every swipe of her tongue. I was frantic with worry…surely Ginger would never walk again if she didn't cease her post-operative care, or more to the point, my husband would return from his latest business trip any moment and discover that her obscenely expensive operation was now added to her rap sheet with no time served.

She and I were still in the doghouse for the mutilation of Grandpa's Bible, so time was of the essence. We were triple-booked for the next available appointment, but it was one step closer to help and bought me some time to plan my next move (which I hoped wasn't out of the house for us both).

We must've looked as pitiful as we felt since the waiting room occupants cleared a path into the examination room the minute I entered with Ginger's battered body. We even skipped the usual niceties and chart updates as the doctor instantly appeared and took over with words of wisdom and the pronouncement that the ER must've been crazy to send Ginger home with exposed sutures. She whipped out a brochure with an astounding array of fiberglass cast colors, and I immediately chose the hot pink. I thought it would bring out the sparkle in Ginger's brown eyes – just as soon as she was able to keep them open.

We exited an hour later with a new list for home care and a cast that completely enclosed her paw from hip to nails. She looked ridiculous but easily turned her new pink accessory into another of her well-honed feminine canine charms. I found myself chuckling upon review of the list, as they felt it prudent to let her get plenty of rest (as if *that* would be a problem) and give heavy doses of attention and love. That seemed easy enough…but wait – there was more.

Hidden in the fine print was another disclaimer issuing the warning to keep all affected areas (including this new hot pink cast) *clean and dry*? The cured fiberglass promised to hold up under her weight while walking, but it obviously didn't meet design specs for marathons or damp grass. The first and only time she tried to race through the doggie door, we found her suspended halfway between with head on one side and the cute little cast on the other.

I headed to the car for a trip to the store…hanging my head in defeat and wondering how many plastic bags and rubber bands I was going to need in the upcoming weeks to keep all affected areas clean and dry. Turning on the radio, I sighed as the weatherman was forecasting a very wet spring.

What lies behind us and what lies before us are tiny matters,
compared to what lies within us.
- Ralph Waldo Emerson -

Over the years, I've participated in many opportunities to discover my spiritual gifts and talents. I keep repeating the process in the hopes that compassion and hospitality will miraculously appear in each new result, but the verdict is very clear: I am *not* a nurse. The spring season of recovery in our home was proof yet again that God has a sense of humor and an ongoing tally of areas in my life that need the most improvement.

My son was still lying on the couch with ailments yet remaining undiscovered by human hands and unimproved by the experiment of a dog's distraction. My hope for a quick mental recovery of mind over the matter of his mysterious fever never happened. A weekend visit by my parents turned into a two-week nightmare when my Dad went into congestive heart failure, and Ginger, by this time, commandeered my own hands and feet as her own. Necessity required a crash course in that elusive realm of compassion, and I found myself formulating a plan for survival. These poor souls were at my mercy and understandably nervous with their personal knowledge of my shortcomings, and I really didn't want to lose anyone on my watch.

My sickly couch potato received a homebound teacher for mental stimulation, as well as a mountain of books and Disney movies for hours of his enjoyment and my chance to be still and remember that God was still actively interested in my progress. Ginger was pacified with a boatload of bananas (her favorite fruit) and the opportunity to be with me 24/7 in her new "mobile ambulance."

It was the result of an early morning brainstorm when I awoke with the inspiration of filling the red Radio Flyer with a plastic egg crate and fluffy pillows. Thankfully, our puppy was still small enough to fit in the crook of my arm as well as the crate, and the constant movement of the wagon from room to room put her to sleep just as a car does to babies. Her cast offered enough counter weight to keep her from jumping out, and she seemed willing and eager to fill the role of spoiled child.

Occasional allowances for her exercise provided comic relief as she lopsidedly careened down the hall with a "click, click, click, thud" as the sound of her nails was followed by the plop of the cumbersome cast. At least I never had to wonder where she was, and it always brought a smile to my son's pale face.

Laugh at yourself first, before anyone else can.
- Elsa Maxwell -

As stressful as the recovery of our little boy and his dog could be there was, of course, the day to highlight my ongoing search for excellence in homebound care. My parents came to visit over Valentine's Day with plenty of heart cards, red hots, and pink-iced cookies, ready to shower their grandchildren with hugs and kisses (and armed with the unspoken desire that their visit would somehow launch our patients into perfect health).

Several nights into their stay, persistent knocking at the bedroom door pulled me from deep slumber as Mom whispered nervously that my Dad couldn't breathe. I threw on a sweat suit, and the three of us piled into their car for a frantic drive to the emergency room. The air was cold and clear and seemed to help his wheezy breathing, but the women in the car knew it sounded serious. We were quite a sight…my parents are both shorter than me, so the driver's seat had my legs somewhere near my chin, Mom had her arms wrapped around my Dad, and he looked like a pretzel with a twisted seat belt precariously draped across his belly. All we needed was Ginger's participation, and the scene would be complete. Even the Three Stooges would've been inspired.

We spent the rest of the night watching the heart monitor bounce an irregular staccato until the doctor on call finally pronounced that he recommended immediate heart surgery. Dad had survived triple bypass surgery and several stint insertions years earlier. My parents knew this drill all too well. Sometimes life only gives you one choice and that is to trust God and proceed. I made arrangements for the care of those at home and joined my parents in a quick prayer for the surgeon's wisdom and capabilities, as well as a miracle for safe and speedy travel through metro rush-hour traffic. Dad arrived via ambulance, but they weren't going to wait on us before proceeding with surgery, and Mom hadn't managed to squeeze in beside him despite her impressive attempts to do so. She rode with me instead, her only support system and means of travel disguised as a confident daughter in a well-worn suburban minivan.

I clung to thoughts of what Ginger would do under these circumstances and came to the conclusion that we should all eat what was offered, look everyone in the eye while talking, circle the room before sitting, and wait patiently for our Master's instructions. While not always easy to follow, her advice proved wise and true as we all emerged days later with healthier hearts and newly forged familial bonds.

There is more to life than increasing its speed.
- Ghandi -

Any thought of return travel before several days of rest was out of the question, so our home became a three-bed hospital as my son, father, and puppy milked their recoveries together. At least that was the plan. The first morning after Dad's release, my husband left for long-overdue work, those who were able got on the school bus, and I settled my son and Ginger on the couch for a morning of Batman movies. Just as I began to assemble the cereal and toast, I heard a muffled cry behind me and turned to find my Mom noticeably shaken. Dad's head was spinning him in circles, and she couldn't get him out of bed. Momentary shock held me spellbound until my brain registered that life was once again taking a detour, and I called 911.

The situation was far from funny, but I laugh every time I think of what must've gone through the emergency crews' minds upon arrival. My addiction to Christmas decorating was out of control at this point in my life, with twelve heavily ornamented trees and enough lights and décor to please the worst of hoarders. With the addition of caregiving duties that particular year, I was still in the process of putting everything away and had placed the last artificial tree into the foyer, considering the possibility of including its presence in a new celebration of Valentine's Day.

As we heard the sirens enter the neighborhood, I threw open the front door and barely managed to shove the tree from the path of an incoming stretcher and a team of fully dressed firefighters as they rushed to my Father's aid. He was still waiting in the upstairs bedroom, so up they all went, collapsing the stretcher on their way to maneuver the stairs and railing. My son's eyes were as big as saucers as he took it all in, and Ginger barked excitedly as she tried in vain to wag her cast-impaired backside and join the procession.

There was certainly no room for me up there, so I went to shut the door and stopped in my tracks. The neighbors would have a field day with this one...gracing our curb was a very large and lipstick red fire truck. I had visions of Dad strapped to the ladder as they wheeled out of the subdivision, watching him grin ear to ear in his position of honor. Surely, they wouldn't use the fire truck to transport him to the hospital...*or would they?*

No, they didn't, but it's a much better visual of the situation than thinking about possible complications with his heart surgery. Several EMT vehicles would soon arrive, and several hours later we returned home with the mixed blessing of a severe vertigo diagnosis with no connection to hearts or hospitals. I placed my Dad at the top of the list for people with the greatest insatiable desire to live and pull out the vision of the fire truck in times of trouble when I'm sorely in need of inspiration.

God's promise of new life sprouted as it always does each spring, as we finally waved goodbye to my parents from a driveway full of happy faces. They were well on their way to recuperation, and I looked forward to the day of discharge for my remaining patients. It was time to focus on reclaiming the couch, as well as my sanity, and we were just days away from the removal of Ginger's cast. Surely, we could discard my son's sickness as easily.

The simplest things are often the truest.
- Richard Bach -

My family is comprised of a long line of athletes and accomplished musicians, orators, and professional college graduates. I flunked my gym class softball throw, play the piano in private, would rather speak to dogs than humans, and only made it halfway through a graphic arts program in my late teens. It was obvious that I was inclined toward a path of creativity, but I had an aversion to organized anything and found life at art school very uncomfortable.

In an atmosphere that encouraged no inhibitions, I stumbled into a world of free everything – except the exorbitant tuition. Aids were still people who assisted others, not the disease we know so well today, but I fear many of my professors and classmates are among those who spread its deadly effects with carefree abandon. I left this career choice behind with regrets and relief, only to see my brief introduction to marketing appear as a blessing years later in the form of a billboard.

In our desire to solve the mystery of our son's illness, my husband and I exhausted all avenues that traditional medicine offered and finally gave up and gave it over to God. With stiff-necked stubbornness, we'd spent months foolishly trying to fix something we couldn't even name. As the scales fell away from our eyes, my husband looked up from driving one day and saw a billboard asking the simple question – "Have you tried everything else?" Yes! We had. I wonder how long that message had sat waiting before we were ready to see. It turned out to be an advertisement for local chiropractors of whom we soon learned the other side of traditional medicine did not accept as a viable alternative.

Reality *is* perception, and it turned me into an open-minded thinker forever. After one week of intense spinal adjustments, our son returned to school without headaches or fever. Never again would a fancy-framed document on the wall from a well-known medical college be able to convince me that it was proof of knowing everything. Only the pages of the Bible can boast that claim, and I began to see the value of surrendering preconceived notions and all judgment to God. I got back to the business of wife and mother, shedding reliance on worldly wisdom in exchange for a firm belief in the power of The Great Physician and independent thought.

An animal's eyes have the power to speak a great language.
- Martin Buber -

Ginger looked forward to the day when she would enjoy her first stretch, lick, and scratch in all those areas denied her for so long. I couldn't wait to see beneath the cast, but wondered – not for the first time, if the saw would cut too deeply or that water had somehow found its way around my carefully designed leg raincoat. I learned to sew as a child, but medical scrubs and dog fashion were never on the pre-printed patterns, and I always had an aversion to coloring outside the lines or thinking outside the box. It's a curse to my organized thinking, though one would think by now that I had improvisation down to a science.

Ginger passed with flying colors, as we left the vet without a cast and headed home to practice solo potty time and re-learn the art of independence. I was filled with hope that my life would soon be back to normal (whatever that was) but now that my mind was free to think more clearly, it suddenly dawned on me that Ginger's recuperation lasted just long enough in the cast to push her past the six-month age requirement for her puppy obedience class. I expelled an audible sigh and wondered if they issued refunds under unusual or extenuating circumstances. I could certainly prove that our lives lately had experienced both and could surely use the distraction of dollar signs in my explanation to my husband during dinner conversation that night.

I admit that numerous years attempting to administer discipline among the ranks of the children had left me with a nonchalant attitude toward Ginger, and it was obvious that someone with objectivity (and a lot more patience) was my next best option. To reinforce my unbelief in coincidence, another company bonus blessed our checking account just about the time I spied an ad in the local paper for a new dog trainer in town. It was Divine Providence at a very high price.

He offered six visits for an obscene amount of money – why didn't someone warn me about the outrageous cost of pets *before* I decided to expand my family? I convinced my husband that this would absolutely, positively, with an asterisked money back guarantee, work to tame our hairy beast, and he reluctantly agreed. I took no chances for second thoughts and began her lessons the next day.

Terry the Trainer was a throwback from the 60's with a longhair ponytail, cut-off shorts, and a rusty Ford pick-up with a beautiful – and well behaved, German Shepherd sitting majestically on the tied-together tailgate. He (the trainer) was late, non-apologetic, and unexpectedly wonderful with Ginger. She took to him instantly, and he had her eating out of his hand (literally) in seconds. I never got beyond having her sit long enough for a treat, but she was inexplicably willing to sit, stay, fetch, roll over, shake, and all but hand over the money at the end of each lesson just for the chance to be by his side. Whatever else he *wasn't*, this guy was incredible with my girl and worth every penny just to see them in action.

He taught me all the standard commands and explained the theories and nuances behind his methods, but I never was able to duplicate the obedience magic between them. I never understood what she saw in him, but it helped prepare me for the years ahead when my children would suddenly become teenagers and start bringing home the new loves of their lives – acne, nervous twitches, and all.

Ginger graduated with honors, giving an award-winning performance on her last day of class, as they both managed to fool us into thinking she'd learned obedience from a master. I think she knew all along how to behave, but stubbornly chose instead to do it on her own terms in front of a sympathetic and biased audience. Perhaps her goal was to drain the finances so we'd rely solely on the power of love. If that was the case, she was definitely making headway.

If you obey all the rules, you miss all the fun.

- Katharine Hepburn -

Too many months of postponed family fun had us all itching for adventure, so we eagerly filled part of summer break with plans for a week at the lake. My folks retired years earlier in their version of heaven with a home in the trees and idyllic life on water just steps from their back porch. My brother's home rested a few miles away on another stretch of lakeside beach, just minutes away by boat. It was a favorite destination for the kids, though I often wonder if news of our intentions met with understandable apprehension instead.

Perhaps Dad's recent bout with heart surgery had the lingering effects of amnesia as well, as they welcomed our boisterous entourage – even with the knowledge that it would include three kids, five bulging suitcases, and the dog. Between both houses, two pontoon boats, and a Sea-do, we'd easily keep the local gas station in business, consume enough hot dogs for major indigestion, and erase the need for bedtime excuses, as the children would fall into bed each night with exhausted smiles and immediate sleep as their heads hit their pillows.

Each morning awoke with Mickey Mouse waffles (my Mom's specialty) and a passionate compulsion to jam as much excitement into daylight hours as possible. Breakfast was too delicious to ignore, but it was obvious that if it hadn't been for those cute little ears doused in syrup, the boat would've been full of hungry sailors. Plates miraculously found their way into the dishwasher unbroken in their haste to begin the day, as my Dad,

"Captain Poppy," assigned all life vests, fishing poles, and seating arrangements. Several inner tubes and tanning lotions later, we pulled from the dock and made our way to open seas for a rendezvous with my brother's family and their equally well-equipped craft.

The objective for my day was twofold - keeping my brood safe and content, while attempting to introduce Ginger to water sports without her knowledge that they included water. Her aversion to mandatory bathing was legendary, and my family is accident prone, so I didn't hold out much hope for accomplishing either. My brother is notorious for elaborate improvisation and teasing of all kinds whenever I'm part of the scenario, which should've given me fair warning for *his* objective.

After finding an empty spot in the middle of nowhere, he proceeded to pitch two oversized doughnut tubes over the side of his boat and tied each securely to its rear corners. My husband and I (both oversized ourselves at the time) were encouraged to take the first spin, and we naïvely jumped overboard to claim our places. Barely having time to kneel and grasp the handholds, the motor lurched into gear, and we began slicing through the waves at a terrifying speed.

At one point, our tubes flared out in opposite directions, only to find themselves careening back to the center and crashing into one another. I was determined to hold on at all costs, even when I began to find myself with the tube still attached to the speeding boat, and under water up to my eyeballs. Only when faced with the choice of being out of breath or letting go did I choose the latter. Both boat's occupants were laughing hysterically upon my retrieval, and I took solace in the fact that dogs can't laugh and pulled myself back to safety beside my straight-faced companion. Ginger looked at me as if to say, "I told you so," and proceeded to lap the water from the puddle at my feet.

A picnic lunch awaited us on what my nephew dubbed Pirate Island a long time ago. Coolers hit the sand just after beaching the boats, and we all tied into the bologna and cheese sandwiches with gusto. Ginger was just finishing her last piece of crust when an enormous flock of ducks descended upon the island. She seemed mesmerized by their curious ways and obviously desired to follow their waddling line into the lake, if only she could figure out how to avoid the water. I could imagine her thoughts of my encounter just moments earlier and felt sorry for her hesitation. Someone suggested giving her a life jacket…if only she knew how to swim.

Necessity is surely the mother of invention, and her look of longing as the ducks were quickly swimming out of sight led to a welcomed solution. Placing the vest on the ground, we inserted her front paws into the armholes and snapped the vest buckles snuggly across her back. I waded in with a secure arm around her middle until instinct took over, and she began to paddle on her own.

She was several yards off shore before she realized what she was doing, barking at the team of swift swimmers (telling them to slow down, I'm sure) and wondering why I was frantically swimming towards her before she swam too far away. Comprehension dawning, her eyes took on a glaze of fear, and she gladly accepted my offer to steer us both back to shore. We were in complete agreement…I would never go tubing again, and Ginger would happily remain a landlubber the rest of her days.

**If you confess with your mouth the Lord Jesus
and believe in your heart that
God has raised him from the dead,
you will be saved.
- Romans 10:9 –**

The split seconds of fear that Ginger and I shared in our harrowing water adventures gave us both something to ponder and produced many conversations and miles of walking on which to expound upon the need for protection on all sides. Water, wind, and the occasional invasive neighbor dog wreaked havoc on our dispositions, and it was obvious that I, in particular, was in need of something omniscient and more powerful than any life vest or overcoat could provide.

After winging it solo through too many self-imposed disasters, Ginger even realized the wisdom of reinforcements and suggested a renewal of my childhood spirit of salvation on the "Roman Road." Our road looked more like a loop, sitting squarely in the middle of a gated community full of millionaires and a few commoners like myself. Ginger and I used that secluded stretch of pavement as a rehab for the soul and spent many an hour exercising our legs and minds.

She was healing from her introduction to fireworks that produced the first in a lifetime of chronic seizures while I struggled to emerge from my own disconnection with survival. Her disease was more a natural result of biology than a product of her disposition or diet. Mine was a consequence of free will on steroids. The love of food, and the fact that eating isn't against the law, made it easy to use Suzy-Q's and French bread as my gateway drugs to food addiction's obesity. I was a very large woman with chronic depression and daily migraines that devoured my joy.

Ginger's prescription for health included walks and fresh air, which unknowingly guided me to the door of improvement for both of us. The Lord used her to drag me back to the living, with stops along the way to smell the flowers or race to the trees. She avoided the use of mind-numbing pills to handle her seizures by massive doses of nature, and I talked my way out of despair with my Savior and (slimmer by the day) sidekick.

I told Jesus many years earlier that I accepted the gift of His life for mine and even said it aloud in front of a roomful of teenagers. The piece of the puzzle that took more time to understand was the part about making him Lord over everything about me. I thought being a loner meant having to be alone, and being unique was a style that each person developed on his or her own. Ginger blew that theory by shattering my wall of defenses and helping me to see that God created me with the precision of a snowflake and that my heart is only whole when shared. I symbolically shed the shackles of my past by walking the loop in the opposite direction, no longer resisting the pull of her leash and embracing the joy of expectations.

**No matter how little money and how few possessions you own,
having a dog makes you rich.
- Louis Sabin -**

All those hours of training and worn out tennis shoes should've amounted to more than a calmer, though persistently obstinate dog. Ginger was obviously aware of my desire for her cooperation but remained steadfast in her ornery stance on contrary behavior nonetheless – a lot like my hair after a storm clears the air of its humidity. She endured quick trips to the vet now and then but wasn't crazy about life on the road. She turned into a real homebody and showed her dislike for my absence during mandatory grocery shopping or PTA meetings by grabbing hold of the toilet tissue and running as fast as she could throughout the house – so much for obedience training.

I only kept her off the furniture when others were looking and actually encouraged her to curl up in my easy chair, hoping that she'd lay there when I wasn't and settle down in the peace and comfort of thinking she was getting away with something. I even started leaving on the stereo with Mozart or Bach playing serenely in the background, hoping in my absence that even if she preferred soft rock, she'd be too lazy to get up and change the channel.

Whatever the reason for her unrest, she was a rebel with claws in the true spirit of my own Irish heritage, discovered only recently by my Mom's foray into genealogy. Imagine my relief to know that my green eyes, reddish hair, and passion for debate really belonged to a long line of patriots looking for freedom, instead of a black sheep among my blond-haired and blue-eyed family of Germans.

It seems that my ancestors, in an attempt to flee Irish authorities, set sail for America and changed the spelling of their last name just prior to coming ashore. If they could be that bold and creative in their desire for anonymity, then surely Ginger and I could find the secret to her happiness and my sanity.

Therefore, I began research into the fascinating subject of dog psychology, only to discover that there are even more expensive and numerous self-help suggestions for pets than there are for people. From pills to dog psychics and back, my exhaustive search ended where it all began in the first place – the animal rescue shelter. The experts believed that another dog was the answer to everything. I wondered if any of them actually had pets themselves, or at the very least, had a doting wealthy aunt with a huge inheritance in their futures. "Oh well," I thought, "with six you get egg roll, so maybe seven will turn into buy one, get one free."

CHAPTER 3

LOVE IS NOT JEALOUS

The average dog has one request to all humankind.
Love me.
- Helen Exley -

After learning to cope with the art of sharing time between child number one and the birth of number two, it became obvious that after going through such a life-altering transformation I could birth another dozen, and the technique would be the same. Fortunately, it never occurred to me that I should test the theory in quite so drastic measures, but I was confidant in my reasoning and felt that I could multiply my affections just as easily to another dog. I was, however, adamant about not starting with a puppy to crate train, with visions of finding a more senior version of Ginger who'd be a good influence and meet the requirements of canine companionship.

After several visits to the shelter (sans children this time) I'd all but given up hope that such a creature existed. Ironically, my husband was the one who managed to stumble and fall crazy in love, with an emphasis on crazy. The object of his immediate affections was a miniature version of a black and white giraffe with a bad case of kennel cough and fleas. Short stubby legs supported his very long neck and body, with wiry hair covering just enough of his eyes to make him appear mysterious. I tried imagining his potential and resigned myself to the idea that we were his ticket out. At the time, I thought he was the luckiest dog on the planet to be coming home with us, but hindsight later revealed that he was, instead, a very clever blessing in disguise.

My husband seemed spellbound by this new little boy and couldn't wait to surprise the kids upon their return home from school. I think he went way beyond surprise and definitely into the realm of severe shock. They begged for years for a pet and suddenly found themselves in the company of two. I fielded all questions by pointing an outstretched arm in their Dad's direction to indicate the source of this newfound treasure. For once, I was completely innocent and reveled in the split second of this phenomenon.

The entire experience seemed to be a pre-packaged set-up, complete with name and instructions included. It was evident that my husband had given this a whole lot more thought than I'd imagined, as he formally introduced us to "Bailey" as if he were a long lost relative with a shared past and royal connection. I was still trying to get past the overwhelming urge to trim the hair out of his eyes while everyone else seemed to accept his arrival without question.

Everyone else, that is, except Ginger. Alerted by her suspiciously silent lurking from beneath the kitchen table, I began to wonder about the merits of our rash decision as I watched her creep up on her new playmate from behind. Surely, she must be in attack mode and ready to pounce at the slightest move. Filled with images of another costly visit to the vet, I quickly bent down to pull her away from impending doom.

Just as I reached for her collar, the most wonderful, unexpected thing happened. She sauntered over to her newly adopted brother and nudged the food bowl his way – this, from a contrary canine who previously was known to inflict bodily harm upon anyone getting between her and a pig ear. I found myself doubting any previous thoughts I might've had about Ginger ever having a jealous bone in her body.

No one close to me has ever discouraged me from pursuing my dreams.
In retrospect, the biggest obstacle has always been myself.
- Tom Peterson -

I have the unfortunate disclosure that jealousy has been, however, a part of my own anatomy from time-to-time. As I've mentioned before, high school was a huge source of anxiety, but instantly provided a source of exotic interest with the introduction of Hilde Svensen. She arrived my senior year as a Norwegian exchange student and lived several farms over, but close enough for her host mom and mine to be acquainted. Their maternal instincts guessed that we would connect as fellow newcomers, even though my trek across the state paled in comparison to her voyage across the sea.

Hilde spoke fluent English, shared most of my classes, and could swing dance in the company of any Ginger Rogers or Fred Astaire. She came equipped with dazzling shoes and the ability to lead, so my shared love of the genre easily placed me in the role of her partner as I learned numerous routines and versions of the Nordic hop. Sadly, all dance steps survive my memory in title only – surfacing years later as inspiration for my beloved Ginger's name.

Our friendship blossomed throughout the year, and I spent many a night dancing with this female partner, blissfully unaware of discouraging social hang-ups that thought two girls dancing appeared somewhat odd. Awareness quickly became apparent, however, on the day that a guy in creative writing class swayed my interest with polished prose, smoothly convincing me that a pair of blue eyes and broad shoulders would serve as an even better partner. I equated his attraction with love, held captive by my adolescent infatuation and became hopelessly oblivious to the obvious.

We'd shared everything else up to this point, so it became Hilde's natural assumption that I wouldn't mind sharing him either. Unfortunately, I turned green and she a certain shade of red, as we parted ways for the remainder of her days in the States (safely ruling out any aspirations I might've had in diplomatic foreign affairs). I regret to this day that I allowed my jealousy of her mirrored interest to lead me into choosing him over her. What I thought was a budding romance didn't last past my stint at higher education, and I'm certain that I'd still have an international pen pal today if I'd only acted *in* love instead of using the excuse *of* love.

> **Folks will know how large your soul is**
> **by the way you treat a dog.**
> **- Charles R. Duran -**

Love at first sight probably fell short of the truth for describing Ginger's reaction to Bailey. It was more like tolerance and resignation. I could relate. With a desperate desire to achieve calm and civility with all members of my household, I was willing to try anything. Ginger's goals were more narcissistic, but if Bailey could keep her warm at night and provide entertainment without stealing the show, we could count her in. Bailey seemed to yearn for nothing more than a place to call home.

It quickly became obvious that Bailey had come from an abusive situation. His eyes shown bright with a longing to love while his body shied away from all sudden movements and unexpected noise sent him cowering to the corner with his face hidden beneath the couch. His skin stuck to his ribs, and his ravenous appetite revealed the suspicion of a previous lack of food. He refused to descend the basement steps for months, opting to wait at the door until one of us took pity and carried him down – or just waited patiently for someone's return instead.

His memories of harsh punishment and banishment to cold, dark places were cruel competition against his desire to belong. We were a family of persistent achievers, however, and accepted his past as fact with a fierce yearning to create a sheltered future. Even Ginger joined in our efforts to pamper and proceed with caution, as she pronounced herself leader of the pack and led him out of the dark and into the wonderful world of possibilities.

I suppose it should've occurred to me that giving Ginger that much power was a dangerous thing, but watching him mimic every move with idolized abandon was too irresistible to squelch. I convinced myself that new carpet and gleaming hardwood floors were nothing if not lived in, and ruts in the nap or gouges in the wood from paws and nails added a certain rustic charm. The route around the kitchen, dining, and family rooms became an indoor short track, complete with an audience to cheer them on. It was a game to see which one's momentum ran them into the furniture first since winning was never in question. Ginger's speed always trumped Bailey's enthusiasm.

Perhaps I was inclined to obsess about the warranty of our floors, but remembering my list of requirements for a second dog haunted me, as I found myself on hands and knees cleaning up one mess after another from Bailey's inability to learn the finer points of personal hygiene. I'm certain that I clearly requested a "senior version of Ginger who'd be a good influence" and was "adamant about not starting with a puppy to crate train."

Bailey *knew* what to do, but insisted on using his influence to do "it" wherever he wanted. No amount of positive reinforcement (or the use of bribes, while showing him where Ginger preferred to go) changed the fact that Bailey was a handful – and I was still on my hands and knees. I felt like a captive at the mercy of a nine-month-old dog and a sister twice his age…wasn't he supposed to be a *senior* version? How had I ventured completely off the path of human in charge?

With the assistance of prayer and probably the influence of too many nagging rants, my husband appeared one day with – what he hoped, would be the answer to my woes. The box contained flags, collars, and instructions for one of those invisible pet fences, guaranteed to bring peace and harmony to every household (my husband's addendum). His strategy aimed at convincing Bailey that potty time was a game to play exclusively outdoors, relying heavily on the assumption that Ginger would buy into his plan and model the collar as part of a new flashy uniform. I admit that my husband's propensity for being right was sometimes irksome, but in this case, I gladly showered praise and removed the case of carpet stain removers from my grocery list.

The indoor track would soon move to fresh air with the discovery of freedom that a doggie door and uninhibited 60-foot radius of fence allowed. Technology supposedly put a man on the moon and paved the way for the small gray box in my pantry that miraculously produced an invisible barrier that kept everyone happy. Ginger and Bailey could now sail around the yard at break-neck speeds until collapsing in contented heaps on the porch floor while I joined them with a book or cup of tea in rare idle moments of bliss. Snatches of heaven on earth are blessings too often overlooked, but my puppies and rescued floors are proof that they exist just the same.

A smile is a curve that sets everything straight.
- Phyllis Diller -

Electricity is undoubtedly my favorite invention of all time. I thoroughly enjoy light at the flick of a switch, hot water, and the use of all gadgets created to tame hair. I learned at an early age to appreciate all of the above with the unfortunate absence of their benefits during the Blizzard of '75 – and no, that's twentieth century – not sometime before the coming of Christ. I was seventeen-something, living with my parents in the middle of several Ohio cornfields and cow pastures, when the snow began to fall.

Meteorology at that point consisted of each family's barometer on the wall instead of fancy computer images on a green screen map, as we watched its needle shift by the hour with a storm veering our way with ferocious intensity. We retired that first evening with extra blankets on the bed and several pairs of socks on our feet, as the wind howled through the bending trees and sent a yardstick of snow pelting into deep drifts against the house.

Morning dawned bright and many degrees below zero with a stillness that occurred to my wakening brain as meaning only one thing: no electricity. Mom had risen hours earlier and already had the fireplace stoked with a dozen eggs sizzling in a cast iron pan. Dad attempted to shovel a path to the woodpile and disappeared from sight within the drifts that towered above him. Aside from the numbness in my freezing fingers and toes, the day held childish excitement for me, as I fondly remembered the advantages of hills to sled or ponds to skate. My propensity for dry boots kept me inside, however, and I opted to paint the scene from the warm side of the window instead. The finished oil still hangs in my parent's foyer and no doubt seems a peculiar choice of subject to anyone but the three of us. I guess you had to be there to appreciate the significance of snow. My parents understood, emphatically choosing to retire many miles *below* the Mason-Dixon Line.

One day without school and the thrill of virgin snow was worth the inconvenience of having no heat or indoor plumbing. *Four* days with only the meager comfort of perpetual fires and enough radio batteries to power our only connection with the outside world is an eternity. I now shared insight into how close Noah must've become with his family of chosen relatives and animals saved from destruction. While I cherish the bond we all formed by our shared survival, I can't seem to summon a fondness for the memories of smoke-filled nostrils, dirty clothing, and unwashed hair. Perhaps this explains why I also chose to move south in my adulthood, and to this day, I immediately wash my hair with the news of impending precipitation.

Twenty years later, the memory of boredom, frozen fingers, and fear of possible extinction remains firmly seared in the back of my head (along with the eyes that my children were convinced I possessed). It seems quite reasonable, then – to me, at least – why I reacted so violently to the discovery that faulty batteries can wreak such havoc on otherwise functioning electricity. Who knew that in order for my miraculous invisible fence to operate, it took more than plugging the cord into the wall?

Blissfully unaware of this crucial piece of fine print, I let the dogs out one morning expecting to retrieve them moments later. Imagine my surprise when they magically disappeared instead, and my morning quickly turned into a mad dash through the neighborhood to discover them before the covenant police did. Armed with a jar of opened peanut butter (their favorite bribe) I scoured all logical routes accessible by golf cart, returning home unsuccessful and doomed to a fate of waiting by the phone for one of my neighbor's inevitable calls.

Several hours later, I heard the beginnings of faint barking in the distance and ran to the door in hopes of catching a glimpse of my wandering convicts. As the noise grew, so did my apprehension, as a vision of adorable puppies returning to their mother's love quickly turned into the horror of their mud-caked bodies barreling toward my open door. Slamming it shut behind me, I waved the jar of peanut butter under their noses and guided them to the rear. Georgia clay turns into red mud when wet and hard as bricks when dry. Apply a liberal dose of both to Ginger's long silk and Bailey's white fur, and you're looking at a natural disaster.

The long shadows of autumn cooled the air this late in the day, but I hesitated mere seconds before taking drastic action and turning the hose on them both. The blast of frigid water seized their attention, as they stood paralyzed in shivering remorse. It took months for their muddy paw prints to disappear from the rear deck but less time than the memory of their perilous flight. A stern warning from the covenant police to keep our pets leashed at all times accelerated the order for fence repair and solidified my desire to move to the country. As Janis Joplin so aptly sung, "Freedom is just another word for nothing left to lose."

A moment's insight is sometimes worth a life's experience.
- Oliver Wendell Holmes -

Ginger and Bailey might just as well be twins, for all the supplies bought in bulk and two-by-two. They were separate in age, size, color, and demeanor, but inseparable in thought and deed. I purchased two little beds for their comfort, lovingly placed on the floor on my side of the mattress and quickly learned to avoid a misplaced slipper on a sleeping mutt, to avoid the loss of life or limb. Bailey's appetite grew exponentially with his body and soon took over both beds. It was yet another illustration of Ginger's miraculous tolerance and love for her fellow "man." She accepted the notice to vacate without complaint and promptly claimed an empty spot directly beneath me, but still within reach of her brother. I could definitely learn a thing or two from her unselfish tendencies that rose above her occasional dips into narrow thinking.

God usually thumps me on the head to capture *my* attention, though I suppose that's more a result of my hard-headedness than His desire for embellishment. He's well aware of my thoughts on electricity and has harnessed its power to alter my direction through amazing displays of nature.

As a young girl, I watched my brother return home from one hot, muggy summer football practice cut short by violent storms. Parking his jeep in the barn, he chose to race across the lawn in the pouring rain rather than wait it out with the smell of musty hay and a leaky roof. The water dumped from blackened clouds in sheets that pelted his body in merciless waves, as I stood at the door, anxiously tracking his arrival.

Just as he cleared the trees and stepped upon the walk, a thunderbolt appeared out of nowhere and chased his hot and sweaty body like a finger of white heat. The force of the current slammed him against the house with a loud crack, and I thought he must surely be dead. Stunned, but alive, he staggered toward the opened door as I closed it firmly on the weather and visions of what just happened. Perhaps too young to comprehend the fragility of life, I stored those thoughts to ponder on another day.

It seems not too much to ask that philosophical matters such as these take a backseat to the daily struggles of a young girl with nothing more on her mind than figuring out how to chew gum and walk at the same time. Nevertheless, God uses all sorts of ways to capture even the attention of the immature with events too dreadful to ignore, bringing the day to "ponder" sooner than I ever expected.

There is no surprise more magical
than the surprise of being loved.
- Charles Morgan -

My Mother is an only child, so the attention that her parents showered on my brothers and me was abundant and undividedly focused. We lived one town "over the river and through the woods" and grew up secure in the knowledge that they thought no other's grandchildren were as intelligent, witty, or beautiful. We saw them weekly, if not days in a row, and enjoyed conversation by party line at least once a day. Ivanhoe 6-3877 (their phone number in the days of switchboard operators) is committed to memory as prominently as ABC's and my very first address. I can't tell you what I ate last Tuesday, but this valuable piece of information kept prominently stored after all these years is a testament to their importance in my life.

Grandma and Grandpa married during the Roaring 20's and celebrated the birth of my Mom in the year of the 1929 stock market crash. Life was hard and precarious during the Depression and formed lasting impressions that they bestowed upon us kids through practical lessons and acres of gardens and fruit trees. They loved me in a way that made me feel as if I was the only little girl in the world. They literally built their own home and fortified my heart with the overflow from their

50

unconditional love. Their memories are vivid and colorful with a warm appreciation for the sanctuary I sought and received from their outstretched arms.

Grandpa was a master carpenter who spent a lifetime working with wood and driving the locals crazy if they found themselves caught behind his office on wheels. He loved to smoke a pipe and undoubtedly chose the non-passing lanes between home and the next job to fiddle with the matches as he crept along at "safe" speeds in his little white Nova. He was never in a hurry and taught me the importance of highway safety and laughing at life. We shared episodes of "Gunsmoke" and Dairy Queen ice cream cones in abundance, and he patiently sat through hours of "comb-overs" while I practiced my dubious barbering skills with the few strands of hair still clinging to his balding crown.

My Mom and I share the exasperating desire to redecorate by removing entire walls or the addition of doorways to a room not yet built, instead of being content with a new pillow for the couch or gallon of latex. Grandpa was famous for saying that "a picture will stand still for anything" whenever approached with our latest outlandish vision, and would make it anyway, forever proving that he *could* build it, in spite of himself. My favorite pair of his custom-made canary yellow Adirondack chairs didn't survive the many moves that would take me across the country, but a miniature hutch and doll-sized table and chairs remain.

Grandma toiled in the local pottery as an accomplished ceramist until the business burned to the ground, turning anything stamped "W.S. George" into an overnight collectible sensation. No one could afford to buy my collection of plates that she designed and decorated by hand…because to me they're priceless. She was the original working woman of many talents, soon becoming regionally renowned for her culinary expertise at a cozy little dive known as *The Bulldog.* Even now, my taste buds tingle at the thought of her signature banana cream pie.

As a young girl, she scraped together enough hard-earned money to purchase a brand new Singer treadle sewing machine. That little beauty would serve her well, feeding seven brothers and sisters, creating entire wardrobes for her, my Mom, me…and then all of *my* children. She mastered quilting, knitting, crochet, and passed on a love for the newspaper's weekly Jumble. I never saw a weed in her extensive flower gardens and long for the days of her melon-sized tomatoes.

Years later, I would become the lucky recipient of her coveted collection of recipes, bound in a spiral steno notepad brimming with folded napkins and torn sheets of whatever was within reach at the moment of her latest taste bud's inspiration. Her secret ingredient to all things wonderful seemed to be sugar and certainly an ample dose of love.

I can't wash or dry dishes by hand or dust the house without memories of Grandma. She and Grandpa never owned a dishwasher or obtained the luxury of a maid. They never saw the need for it when there were three strong grandkids to pick up the slack. I'm doubtful that my childish attempts to hit the nooks and crannies of their prized possessions were up to par with her standards, but all I remember was a constant stream of complimentary praise and warm hugs and cookies upon completion. Grandma hummed a continuous unidentifiable tune throughout her day, and I still find myself caught in the record's skip of a similar haunting melody whenever deep in thought in the mopping of the kitchen floor. She and Grandpa were my shining examples of what happens when you work hard, live right, and love always.

Each moment is a place you've never been.
- Mark Strand -

My parents illustrated *their* parents' example every year in their participation with the local high school after-prom party. The Women's Club, of which my Mom (and Dad, since he owned all the tools) was a member, was in charge of funding and creating this extravaganza. It was a pre-curser to the elaborate and expensive catered limousine parties of today's generation, and in my humble opinion, was their creative superior.

During each season of party preparations, my parents immersed themselves in late-night meetings to paint and plan, while the rest of us pretended that we loved TV dinners and counted the days until we'd finally be old enough for the invitation to first glimpse the fruits of their labor. Both of my brothers were inching closer and at least rated the status of free labor, so they ranked among those who now swarmed the cafeteria like bees, hoping to transform this normally sterile environment into something more closely resembling this year's theme of exotic island paradise.

Upon reaching the age of limbo – ten years' experience, but still in need of wisdom and guidance, my parents reached a point of compromise and trusted me to the solitary comforts of home. At everyone else's disappearance to the school, I found myself in charge of feeding the cats in between chapters of Nancy Drew, wondering how it would feel to grow beyond the age of ten and find myself embroiled in detective endeavors. I was just nearing the end of the book after a lunch of re-heated leftovers when the phone rang, and I rejoiced to hear my Grandma's voice. Having the freedom to stay by myself was something I dearly wanted, but I confess to feeling immense relief at being able to talk to someone besides the four walls.

She asked to speak to Mom, then my Dad…anyone else but me. I kept telling her that I was the only one home and couldn't understand why she sounded so strange or why we weren't talking about usual things, like my week at school or latest report card. Her voice wasn't even the same. It had a quiver and catch that eerily reminded me of how mine sounds right before I'm about to spill over and cry.

After a very uncomfortable silence, she took a huge breath as if to fortify her weary bones, and delivered the news that my Grandpa lay crumpled in a heap on the kitchen floor, where he breathed no more. She choked out an explanation of trying, in vain, to shake and cajole him back to life, but eventually gave up the fight when it was clear that his body was still, and his heart had stopped beating. Neighbors had summoned volunteers from their small but mighty firehouse, but no one could revive him, and the county's coroner was on his way.

What could a ten-year-old say to her cherished Grandma about the sudden death of her beloved Grandpa? Words are few when you hurt too much to think. Perhaps our shared silence was comfort enough, but at some point, she was able to summon the courage to ask the impossible. Could I find my Mom and tell her…tell her that her Mother needed her…that her Father was gone.

Somehow, I managed to hang up the phone and found myself in an awful position. With no adults in sight, no cell phones to call for help, and no previous experience in cataclysmic disasters, how would I follow through? Grandma was asking for the moon, but I knew I wouldn't let her down. I was the child sent to do a giant's errand. I was David without his slingshot. I was low on options but coaxed myself to think, think…*think*. Even as a pathetic ten-year-old, God used what I had – two strong legs and a shiny new Schwinn standing at the ready in our garage.

My goal was to reach the elementary school, which seemed miles away to a desperate youngster on a mission of impossible proportions. We lived at the end of a very long street that crossed the tracks and made its way to town through a series of stops and turns that seemed to grow even longer to a frightened and sobbing little girl pedaling her bike as fast as adrenaline could take her.

Finally, the rise in the last hill had brought me to my destination. I slid sideways into the parking lot and made my way inside. People were everywhere, busy with noise and confusion, oblivious to my distress. Nonetheless, I felt led in pursuit of finding familiar faces and eventually came upon my Mom. Looking up from the assembly of papier-mâché palm trees, our eyes locked, and she knew something was terribly wrong. My face held streaks of dust and tears while my whole body shook with emotion. She patted me down, checking for broken bones, having no way to know or prepare for the news I was about to deliver.

In my haste to arrive, I hadn't given thought to what I was mindlessly propelling myself to do, and once I got there, had no idea how a person could ever gently share that someone was gone and never coming back. I was just a kid, and fumbled through the horror by shocking her senseless with blunt – and brutal honesty. I watched her collapse into the arms of my Dad, and remember walking to the car, with the ridiculous notion that someone should go back for my bike.

Moments like those change a person's life forever. My forever just got started earlier than most, as I began to collect snatches of wisdom from each event and put them in my proverbial pocket for future use. God chose to place particular people and my dogs and I together for a reason that I can't quite explain, but it really doesn't matter, as long as I keep my thumb on the pocket's button and pull tight on its thread. Grandpa's absence left a gaping hole in my pocket, with life and circumstances fraying the edges, as I grew older. Grandma mended both of our broken hearts with her perfectly placed stitches until she would eventually leave her needle and thread to Ginger. Together, they created a set of patches for me that would make quite a crazy quilt of safety and solace.

CHAPTER 4

LOVE BEARS ALL THINGS

Enjoy life – it has an expiration date.
- Bumper Sticker -

I shared the conclusion of high school with the bicentennial of our country and dreamed since childhood about all the grand celebrations in which I would be an excited participant. The nation prepared with countless parades, ceremonies, and banners proudly proclaiming our precious birth of freedom with prayers of thanksgiving and fireworks too awesome to describe. I couldn't think of a better time in history to be making my mark from wading through years of educational preparation into the exciting world of adulthood and independent thinking.

My dreams included the naïve notion that everyone on the planet would be as excited as me to sit through hours of tedious speeches and lines of fidgeting graduates as my name was finally announced – and pronounced correctly. They would follow me home to a catered luncheon with a pianist playing in the background, with standing room only surrounding dozens of tables laden with fresh bouquets and freshly pressed white tablecloths.

I'm the youngest of three children and third from the last in a huge flock of grandchildren on my Dad's side, so I understood the lack of interest and novelty in this year's predictable graduation invitation. I'm sure of their collective pride that another family member had reached our perfect score for completion, but thoughts of guaranteed boredom dwindled the adoring masses in my head to only a few. The loyal and true included my parents, Grandma, and probably my brothers – though I can't seem to recall if they ate a piece of cake *that* day or from the freezer on their next visit home from college.

Thoughts of thwarted expectations swam in my head upon the rapidly approaching day of that same milestone for my daughter. Eighteen years flew by at the speed of light, and now I faced the challenge of letting her go, pushing her forward, and preparing the house for seldom seen relatives, all at the same time. I have the tendency to overcompensate when stressed, so it came as no surprise to my family that I chose to wallpaper three rooms, shampoo the carpet, and re-design the flowerbeds within the span of two weeks.

My husband left suspiciously early for a business convention that flew him safely out of state, while the kids managed to disappear with friends or mysterious last minute school assignments. It should've occurred to me that history was repeating itself with my visions of grandeur, but the house was quiet and I relished the chance to get this right on my second try, regardless of my daughter's requests to keep the affair simple.

The wallpaper order encountered a glitch with news of backorder status until five days before graduation. Ok…if I ordered pizza and omitted sleep from my calendar, I could still manage to cover the walls before the first guest arrived. Thoughts of cleaning the carpet moved to the bottom of the list, as the dogs and I moved our assault to the front yard. With ten days and as many flats of flowers, I began the conversion of dull earth into carefully planned plots of color.

Ginger and Bailey were contented companions who took my flurry of activities in stride. They napped in the sun with one eye open and kept watch on my progress as the day turned warm and cloudless. I've never achieved the ability to stay clean and dry when painting or working with dirt, so they were used to seeing me with a face streaked with mud and overalls turned a reddish-brown. They loved me just the same. I even had a neighbor who once asked me for a business card when she mistook me for our lawn guy instead of the owner who lived next door. Ginger thought my natural look was very becoming and shielded me with incessant barking, discouraging any curious neighbors who dared to slow down to monitor my latest planting fiasco.

After the completion of one such attempt to honor my current landscape design, Ginger sprung to the driveway and I looked up from my labors when Bailey joined the chase. A car was pulling in, so I rose from my knees with suppressed irritation. I didn't have time to chat, and it was too late to avoid a sales pitch for makeup or a new set of plastic containers. I adjusted the brim of my dirt-caked visor and jammed dirty nails into my grimy pockets. Quickly preparing a polite speech to expel them from the driveway, I stopped in my tracks when the wife of my husband's boss emerged. What was *she* doing here? It wasn't time for our annual Christmas party, and she was too early for graduation – even for her prompt standards. I couldn't remember anything that I'd forgotten and surely looked pathetic next to her very clean and stylish ensemble.

The dogs had better manners than I did at that moment, as they took it upon themselves to welcome her with great enthusiasm. Luckily, she accepted their slobbering attention with dog-loving understanding, and I breathed a sigh of relief that I wouldn't be the cause of any mark against my husband's record. She seemed to take pity on my disheveled appearance and befuddled thoughts, and suggested that I take a break in the shade on the back porch. All four of us retired to the wicker seating, for what, I couldn't imagine…understatement at its best.

Don't resent growing old.
Many are denied the privilege.
- Unknown -

Our guest refrained from small talk and moved right into the reason for her visit with a question about my answering machine. I didn't see the relevance of whether or not I'd talked with her husband that day, but I humored her with my own small talk until her body language begged me to stop. She was trained in psychology with a gift for always knowing just the right words to say, but at this moment I could tell that "right" was going to seem very wrong. The dogs even sensed her mood and lay quietly at my feet while she delivered the shocking news that her husband found mine earlier that morning, dead in his hotel bed.

Time stood still. The mind has an uncanny way of searing the horror and aching pain of something like that indelibly into the wall of your brain. Every sound, smell, and emotion still triggers a visceral response. It's something that fades with time, but never goes away. I remember that she took both of my hands in hers, dirty nails and all, and eventually wrapped me in her arms as my stunned silence inevitably turned into wracking sobs. After the onslaught of tears, she gently led me to the shower, turned on the water, and gave me instructions to get in, take my time, and get ready for…whatever came next. The water turned muddy as the garden dirt disappeared down the drain, and I slid down the wall of wet tile in thoughts of going down with it.

How could a person who I kissed goodbye only yesterday be gone forever? His just-pressed suits lay hanging in the closet waiting for his return. The last piece of his favorite pie sat safely wrapped in hiding for his welcome home. Bailey always abandoned his own bed to sleep on his master's side until his return…something that would never happen again. I began a mantra of "what do I do now?" until abruptly silenced with the reality of needing to share this devastating news with the children. Lord, help me.

A happy family is but an earlier heaven.
- Bowring -

I'd spent many an hour since childhood contemplating why fate had given me the horrible task of transporting the news of my Grandpa's demise at such a tender age. Here I was again, faced with an unspeakable task and finally able to put myself in Grandma's place and realize what a burden she bore. Now *I* had to be the adult who delivered the message of doom, and though God had seemingly prepared me for this moment, I still live with the regret of not being any more capable of softening the blow now, as she and I were then.

Calling the school for altered dismissal, I managed to steer the kids home before football practice and bus lines had a chance to claim them. The two eldest arrived home first with exasperation and curiosity in their eyes. Tossing backpacks aside at the awareness of the unusual guest in our kitchen, they smothered their questions and welcomed the wife of their revered Father's boss with manners that would've made him proud.

After the formalities, they looked from one face to the other, much like a tennis match, and finally settled on mine with an intensity that riveted me to the floor. Intending to wait until all three were gathered, I broke my resolve under pressure and shocked them with the news. Just as one son was escaping the scene out the back door, my youngest was coming through the front. He caught just enough of the lingering fragments of my pathetic explanation to understand that his Dad was gone, and give him enough reason to hold his Mother responsible for that, and so many other things to come.

The children took solace in their bedrooms after hours of riding the cart paths with friends and a pizza, rather than occupy the same space with well-intentioned neighbors or me. The pastor, my psychologist and her husband were the last to leave the house, and the overwhelming quiet made it clear that my journey was going to be lonely and long. I clung to the hope that two dogs and a willing spirit would be enough to mend our broken hearts and heal a fractured family.

Thinking that the comfort of routine would somehow ease the burden of not knowing what to do next, lights went out as usual as we all lay down to seek the solace of sleep. Not but a handful of minutes passed before my youngest stood at the foot of the bed, asking to climb in beside me. I don't think any of my children had ever sought more than a drink of water at bedtime, so this request meant much more than its words. We lay in the dark for the longest time, listening to the steady snores of the pets beneath us, and grieved together in silence. He was the last tangible gift that my husband and I had created together. I was the last link to knowledge of the things he'd never know about his father. Sadness engulfed the room, and the weight of it all eventually claimed my son in merciful slumber. I wasn't as fortunate and finally conceded that I might as well get up and face the darkness head on. Two precious companions followed closely behind.

Memories swirled like the ice cubes in my glass of water, as I played a swan song to our life together. I met my husband on a blind date, where he took me to a college basketball game in which we sat directly behind the bench. I spent the entire game trying, in vain, to get ourselves onto the television broadcast, so my parents could see firsthand the man I could easily fall in love with. Why wouldn't I want to let the *whole* world know?

He wined and dined me and set us on a two-year course of courting that would drive me insane with anticipated waiting. After sending a barber shop quartet singing "Let me call you sweetheart...I'm in love with you" just weeks after meeting, I was understandably vexed by his cold feet and procrastination. Twenty years later, I could only admit to full disclosure before I married him. The only thing predictable about him was his unpredictability.

I spent the rest of the longest night of my life wrapped in the shelter of my husband's recliner with Ginger and Bailey snugly resting on my lap. We'd experienced many a night without him before but always with the confident knowledge that he'd be returning at the end of each trip's conclusion. This wasn't the way it was supposed to be. None of us had signed on for this. Moms and dads are supposed to be able to fix anything, but mine were hours away, and I, as the sole heir to this parenting nightmare, wasn't capable of fixing a sandwich, let alone the permanent disappearance of the head of our household.

Bailey didn't understand why intruders occupied his Daddy's chair with lumpier laps and no room to stretch. Ginger balked at the idea of sharing with anyone, but finally settled for jamming herself against her brother's hip and my elbow. Donned in one of my husband's old sweatshirts, I pulled the collar to my nose in an attempt to breathe in his scent and somehow will his presence into the room. My companions fell into an enviable state of fitful slumber as my legs fell asleep in lieu of my conscience.

What was I going to do without him? How could he leave me with three teenagers, several mortgages, and an empty bed? We had one son just beginning young adulthood, another which was mere months from obtaining his license to drive, and of course, my daughter's graduation, which loomed so close now; we could measure its arrival by the clock's second hand.

I hadn't received a salary for work outside the home since the birth of our first child, so prospects for my dusty secretarial skills were limited at best. My husband was a planner to the first degree, but I had no idea if our futures would survive his good intentions and my lack of employability. Our daughter was planning to enter college in less than two months, the oversized first and second mortgages were due in two days, and I found out quite by accident that our health insurance didn't even last two hours after his death.

The steady breathing of the dogs seemed to echo in the soaring expanse of the vaulted ceilings, and I found myself shrinking inside the walls of this monstrosity that I no longer viewed as home. I'd exhausted all the issues I could see, smell, and touch, as silence rendered me defenseless and forced me to confront a host of unbidden thoughts. Everyone, no more than I, sought answers to why now, to what purpose, and when exactly the breath of life ceased to exist for the man with whom I'd chosen to share everything. Even in that, God had given me a subtle communiqué from the two beings I trusted most, left behind to herd me forward as I desperately sat struggling with agonizing truth and horrendous consequences. The answer to one question at least lay within my own memory, as an image appeared from just 24 hours prior, catching me by surprise and sticking in my throat like cherry cough drops intent on soothing with sugar what is otherwise painful to swallow.

The coroner's official time of death was one in which I concurred, substantiated by my two furry friends huddled together in sad solidarity. At exactly 4:42 am in the day's wee hours, Ginger and Bailey woke me from a deep sleep with unearthly howls and growls that instantly alerted me to unseen danger – or what I thought at the time must be nothing more than the deer that was persistently devouring my edible shrubbery. I threw back the covers and proceeded to the front door with dogs at my heels and a verbal assault aimed at the cause for my interrupted sleep.

I opened the door to darkness and a vacant front yard, while the three of us stuck our heads out just far enough to create a strange looking totem pole of inquiring minds. None of us seemed willing to chill more than the end of our noses, and it struck me as odd that neither one had ventured beyond my post of safety in a wild chase of suspected intruders. After a few moments of expectation, it seemed reasonable to believe that we weren't in any danger of losing anything more than my precious sleep, so we abandoned further surveillance and went back to bed.

They knew then what I would learn later, and I had to wonder how many other premonitions I might've previously mistaken irrelevant. I really needed to give more thought to the signs and wonders of the animals gifted into my care. They couldn't change or prevent certain outcomes but might cushion the glancing blows of life.

I entered into the holy bonds of matrimony never once taking into consideration that "till death do us part" was an option that might occur unannounced, unwanted, and uncontrollable. Wasn't it something that happens to people who share their whole lives together and end up with gray hair and matching rockers on the front porch? This wasn't the future we'd talked about on the nights when our babies couldn't sleep and surely wasn't in any brochure for estate planning. I had no idea what to pray for but gravitated to the comforting thought that surely someone else did and finally closed my heavy lids to a merciful reprieve.

Attitude is a little thing that makes a big difference.
- Winston Churchill -

The children chose not to avoid school or questions from classmates, as they wandered through the day after, in a courageous attempt to appear normal. I stayed behind to man the phone, spending the next several hours in an emotional stupor as I fielded calls from friends and loved ones in between a forced audition for my very own reality show.

CSI: Las Vegas had just shown up in my living room, uninvited through the telephone line, and asking questions right out of a script so compelling, it was hard to believe that it was happening to me. I miraculously answered their questions while calmly listening through the receiver instead of throwing it against the wall. Yes, we'd been married for twenty years. No, I had no reason to believe that this family man was involved in underworld crime or prostitution, or that it ever entered his mind that anyone would ask his wife such incredibly offensive questions. My vehement answers – and possibly the occasional pause while I collected myself from the latest onslaught of tears, must finally have convinced them that my husband really did have the misfortune of dying a virtuous man on legitimate business in a city known for the pleasures of sin. After hours of seemingly senseless interrogation, they finally moved on to the next poor soul. I sincerely hoped they'd somehow learn from me and decide to spare them from the same cruel advances. If life imitates art, that's as good a reason as any for why I no longer watch much TV.

I fled the house with Ginger and Bailey in tow, desperately trying to distance myself from the foul taste of Hollywood's example of how the other half presumably lives. It's a shame that life doesn't come with a handheld remote cleverly programmed with the option to delete on demand. My trusty sidekicks quickly picked up the pace and matched my angry strides in an attempt to keep up. I cried the full measure of our usual loop, in what would become a ritual in my need to heal.

My pastor once wrote that time really doesn't heal all wounds; rather the *discernment* of pain merely diminishes. It would take weeks to discover but time would eventually allow me to talk myself into the idea that everything, somehow, was going to be all right. It's amazing how one day I could sob with grief and days later make it through with a smile and somehow fix my eyes on the horizon. Ginger and Bailey got the brunt of my transformation, listening patiently to conversations ranging from anguished cries of "why?" to prayers for guidance and the occasional shout out to my husband whom I was sure was looking down from somewhere above.

They never questioned the outbursts and became sure and steady escorts in my fragile struggle each day around the bend, down the valley, and up the hill to whatever came next. My dogs never smiled with their teeth, but rather, grasped every opportunity to include their whole bodies to convey pleasure or excitement. With a few barks thrown in with their leaps and bounds, I knew they were as delighted as I was, in my baby steps towards contemplating what life looks like beyond the shadows of grief.

We buried my husband beside his father, the war hero, on a frigid windy day in May. The logistical nightmare of transporting his body from the convention's hotel in Las Vegas to the cemetery that lay in Ohio and flying our dwindled family of four from Georgia to the funeral all at the same time was arranged by friends with airline – and Godly connections. The casket no doubt traveled simultaneously in the belly of another jet while we waited standby. Miraculously boarding on time for the first flight of the day, we were ushered into first class seating. None of us had ever done more than walk *through* that area on our way to the back of a plane before and would experience the same luxury on the return flight – yet more proof of divine intervention. It's a shame that we weren't headed for fun in the sun instead.

Our itinerary was sandwiched between the earliest possible time for the funeral, the schedule of the minister who had married us and baptized two of our children, and the graduation festivities and final exams that would occur the next week. I resorted to begging, and what everyone said could never happen, did. We flew in and out within a weekend, and returned hollow and spent to a house that echoed with my husband's absence, the only bright spot delivered by the warm noses and tongues of our kennel-rescued pups. They were the only reason it was good to be home.

Bailey planted himself at the top of the stairs that led to his dearly departed companion's realm of business, a technological state-of-the-art home office placed in a corner of the basement of which he'd just recently conquered his fear. His steadfast vigil for the return of his idol would sadly prove unfruitful and aptly portrayed what the rest of us were feeling but couldn't put into words. He mourned and grieved with childish honesty and

68

reminded me each time I passed his poor little forlorn face, how desperately we all wished and waited for the same thing. Maybe it was time to wait expectantly for something that could actually happen.

Friendship isn't a big thing – it's a million little things.
- Anonymous -

Did you ever do something, that at the time you had absolutely no idea why you had? Several months prior to finding myself in the black hole of widowhood, I'd enrolled in a group at church that was "Experiencing God." Weeks into the study, I felt no closer to the God I read about in all the designated scripture lessons than when I'd started. I began to wonder if I belonged in a place of worship with a bunch of people who obviously seemed to know and understand this whole idea of the study's description about transformational experiences touted in the church bulletin. I kept waiting for a prophetic moment, or *something,* that would reveal at least a hint of the mysteries that plagued me about my role in the universe, or even just my family. I was clueless and quite unaware of the precious gift He was giving by simply placing me in that position, at that time, with that particular group of women.

We were an odd assortment of married homemakers with a rare span of consecutive Wednesday mornings available and free from the responsibilities of children, husbands, and chores. We hailed from various states, both north and south, with diverse backgrounds, educations, and denominational childhoods. Conversation was lively, though not always on message, and I found myself opening up to the possibility of venturing into the scary realm of friendship again. I gained very little from the purchase of the study's carefully crafted materials but received instead a priceless reward for my efforts in the form of this faithful group of followers who took the Bible's call to help all widows and orphans quite seriously. God knew that I couldn't face the future alone, and I humbly accepted the fact that I wasn't in control of anything and welcomed the help of all who would offer everything.

With the daunting task of getting through a graduation that we formerly anticipated with great joy and now lay clouded with suppressed emotion, I swallowed my pride and gratefully accepted their offers to help. After spending a lifetime under the thumb of self-imposed perfectionism and doing everything myself, that was undoubtedly one of the hardest tasks I've ever relinquished. With the support of neighbors, and the loving guidance and organization of my new friends (and family, of course), all offers to bombard us with food that we would never consume were delayed from the customary post-funeral days. They became, instead, the makings of a buffet that would cater to the celebration of life for our daughter's accomplishment, held less than a week after leaving her father's grave.

I issued a request that no one arrive without a smile for the living and memories of one who had passed, as we managed to get through the social meet and greet with minor bruising and pasted on smiles intact. Our kitchen table overflowed with the universal gift of love – heaping bowls of fried chicken, mashed potatoes with gravy and biscuits, and my personal favorite – the largest strawberries I've ever seen drenched in rich dark chocolate. Food comforts the soul, even at a time when everything tastes like sawdust.

The graduation ceremony afterwards took place outdoors in the light of a full moon that shone brightly on the empty seat beside me. The dark sky was as full of stars as my heart was of sorrow, but the vastness of it all reminded me that one greater than I had made everything for His good and wasn't about to give up on me now. Just months earlier, my husband and I spent a glorious week alone in the celebration of our 20th wedding anniversary with the red rocks of Sedona and vastness of the Grand Canyon beginning my journey towards the realization that God is bigger than anything or anyone than I can imagine. He gives proof in all that surrounds me, from the tiniest flea to the endless skies that reach far beyond the horizon. In my case, that's often no further than the end of my nose, but tragedy has a way of honing in on clearer vision.

The future is as bright as the promises of God.
- Adoniram Judson -

My parents extended their graduation visit to help with the formulation of a plan. We humans seem to have a plan for everything, except what might be good for us (as in broccoli or exercise), and there was nothing "good" about planning a life without the love of mine. Nevertheless, my checkbook balance wouldn't cover more than a summer's worth of house notes, let alone the groceries or dog food bills, so it was clear that my options were limited.

Mom and I headed for the attic to begin major liquidation from the top floor down, for a garage sale of mammoth proportions while Dad retrieved the phone book and settled in to who knew what. He was famous for getting on the "drawing board" and producing elaborate sketches of his latest project or invention, but that didn't usually involve the simple movement of his fingers walking through the yellow pages.

We re-grouped at lunchtime, dripping with sweat and already exhausted from the stress of finding Christmas presents cleverly hidden in the eaves by my husband for future family fun that we'd never be able to enjoy together. I was tempted to go back to bed and pull the covers over my head in a fruitless effort to nod off and wake from this recurring nightmare. Dad, however, seemed energized beyond comprehension, so curiosity got the better of me as I absentmindedly forked the uneaten morsels on my plate in patient anticipation.

Our disjointed efforts that morning to connect the dots in an effort to move forward suddenly began to make sense as he excitedly outlined his latest brainstorm. He'd spent *his* morning in conversation with a local auctioneer who guaranteed services that could wrap all my troubles in a pretty bow and produce a one-day solution to my woes. Dad was confident in his discovery and announced that the guy would be arriving that afternoon for my consideration.

We talked for hours about the intricacies of liquidating twenty years of marriage in a single day. My mind spun with the knowledge that within a span of thirty days, I could be relieved of my obligation to the bank, purge my life of accumulated clutter, and move away from all the constant reminders of our loss. Of course, this would also mean spending hours sorting through memories and preparing an already traumatized household for a sale to strangers. The auctioneer finally rose to depart, leaving me with the advice to think it over and give him a call. I felt certain that my Dad's intervention must surely be the latest bullet point on God's master plan and asked to sign his contract. He turned from the doorway with astonishment that I would make such a rash decision, but my parents and I shared a knowing look, and I smiled as I signed on the dotted line.

Love Never Fails

You can't have everything. Where would you put it?
- Steven Wright -

With the dubious distinction of having garage sale genes flowing through my veins, it didn't surprise me that I awoke on the morning of the auction with a generous portion of anxiety laced with an eerie sense of excitement. A month of 18-hour days left me depleted and weary, knowing that the next twelve hours would determine our future. I kept wondering what we'd do if the house didn't sell or if the furniture was left strewn around the yard when no one bothered to appear and bid on the treasures of my former life. I'd lived in a self-induced fast forward for so long in an attempt to avoid the consequences of what was about to commence, that the actual morning of the sale had me scared simple.

After spending several minutes in a pep talk with the bathroom mirror, I fell to my knees and finally filled my spirit with all I needed. Ginger appeared to remind me that I wasn't alone, and that more importantly, it was time to walk her and Bailey down to the neighbor for a day away from our impending chaos, toward the promise of virgin territory to smell and greener grass to explore. I was tempted to join them, safely hidden within the confines of this friendly backyard fence, but I patted my charges farewell instead and unleashed them to their unrestricted freedom. They didn't even spare me a backward glance. How I envied their disconnection from responsibility and turned homeward bound, heavily laden with my own.

Upon my return, the yard was buzzing with activity as the auctioneer's team carried box after box of itemized goodies to form a line for systematic selling. Twenty years of antiquing, Christmas toys times three children and enough pinball machines to fill an arcade gave the illusion of wealth to the surreal setting. The massive accumulation of *things* put the sorry state of my worldly existence into perspective, and I promised myself – on that very morning, never to keep boxes full of boxes or place the importance of minutia over the sanctity of life again.

The idea that it takes a village to raise a child became a reality for me throughout the process. I'd marooned myself on an island of independence and found rescue boats aplenty in the eyes of an unlikely assortment of sailors who coaxed me into unknown waters with gentle encouragement and small, profound acts of kindness.

One fellow football mom organized a food wagon (and her son's entire baseball team) to supply the hungry masses that we hoped would come, later bestowing a donation of their proceeds in honor of my husband. A next-door neighbor offered their driveway for the parking of the few things we *weren't* selling, as another friend appeared to provide moral support throughout the day. Just days before, I'd returned a lawnmower to friends around the corner who offered their brand new machine when hearing about the sudden demise of our old clunker. My parents erected a silent force field to shield me from invasive questions from curious bystanders and a handful of unbelievably ruthless buyers as my children busied themselves with the removal of multiple sofas and big screen TV's.

I shamelessly escaped to the only room without furniture to sell, firmly pulling the door shut and turning the key. It was tempting to throw it away until it occurred to me that none of this endeavor would've been possible without the love and compassion of others. How foolish and selfish I'd been to think that I was ever alone. I was minus one, to be sure, but plus a whole lot more. Strengthened by that realization, and fortified by the necessity of a successful sale, I emerged from hiding and reluctantly answered the man in charge with a summons to the auction block.

In a cruel and humiliating exercise, I stood bravely in view of all who wished to bid on the lumber and bricks that had been our home, despite my fervent desire for invisibility. The auctioneer held the uncompromising opinion that the house would sell for more if potential buyers felt sorry for our circumstances and paid more just to put me out of my misery. He was right about the misery, but the auction itself ended without results on the first pass, and rumor went rampant through the crowd that the house hadn't sold.

I was blissfully unaware of the drama unfolding above me, having fled the scene to the solitude of an empty basement as soon as I fulfilled the auctioneer's excruciating expectations. I just assumed the bids were still flying as fast as my hasty retreat and that someone would find me when we finally had a buyer. The frantic auctioneer did find me, in the last place he looked, chastising me for my lack of participation in his orchestrated coup and proceeded to lay out a proposal from the person who'd placed the last highest bid. They were interested, but it stood way below the line of my bottom dollar.

I began this journey with peaceful assurance that all would work together for *His* good and held firm in my resolve to see it through *His* way. The peace that passes all understanding didn't extend to my auctioneer, however, and he emerged from an intense negotiation process sweating profusely and visibly shaken, and producing with considerable awe, a final contract that would send me on my way with enough and then some.

Making haste to share the news, I found my Mother in tears and several anxious friends gathered around my Dad, unfortunately oblivious to the transaction that had unfolded below. They must've thought my smile indicated lunacy instead of good news to come, since it took several repeated explanations before they were able to comprehend that I held the deal of the century safely tucked in the grasp of my hands.

Miracles really do happen to ordinary people. Trust and obedience produce results, and in my case, a voracious appetite. Piling into a mass of cars that were bound for yet another friend's backyard; we devoured all-you-can-eat pizza and celebrated the blessings of our labor with cool water from their baptismal pool of concrete. The meager remains of our household packing would just have to wait for another day.

> **Look at everything as though you were seeing it**
> **either for the first or last time.**
> **- Betty Smith -**

When my husband and I married, we merged the contents of two zealous antique buffs who'd been single long enough to amass separate collections that required the necessity of building another room just to house the overflow. A job promotion materialized two months after the ceremony, before the last box was even unpacked or the remodel sawdust could settle. The move would take us to New England territory and the land of weekly "junking," which only served to amplify our mutual obsession to collect. I was addicted to the lure of patriotic linens and things, while he gathered a hoard of pre-electricity vacuum cleaners and tin toys that were supposed to become the inventory for that shop he'd never open. It was wall-to-wall furniture in a forest of oak and walnut, with china closets full of cherished heirlooms and breakables from unknown families of the past.

We began our own family within that cluttered atmosphere, adding ancient strollers and a clever settler's "bouncy chair" to our baby daughter's nursery. We quickly began to bulge at the seams and jumped at the chance to relocate to warmer climes and the promise of lucrative sales bonus opportunities. Our growing needs were only due in part to family expansion and held more to the conclusion that the house had shrunk.

My husband's company desire to promote from within generated many second thoughts after one look at the exorbitant moving company estimate – and our bulging chest of treasures. It wasn't their experience that young, newlywed families with one infant would have more accumulated possessions than a near-retirement family of five. Nevertheless, moving day arrived, and our household was transported several states southward, split nearly down the middle as half moved into a rental, and half went promptly into storage until we built the house of my dreams.

The idea of building from the ground up seemed like a good one at the time, but hindsight left me with no option but to agree with my Grandpa when he'd remind all of us decorating visionaries about a picture standing still for anything. It just doesn't always factor in things like the reality of square corners, square feet requirements, and good old common sense. Years of pouring through magazines had produced quite a folder of ideas. It had our builder dazed and confused during pre-construction discussions about tweaking his own mundane plans on paper. He didn't share my vision for a gingerbread Victorian with five different colors of paint, installation of vintage lighting, and the placement of a centuries old fireplace, staircase, and doors. He never understood my love for "gently used," causing frustrating delays while his crew dealt with learning how to think outside the box and build a home around pieces of history instead of prefabricated plywood.

Living out of boxes for months on end, while I fought stubbornly for my home sweet home, diminished my memory of the packed floor-to-ceiling moving vans that had pulled out the drive a year before, but the day of their long-awaited arrival was finally here. My husband's knack for disappearing out of town on convenient business required the need for reinforcements.

As I stood atop the new front porch steps with an energetic two-year-old on my hip and flanked by the able assistance of my Mom and Grandma, I couldn't help thinking how blessed I was to have such support in the face of such potential disaster. They were veterans in the realm of moving and remained by my side despite mosquito bites from the lack of backordered window screens in the heat of a Georgia August and an incompetent air conditioning installment the day before. We're a tight-knit clan known for finding humor in the absurd, which was convenient in light of what was presently making its way down the street.

Two packed moving vans had mysteriously turned into a caravan of boxcars lying on flatbed semis, strongly suggesting the resemblance of a traveling circus from days gone by. New neighbors dotted the lawns on either side of the road to watch the procession of precious cargo arrive in all its glory. For all they knew, lions and elephants could emerge from the padlocked storage containers; but my embarrassment was complete as they disappointedly drifted back indoors at the sight of nothing more than a steady stream of harmless chairs and boxes that seemed to have no end. The three-story house that hours ago seemed cavernous and empty now bulged at the seams with furniture and mountains of boxes that held the collection of hopes and dreams I'd pondered for so long.

Here I was, many moons and another move later, standing on the steps of a different home, waiting once again for new beginnings. What seemed so important at the time had gone through liquidation in the blink of an eye. Priorities had replaced the need for multiple professional moving vans with a band of loyal friends and the largest U-Haul trailer we could find. Husbands of my church ladies chose a day of labor in lieu of a day's pay to stack and haul the diminished selections too precious to part with. Their sons and daughters joined my children in a young army of strong backs and willing participation. Dad kept the steady flow of human traffic organized, while Mom and I joined the other females in maintaining sustenance in the form of food, water, and prayer. Two crammed loads and many hours later, the last broom was sweeping the bare floors and all that remained was an empty shell and the unclaimed refrigerator sold at auction and scheduled for pick up the next day. This last remnant of a well-worn past would soon become the cause of an unforeseen (and inconceivable) future.

CHAPTER 5

LOVE BELIEVES ALL THINGS

**Our attitude toward life
determines life's attitude towards us.
- Earl Nightingale -**

I relished the predictability of my first fifteen Christmas mornings and the comfort that comes from living in the same house, spending sleepless nights in the same canopy bed, and reassurance that Santa would always know where to find my stocking. Our move to parts unknown, at the gawky stage between believing and doubting everything, didn't lend any luster of mid-day to objects below, but I still found myself giddy with the prospect of finally achieving a long-held dream of choosing the largest tree in the forest to fill an unfamiliar room with cheer. Our new home was actually a big red barn (minus silos or hay) with enormous windows and ceilings that reached to the sky. They could easily accommodate the twenty-foot tree that I had in mind, and the one that made it atop our vehicle was only shy of that height by a few inches.

The stash of decorations we previously considered abundant fell short of reaching halfway up and twice around. All strands of larger outdoor light bulbs were confiscated and stretched throughout the front and sides with only the neighbor's cows to complain at the tree's bare backside. One of my brothers, home early from college and bored enough to care, took pity on my feeble attempts to lavish the tree with ornaments of sudden miniature proportions and set his architectural expertise to work on a new set of finery to scale. The tree now filled the room with its regal adornment and heady scent of pine, becoming the inspiration for a season full of surprises – and a refrigerator box wrapped in newspaper comics with a tag from my ornery brother to me.

There was nothing in the large red bow or suspicious holes punched at uniformly spaced intervals that gave even a hint of its contents. It became the center of attention and great speculation, providing endless opportunities for teasing me into a constant state of frenzy. With well-timed moments of shaking the box and emitting growls and undefined noises, I was certain that it must contain a pet of some kind but my overactive imagination (from years of short sheeting and pranks) dreaded the discovery of just what species. Love believes all things, and in this case I believed in the power of their suggestions.

They kept the box until last for a grand gift-giving finale as everyone began to roll their tongues in a band of drum rolls. With my eyes half-closed and teeth clenched in anticipation, I carefully peeled away the paper and opened the box…to a huge fern suspended from a hook and dowel. It was a fern…all that for a big, bushy *Boston Fern*? They'd managed to center an entire Christmas season around one illusion of anticipation. Perhaps not then, but certainly now, I can appreciate the brilliance of it all, and be comforted by the promise – certainly not an illusion – of Jesus' anticipated return.

**In times like these, it helps to remember
there have always been times like these.
- Paul Harvey -**

The anticipation and accomplishment of our unprecedented neighborhood sale of the century was finally complete. This was it. All those days of working late and rising early had emptied our former home of its heart and soul, and it broke my own heart to gaze upon the last tangible evidence of our tenure. Cartons of milk and dozens of eggs made the transfer hours ago into their new roomy residence, complete with ice and water on the door. Oh, if only it was that simple to move my tiny band of human nomads into the comfort of climate controlled vegetable bins and take for granted that electricity would power their needs. A flash of memory for that crazy refrigerator box from Christmas long ago reminded me to laugh at the irony of God's repetitive use of mundane objects to grab and hold my attention. I guess the big beige appliance standing before me was as fitting a symbol as any to be the last to let go.

A man arrived at the door with a professional-looking hand truck and a receipt for the collection of his auction prize that stood prominently in the middle of my soon-to-be former kitchen. With bittersweet resignation, a long sigh, and shrug off my shoulders, I motioned him in and watched the old relic strapped in and carefully pulled down the steps and toward its destination for parts unknown, leaving all keys on the counter and shutting the door before I was tempted to look back.

With the distraction of so many memories and a million other details, the absence of multiple moving men waiting in the driveway didn't occur to me until I pulled up short upon arrival at the end of the sidewalk and noticed that there were no more able bodies waiting to assist. I don't know how much a refrigerator weighs, but a recently widowed and weary mother of three and one man half my size were no match for hefting its bulk up and into the rear of his truck.

It was nearing dusk, I hadn't thought to enlist the help of even my boys, and the locked front door wasn't going to allow re-entry for phone support. I was amazed at his assumption that the two of us could do the job of four burly men, but even more incredulous that in my haste to complete the mission I would abandon all reason and agree.

Several minutes of maneuvering had the bulky mass teetering halfway against the tailgate and several feet above the ground. One more thrust pushed it far enough to pull its own weight the rest of the way over, but unfortunately for me instant excruciating pain indicated the possibility of internal organs going with it. I actually heard my body tearing apart and belatedly realized that I should've known better. The reason why I'm able to speak with authority when counseling my children about things they shouldn't do that will harm them is because I have a ridiculously long list of previous experience from which to draw.

After spending the night in our new home, with the smells of fresh paint and deep-heating lotion, it was clear that unpacking without the ability to push or pull in the absence of agony, was in desperate need of postponement. One visit to the doctor and another opinion for good measure indicated the necessity for an operation. The body is a miraculous piece of God's creation, but its limits apparently include the misuse and abuse of stubborn women who unwisely insist on using body parts never intended to be bionic rubber bands.

To date, my hospital experience was limited to three overnights for the birth of my babies, so hysterectomy surgery sounded reassuringly simple by the doctor's explanation that routine and 99% probability for success would have me home the day after. My stupidity got me into this mess, and I hoped they based *their* educated guessing on a much higher learning curve. Ordinarily that would probably hold true, but I'd soon discover what it means to be in the unfortunate group that makes up the 1% minority.

> **Nobody can be in good health if he does not have**
> **fresh air, sunshine, and good water.**
> **- Flying Hawk, Ocala Sioux Chief -**

In another life, surgery of any kind would've been something that I encountered, analyzed with calmness, and bravely endured. However, I never planned on the story of "what I did on summer vacation" to include my husband's funeral in May, auction in June, move in July, back to school for the boys and my daughter's initiation into college in August – to permanently losing my ability to reproduce in October. Half a year vanished, along with the naïve assumption that life takes care of itself, and I found my days consumed with planning not only where to place furniture and photos, but also living wills and estate distribution. The hospital was a stickler for detailing the future, with fine print that eliminated their liability and forced me to contemplate mortality at the same time I was placing sticky note reminders in book bags for tomorrow's teachers.

Ginger's experience with reproductive engineering was messy, but manageable, missing her carefully planned spay surgery by one day and marking her entry into "womanhood" with red streaks across my white carpet on her hormone-charged craze throughout the upstairs. At the time, I dismissed it as rotten luck, but perhaps she and I really are soul sisters and destined to share more than bananas. I would finally know how she must feel about being restricted from the company of mothers who conceive and multiply. We made *her* decision for her, but *I* sealed my own fate by a desire to place expediency above life. I continue to make choices that surely cause heaven to gasp but am forgiven just the same. What a deal.

This new bond of solidarity found Ginger and I engrossed in even more girl talk than usual as we formulated a plan for life before the scalpel and everything after. I decided to make a list of everything I always wanted to do but was either afraid to try or previously seemed frivolous to a wife and mother bound by the dictates of her brood. With Ginger's free-spirited approach to life as my guide, I discarded all former notions of priority as easily as the cellophane enclosing her individually wrapped treats. I don't know if I just imagined her resounding approval of each possibility or if the shaking of her head was merely a response to pesky flies, but the process became a welcomed diversion to otherwise daunting circumstances and "The List" was born.

The biggest enemy of creativity is lack of courage.
Creativity involves risk.
- Sue Monk Kidd -

My fascination with the beauty of the human body is responsible for watching many an old black and white movie with grand musical productions including extravagant dance numbers and the occasional aquatic ballet. Graceful movement and the sway of shimmering fabric always leaves me with a sense of nostalgia and never fails to spark a desire to grab a pair of heels and lose myself in the music (or faded memories of high school dances). I'd tried all the usual childhood requisites of tap and ballet but never got the hang of those toe-shoes that cut the circulation from my legs or spun out of control during pirouette practice. Grace and sway were never my strong suits, but my body was willing, and my mind could still imagine a ballroom full of vitality and me in it.

As a result, top of the list became "learn to dance with confidence in a room full of strangers." With the encouragement of fellow basketball parents and one of their single co-workers, I had just enough time before the hospital would claim me to sign up for a six-week swing dance session at the local rec department. The co-worker was just as uncomfortable as I was in our pairing, but my aversion to much younger male strangers and his phobia of being in the company of anyone female was no match for our mutual desire to learn…and the requirement for couples only. With his gracious cooperation, I was able to stick my toe back in the water of single society while he mastered the ability to lead and eventually dance his way into the arms of the girl at the water cooler whom he previously felt too intimidated by to date.

The finale for our diligent efforts in class participation (and dubious reward for those of us with questionable rhythm) would highlight our "finely honed skills" at a dancing meet-and-greet held conveniently on the weekend prior to my surgery. Even though the thought of dancing in front of a roomful of strangers still raced my pulse to dangerous levels, it was a perfect way to prove to myself once and for all that I really did want to get a life.

Still getting used to the idea of arriving at *anything* solo and fidgeting with the concealment of the hospital bracelet removed only by penalty of law (or a sharp pair of scissors), I appeared to be the only strapless ball gown in the midst of a sea of cowboy boots and flannel. The situation was too funny not to remind me about taking anything – especially myself, too seriously, and I ventured into the room instead of fleeing the scene in mortification. Our instructor had conveniently omitted the fact that our meet-and-greet was actually a western line dance party where our small band of swing-dancing wannabes was to be the nightly intermission's entertainment.

Ginger and Bailey would seize this unique opportunity to shine in the spotlight and dance their way into the hearts of the crowd. I decided to do the same and learned that shining with shimmer is simply a state of mind for those who choose to embrace it. My dogs were creative geniuses that I would definitely need to study more closely.

Friends understand each other's thoughts
even before they are spoken.
- Susan Polis Schutz -

The next morning arrived without fanfare and thankfully flowed smoothly with the benefit of preparation and carefully planned diversionary tactics. Thoughts of sweaty palms and sore feet from my night of dancing with the stars helped to distract attention from the fact that I was dressing for success in the operating room and leaving the children in the care of my dogs. Or was it the other way around?

Regardless, I two-stepped my way out the door with warm, fuzzy socks and a goofy looking pair of back-up glasses that didn't provide sufficient vision to drive but would get me through the hospital without walking into any walls. I assured myself that one night away from home would be good for us all and took the doggies' sad eyes as an indication that maybe they'd even miss me in the process.

My designated driver was the leader of my group of ladies at the church who instantly became my rock of inspiration the moment she shared with us about losing a child through miscarriage many years ago. She never let that loss define her and eventually became the mother of two beautiful children with a loving husband and passion for Christ and gift of prophecy that held me riveted to her revelations. It was tempting to envy her ability to juggle wife, mother, sister, room mom, teacher, and friend; but she taught me the valuable lesson that we all have a very unique path to follow and that God doesn't define "super mom" by the number of positions we manage to pile on our plates.

In characteristic fashion, she still rated super status to me as she tied the skimpy hospital gown in places I couldn't reach and held my hand as we prayed in the sterile surroundings of my holding cell. In the meantime, she became a fitting surrogate for my husband who no longer existed, my mother who found herself torn between caring for an ailing spouse and being there to hold my hand, my boys too young to saddle with this responsibility, and my stand-in for moral support of the daughter unfortunately forced to take it on.

As my only living adult relative within a 350-mile radius, my daughter was the only one who satisfied the hospital's requirement for legitimately signing as the responsible party in charge of my affairs should the unlikely 1% complication happen to arise. She would arrive long after surgery would begin, after completing morning mid-terms and a mad dash through traffic. My heart longed to change the ugly reality of this vulnerable situation, but the physicians warned me not to delay the inevitable, and my little-girl-grown-up assured me that she was her mother's daughter and could handle most anything in the wake of what we'd already endured.

My stalwart friend promised to remain rooted to the waiting room floor and glued to my daughter's side, with assurance that she already had their seats warm and the coffee hot for the duration. With a squeeze of my hand, we parted ways as they wheeled me down the corridor, and the vision of her smiling face faded into anesthetized calm. The last thing I remember was thinking that someone really ought to turn up the heat and fire the guy who insisted on telling bad jokes as he was sticking needles in my arm.

There are no shortcuts to anywhere worth going.
- Anonymous -

There's a lot of hype these days concerning near death experiences and ethereal stories of heaven, seeing long lost relatives, and blinding white lights that beckon to places we yearn to discover. I believe in heaven and hell, admit to a keen interest in their stories, and have always imagined my final destination as a place with incredible color, promise, and lots of bright light.

Nevertheless, *I* awoke from my own near death experience with my surgeon hovering much too close to my face and asking the laughable question of "How do you feel?" I answered in what was probably a slurred sarcastic retort, "Like a truck just ran me over." She smothered a nervous giggle and proceeded to explain that my routine hysterectomy didn't go as well as planned and that I was now to be the proud owner of a scar reaching from one hip to the other.

Whatever happened to blinding white lights and feelings of peace so overwhelming that you don't want to return to earth? All *I* could remember was the irritating guy with the needles one minute, and the smell of the doctor's hairspray and mouthwash the next. I had no memory of the multiple missing hours in between that included emergency C-section, interruption of numerous tee-times for doctors on call, and noisy monitors going blank. Evidently, my body decided it didn't appreciate manipulation and nearly bled itself to death while a swat team of medical tailors tried desperately to sew me back together. I guess I wouldn't be going home the next day.

Make a nest of pleasant thoughts.
- Unknown –

The meandering path through mazes of echoing hallways took me several floors up to the room that would become my home for the duration of this sudden extended stay. I struggled to gain consciousness over the overwhelming desire for surrender back to blessed sleep and focused on the count of fluorescent ceiling tiles and bells of the rising elevator floors from the perch atop my bed on wheels.

I randomly wondered if hospitals double-booked their rooms as the airlines do, making it a bit crowded when people like me wander in unexpectedly. Suspecting the possibility of being confused with the patient next door, I did a quick inventory of my new digs for future insurance bill verification, nodding on and off between calculations. The volume of tubes and machines indicated the lack of need for bedpans or walkers since they securely fastened me to the wall in a way that wouldn't allow free access about the cabin. I didn't intend to pay for multiple boxes of tissues either. What absurd things to ponder on the aftermath of averted mortality. I chalked it up to the bag of morphine dripping into my veins from the apparatus by my side and must've drifted off again to happier times since I later shocked back to life at the sound of my offspring loudly making their way through the door.

Pitch dark through my cubicle window signaled the late time of day, and I breathed a sigh of relief that my children weren't skipping school to witness this feeble excuse of their extravagantly drug-induced mother. Understandably avoiding the reality of nearly losing their only remaining parent in less than a cycle of months, their chatter was quick, constant, and clever in an attempt to divert all conversation from the fact that their mother lay helpless in a sea of tubing with a death grip on the clicker that fed the morphine machine.

They found great humor in watching me pitch the clicker aside in my impatience with its lack of ability to ease my exploding pain. Their hilarious laughter was contagious, and though I loathed seeing them depart, it hurt even too much to form a smile, and I begged them to leave. The tears that trickled down my cheeks would have to suffice for this night's humorous outlet and could play a dual role with the heartbreak working its way through my vulnerable soul.

I'm an avid reader of historical romance novels and had packed my overnight bag with plenty of material that I foolishly imagined to finish during my previously anticipated overnight stay. The night nurse kindly pulled a selection from the zippered pocket and placed it between a tray of ice water and the vomit pail. It was my fervent hope that I'd only need two out of three as the night progressed. As I read the same paragraph for what seemed like the twelfth time, it eventually crossed my mind that my body was buzzing from head to toe as if all my nerves were on top of my skin and standing at rigid attention. I couldn't relax long enough to concentrate on anything more complex than knowing that something was horribly wrong. Someone's thoughtful prediction that things like this happen made it protocol to place the nurse's call button just beneath the only unrestricted finger left, and I mashed an urgent call for help.

91

Is not life more than food?
- Matthew 6:25 -

God has always gotten my attention with food, whether it was through nursing guidance when dealing with baby number two (born the size of a normal three-month-old with the grip of a steel trap) or much later, when I found myself drowning from too much of what I thought was a good thing and a sinking ship of food-induced depression. In any case, He always seems to know what will stimulate my immediate positive reactions.

He corrected the first situation with the use of a handy – and very thick, rubberized contraption that placed merciful distance between the jaws of my hungry newborn and my ravaged skin. This blessed answer to anguished prayer began my personal encounters with The Big Guy in the intimacy of the shower. I suppose this choice of venue owes more to the fact that it confines me in a wall of water until washed clean than the truth that distractions that keep me from hearing Him more clearly await on the other side of the door. He communicates in short one to three word phrases such as "trust me," "be still," and "thick, rubberized contraption." By keeping it simple, I have no chance of misinterpretation or time to hide under the bathroom rug.

God handled the second situation with the ironic assistance of my steel trap, who by now was many years older – and much wiser than his mother seemed to be. Having instilled a love of reading in all of my kids, this epiphany happened in a bookstore on a day that also found me frantically searching the 7-Elevens for the last of my favorite non-alcoholic six-packs in town and bouncing from one mood to another in an unsettling and embarrassing display of volatility.

My poor son's requirement for school reading must've

outweighed his desire to avoid me for the day as we perused the aisles together and managed to lose ourselves in the pages of someone else's reality. Random selection brought my son and a particular book to my side in what proved to be one of the most profound discoveries of my life. He thrust it under my nose with the prophetic statement "this sounds like something *you* need, Mom." Its title held promise for an alternative to my own pitiful reality with the words "Potatoes Not Prozac." Having taken the little green pills for depression for months – without noticeable improvement my son might add, the food reference speared me with interest – as God knew it would.

After reading the first paragraph, two questions immediately came to mind. First, how did this author know me so well? Had she caught me on camera hiding in the pantry with the door closed while I gulped down that last piece of cake before anyone could discover my shameful secret? How did she know that I couldn't rest until consuming the entire half-gallon of ice cream I'd just purchased and taken straight from the car or devouring every crumb from the bag of cookies left from last night's supper? She'd managed to condense my dirty little secret into several hundred pages bound neatly between the covers of her research on food addiction…so that's what it was.

All these years, I just thought I was doomed to live in a pear-shaped body with a predilection toward all things containing dough or sugar sprinkles. She offered hope by naming this phenomenon "sugar sensitivity," and urged me to back away from the refrigerator and dispose of all foods containing the color white and to replace them with my new best friends brown and green. After embracing the color wheel and her book of theories, which after exhaustive experimentation actually worked for me, I bid a tearful farewell to my last can of soda and the wonderful world of sugar.

In addition, lest I forget, the second question I had after reading the book's opening salvo involved the nagging suspicion that Ginger had somehow traded information for treats. I decided to forego a tendency towards conspiracy theories and chose instead to believe in her genuine desire for my health and well-being. I guess it didn't matter why, what, or who changed my life, as long as it was for the better. My family could finally expel a collective sigh of gratitude and as far as Ginger was concerned, I could return to a focus of nothing but her – and occasionally, her and Bailey.

Listening is where love begins.
- Fred Rogers -

After spending the night turned on constant "high," the haggard bunch of twilight nurses turned into a new crew with the light of day, and I told anyone who'd listen about the strange sensations that were pulsing throughout my body. I hadn't slept since awakening from the anesthesia half a day ago, and it seemed only logical to be asking for answers to a question that had never arisen before. This "one percent" patient was alive and trying to get well, although running out of patience and inventive ways to attract *someone's* attention.

The nurse's station had long past decided that I was "one of those" patients adversely affected by drugs and relegated all response to my repeated summons to orderlies randomly grabbed from the hall. I resorted to desperate tactics with the only means in front of me, with creative manipulation of the daily menu one of them just dropped within reach. I'd written "no sugar" in bold capital letters across all the pre-op paperwork pertaining to allergies, and decided to try enlisting the help of at least the lunch crew in my desire to stay on track with food. Bingo! Those two little words must've finally caught the attention of the liability police with their nutrition expert appearing in the doorway quite out of breath and suddenly willing to listen to the loon whom they hoped wouldn't sue for food poisoning or anaphylactic shock.

I finally had the ear of someone who cared. And at this point, it didn't matter to me whether money or my health was the reason. I downloaded my symptoms in nauseating detail and waited to hear the usual, "I've never heard of that happening before." Imagine my surprise when she began to investigate my chart and all the tubes running in and out of my appendages and suddenly held up one of the bags of fluid and let out a triumphant "Ta-da!"

Evidently, someone with a license to practice medicine *without* exemplary reading skills and attention to detail, had overlooked my explicit warning to avoid the sweet white stuff, and was pumping glucose into my veins with stunning ignorance. Armed with newfound knowledge from my trusty "Potatoes Not Prozac," even I, with limited medical expertise, now knew that a person with sugar sensitivity reacts to glucose in much the same way as drug addicts reacts to cocaine. That information, coupled with losing enough blood just this side of needing transfusions, indicated this was *not* a good idea.

At least now, I knew that eighteen hours of a drip-line high was the culprit that had elevated my blood pressure that sent me into hyperactive drive and not a sudden attack of insanity or some weird desire to rail on the help. The nutritionist replaced the glucose with a simple saline solution that hydrated without turning me into a zombie, and I think I fell asleep before she even got the door closed behind her.

It took four days to convince damage control that I was finally able to function normally, cleverly disguising the fact that several minutes expired each time I shuffled from my bed to the bathroom, and that I'd been subsisting on smuggled food alone, and not the Cafeteria's one-size-fits-all cuisine. They still didn't seem to grasp the concept of sugar sensitivity, insisting on serving hefty portions of sweetened lime Jell-O and mashed potatoes swimming in greasy gravy. What I wouldn't give for a warm bath with bubbles and a piece of homemade bread.

This environment did nothing for digestion *or* a good night's sleep, and I felt certain that my recovery hinged on escape. This came in the form of release papers on a Friday afternoon just prior to another shift change and thankfully before the evening meal. I use that term loosely, since it happened to be chicken surprise with a side of guess-what-flavor Jell-O. The requisite wheel chair and candy-striped volunteer provided a competent bon voyage, as I sent a grateful thank-you to heaven above and basked in the sight through the exit doors to my right.

Three of my husband's most prized possessions stared back in an unlikely welcome committee of two teenage boys and the 1975 Olds 442, gleaming from a recent wash and wax. I assumed all three benefited from the wash, but hoped the wax was only on the car. This particular model included massive steel doors and swivel seats, both options I'd previously dismissed with ambivalence and now humbly accepted for their generous ease of entry.

The muscle car of his dreams had more history with my husband than I did and proved my nemesis for years. Every time we seemed to garner a little extra cash, it mysteriously moved from my decorating budget into a category generously named "restorative parts." It was the first new car he had ever owned, driven to pick me up on our first date, and passed on to our son who willingly accepted the testosterone-based tradition of continuing to sink massive sums of money into its equally massive parts of steel. Defeated by the acceptance that there is a strong brotherhood devoted to all things male; I made the painful transition from wheelchair to my awaiting chariot and thankfully headed for home.

What I'm looking for is a blessing that's not in disguise.
- Jerome K. Jerome -

Oh, how I'd missed Ginger and Bailey…and how much it hurt when they jumped at my battered body with unreserved glee. New ground rules emerged immediately, as I checked bandages for bleeding and administered attention to all fresh scratches within reach. The boys disappeared to their rooms with a pizza in one hand, and the remote in another. The dogs and I headed to bed.

It was heaven. No annoying machines, tubes, or needles, and there were plenty of pillows and blankets to accompany sole possession of the thermostat control. I gingerly discarded my "going to the hospital" uniform of zippered sweats and left them in a heap on the floor, resigning myself to the conclusion that any habits of order and cleanliness vanished with my ability to bend at the waist.

Bailey assumed the pile was one of his, sniffed at the anesthetic odors, and disappointedly abandoned them for the comfort at the foot of the bed. Ginger already lay at her staked claim beside me, but sensed the need for an invisible force field by my unspoken request for space. Well, maybe it had more to do with the fact that I lay stiff as a board on my back, with both arms guarding my sutures and legs bent at the knee for additional fortification. In any case, this was where you'd find us anytime in the near future, and I was more than happy to trade their occasional snores for the wretched hospital ambience of my recently vacated room.

My surgeon was highly competent and very astute in her supposition that my pain throughout the next several weeks would far surpass the "frowny-face" on her comfort chart, and prescribed extreme doses of narcotics designed to either reduce my limbs to useless stubs or knock me out completely – whichever came first. As wild hallucination after another presented themselves throughout that first night, it was only the warm reassurance from the doggies beside me *and* the fact that movement of any kind sent nauseating waves of pain from my toes to my exploding brain, that kept me immobile and sane.

I quit taking pills sometime in the dark of night, and dawn brought me lucid and ready to strangle anyone in a white lab coat. A plea to the doctor on call managed to open a line of communication with a nurse in some remote location (probably the comfort of her own home) who offered a different prescription – *if* I'd be willing to make the 60-mile trek downtown – and arrive before noon. Well…I couldn't even make it to the bathroom, let alone the garage, so that nixed that idea. Neither was I sending my 16-year-old with a brand new driver's license into the accident capital of the world. The nurse was adamant about not allowing my local pharmacist to provide the paperwork necessary for changing a legally regulated substance, which was probably readily (albeit illegally) available on any of the city streets she suggested my son travel, so I reluctantly chose to spend the remainder of the weekend without hallucinatory drugs.

This choice might seem to hover dangerously close to cruel

and unusual punishment, but actually rates in the top three of my most liberating decisions to date. First, of course, would be accepting Jesus Christ as my Lord and Savior, then the freedom of finally discarding my wristwatch for the possibilities of life without self-imposed timelines. The decision to live through excruciating pain and savor the victory with a clear head when it was finally over definitely slides in at a close number three.

I think the devil has a major in marketing and a minor in advertising, the way the world has swallowed the idea that pain of any kind disappears by popping a pill. I don't have any higher threshold for pain than the next person, but I can tell you from experience that the human body is equipped with the capacity to endure what the mind has convinced impossible. By choosing to go it alone those three little days in the span of a lifetime, I set myself up for a future of healthy alternatives that continue to serve me well. I did that for myself, but how much more awesome it is to think about Jesus doing that and more for all of us.

The medical community that pulled me through peril wasn't impressed with my steadfast plan but decided to keep my chart on file and monitor my progress anyway. They became observers in what they deemed a futile experiment but reluctantly admitted eight weeks later that never before had a patient bounced back to normal with such speed and miraculous healing. I tried to share with them about how all the home cooked meals prepared to my dietary restrictions, chauffeurs to doctor appointments when I couldn't drive, walking the dogs when I couldn't, and the constant prayers for a widow and her children were the recipes for success, but they didn't understand what appeared to them old-fashioned and unbelievable. We just didn't read the same non-fiction. They buried their heads in medical journals while I preferred the Bible.

CHAPTER 6

LOVE IS NOT BOASTFUL

**What if you woke up today with only the things
you asked God for yesterday.
- Erin Clarkson -**

I once ran across the lovely French phrase "wit of the staircase" which refers to all the things you think to say while *leaving* a party that you wish you'd thought to say while you were still there. Spending eight weeks after surgery doing nothing more physical than healing, reading, grieving my dearly-departed husband, and keeping doggie tails out from under my rocker, I experienced meditation on steroids and the condensed version of grief management without the benefit of life's normal interruptions. This abundance of time to devote to thinking alone produced more than enough "wit" for the staircase that I wasn't even allowed to utilize until driving rights and the keys (my son hid weeks ago) were reinstated.

I re-wrote the scene a hundred times in which I bid a fond farewell to my husband on the last morning I looked into his eyes and kissed him goodbye. Those are such common occurrences in the span of a marriage, yet convey everything you need your loved one to know. I could've told him how much I appreciated his laughter, our children, or his indomitable spirit of provision, but chose instead to give him a little sugar and send him on his way so I could go hang the new bedroom drapes.

Those drapes now hung in a new room in which I read myself to sleep each night in a bed too large and empty, despite Ginger and Bailey's attempts to fill it abundantly. Often waking too soon to start another day, many an hour passed with the draperies parted to the light of a moon that never seemed interested in my lonely conversations. It is sage advice never to put off for tomorrow what you can do (or say) today, and life is always full of opportunities to choose. I choose life…and it was way past time for me to create a new one.

It'd been weeks since I first embarked upon this journey of nearly losing my life, but "The List" of things I always wanted to do if I ever got one (a life, that is) was still buried somewhere beneath the growing stack of bills. I viewed the checklist with fresh eyes and hopeful importance. My days of dancing might be a thing of the past, but by now I was way past eliminating fear of the unknown, so this was going to be fun. I believed in the theory that knowledge is power and subscribed to several newspapers with society columns and cultural interest reviews. I wanted to see museum exhibits, listen to symphony orchestras, peruse the aisles of antique markets, and dine gourmet. I wanted to purge my wardrobe, color my hair, and buy a convertible. I even went to Section C and contemplated season tickets to pro football – or maybe even hockey or horses.

The list was endless, and I found myself exhilarated with its infinite possibilities. I pulled out the calendar and marked all the dates for upcoming events through the end of the year. All those pages of empty squares with an occasional school function or doctor visit now registered concerts, salon appointments, and fascinating exhibits of art.

I ordered two tickets for everything and opened the mail with the excitement of Christmas morning the day my treasure arrived. I lay them on the table, each sitting next to its corresponding date on the calendar, and gazed upon the itinerary before me. I caught myself holding my breath in the sheer anticipation of what I was really getting ready to do…until it hit me that in my ascent into this brave new world I neglected one tiny, albeit important, detail. Two tickets, only one of me.

I would have lost heart, unless I had believed
That I would see the goodness of the Lord
In the land of the living.
- Psalm 27:13 -

Ever since I was old enough to have an opinion, I can remember wishing for several things – looking out from the crown of the Statue of Liberty, standing at the foot of the Redwoods, and driving the stick shift of a little yellow Triumph. The year I turned sixteen, I came home from a birthday lunch to an opened garage that revealed my yellow dream. She was a beauty, complete with a black ragtop and a dent in the rear bumper that gave me comfort that I wouldn't be the first to give her a scratch. I'll never forget the simultaneous shift from elation to deflation as I slid into the driver's seat…and realized I had no idea how to manipulate a manual transmission, let alone get it started. It took weeks to master all my brother taught me about the art of stick shifting, but it left an early impression that love really isn't boastful. To think that I manage to achieve anything without His grace or someone He's sent me is foolish.

It would appear that I'd require several reminders of this same lesson as I stood looking at the multiple pairs of tickets with a stupid look on my face and neck pain from shaking it side to side in dumbfounded comprehension. Forward momentum always comes to a screeching halt when I fail to include others or pay attention to the driver's manual.

You'd think that my Triumph, at least, would've taught me a lesson or two. One, don't buy a temperamental foreign car for use in heavy weather without a permanent set of jumper cables in the trunk or able-bodied chaperone to push you downhill for each running start. Two, never leave home without working wiper blades when the forecast calls for monsoons with tornado activity and you're heading toward large bodies of water. And three, a colorful exterior with cute lines is no substitute for the reliability of a clunker with great gas mileage.

My mission was clear. Enlist the help of others, and be careful not to overlook the "clunkers" in my search for a new seat partner. I vaguely remembered a friend giving me a flier for some highly touted dating service during my recuperation. At the time, I'd tossed it into that ever-growing stack of bills and accumulated junk mail on my desk, thinking something like that would never be necessary. OK, so I was wrong. The ad for navigating the single scene suddenly took on new meaning, and I hoped that it included someone like me and not reserved solely for the young and looking for love.

All the married couples I formerly hung out with took turns including me in their own versions of happiness, but being the "odd man out" created confusion in restaurant seating and often left me sitting by myself at a table for two or in the extra chair jammed into the aisle at the end of the table. I appreciated their willingness to get me out of the house and into the company of adults, but they already had their two-by-two things going and it no longer included me. This was definitely a consequence to my aversion for making friends outside of my own household. Unfortunately, Ginger didn't meet height or dress code requirements for the places I wanted to go, and I craved the opportunity for a two-way conversation that involved more than patient adoration and a warm nose on my knee.

The whole idea of heading downtown for a videotaped

interview that would debut in a dating service client base by morning was daunting. I was a mid-life crisis mom with two dogs and a preference for the comforts of home. This was so far out of my zone that it had to be God's plan, but that, and the fact that all participants participated in the same criminal background check, gave me the courage to leave my car in the parking lot and finally make my way inside the agency's door. I flipped through several books filled with glossy photos of hopeful contestants in this bizarre game of chance and belatedly realized that my own "deer in the headlights" mug shot would soon join their ranks.

Whatever happened to the good old process of girl meets boy at the diner, waiting in line at the movies, or hanging out at the mall? I met my husband on a blind date, which of course (why didn't I think of this before?) included the help of a co-worker who "just knew we'd be a perfect match." I left the work scene three teenagers ago, so that fleeting thought fizzled before it even began. It all seemed so surreal, especially with it happening on the day of what should've been wedding anniversary twenty-one. That thought alone made me want to cry and harangue my husband for his absence all at the same time. Being single wasn't much fun, and at the age of forty-four it never occurred to me that this would be the life I was living. I told myself to get over it and managed to proceed when summoned to the nearest cubicle.

The process was very tedious and obscenely expensive – a lot like Ginger and Bailey's maintenance. The interview consisted mostly of reams of paper with questions ranging from intrusive to absurd, with lots of pencil pushing and filling in the squares. I have the awkward inclination to say aloud what my mind is thinking and came away hoping that my old-fashioned opinions about their "state-of-the-art" matchmaking didn't escape too loudly.

They took a few pictures, deposited my check in a drawer bulging with all the others and sent me out the door with instructions to buy a new wardrobe suitable for nights on the town. Evidently, my matching two-piece church pantsuit didn't produce waves of excitement for my prospects, and they warned me to "be patient." I lived outside the customary driving range for their dating pool, was too young to be a logical choice for most widows, and too old for most everyone else. With a hole in my budget the size of my audible sigh, I headed back to suburbia and those soothing unfashionable comforts of home.

> **If you ask me what I came to do in this world,**
> **I, an artist, will answer you:**
> **I am here to live out loud.**
> **- Emile Zola -**

Patience is the virtue that I mastered long ago on the bleachers of too many practice fields to remember but always seems easier to sustain when it pertains to others. The phone seemed to ring only with telemarketers still trying to sell useless articles to my deceased husband and not with the strange voices of new people who longed to meet me. Refusing to give up before losing my nerve, I began to shop in earnest for clothing, that perfect shade of hair dye, and a new convertible to cruise around the block just in case that's as far as I'd ever go.

I ventured into virgin territory at boutiques named for adult women instead of places with rows of shopping carts parked at the front door and filled my closet with the latest fashions despite the unshakable habit of making a bee line to the nearest clearance rack upon entering each store. With the encouragement and guidance from my daughter's vast knowledge of dating attire, I reluctantly emerged with a much lighter pocketbook and great looking hair a la Salon Fifty-Four.

The convertible on my wish list definitely took the biggest bite from my budget, with a trip north to the big city and the assistance of our family moneyman. His credibility for producing the impossible was fresh in my mind from having just navigated me through mountains of estate settlement papers and the reassurance of insurance checks in my hand. I had no doubt about his touted connections with the largest auto auction in the south.

Nobody needed to convince *me* that this was another part of The Plan. Where else could I drive a loaded monstrosity of a conversion van (that no longer hauled more than the dogs and a few bags of groceries) into one lot and drive away the same day with a gently worn ragtop Beamer with extended warranty to boot? It wasn't yellow, brand new, or decked out with sporty trim, but I felt like a new woman and ready to take on the world in this five-speed blessing. The world would have to wait as I picked up my boys instead, and we celebrated by driving to dinner with the top down – which unfortunately decided that very evening to stick in place and necessitate immediate examination of how extended my new warranty really was.

Perhaps this was an elaborate scheme to build my virtue and character. Whatever the reason, waiting for car repairs *and* dating replacements had me edgy and more than ready to move on. I'd just spent months sitting under house arrest while recuperating and wasn't about to wither from lack of locomotion. Ginger and Bailey were quite content with my recent return to homebody status, but even *I* have a limit to the number of times I'm willing to scratch bellies and wait for the cows to come home. It wasn't even that I looked forward to the prospect of having to dress up and make polite conversation with people I didn't know. It just seemed a pity to waste all those clothes and forward momentum to lousy luck with cars and a fickle group of men who happened to be as single as I was.

Many a night would find me stationed on the front porch steps staring at the vast open sky and wondering if my husband could hear me amidst the crickets and car horns in the distance. After falling into a routine of dinner, homework, and dishes, then giving up on TV after going once around the dial, the porch offered a place to think with just enough nip in the air to my freezing nose to remind me that I could still feel more than an empty heart. Bailey had always retired early and rarely joined Ginger and me on this nightly ritual, so it became a new therapeutic twist to girl's night out.

Poor Ginger had to hear me rant at the moon and commiserate about lonely days, endless nights, and overall frustration with life. She was a body to lean on and fur to stroke while I cried my tears and shared a mountain of impossible dreams and ideas. We could've built a city with all the plans we put together, but by that time of day neither one of us aspired to go much further than the end of the driveway, and we always seemed more willing to retreat to the warmth of the bed Bailey so thoughtfully preheated hours earlier.

I don't believe in luck, destiny, *or* fate. God has a plan – it's as simple as that, and all the fretting in the world won't make the phone ring any faster or the car appear in the driveway the day before it's due. One day just finally arrives and blesses us with results – easy to say, *after* it happens. Nevertheless, my vehicle miraculously appeared just in time to meet contestant number one in this crazy scheme for simply finding someone to use all those extra tickets. Only time would tell if I, or the scheme, was the crazy one.

We are always the same age inside.
- Gertrude Stein -

All those words expelled from the front porch must've made their way up, since it wasn't long after that they fell back like gentle rain on the fields of my sorrow. Church offered a well-timed sequel to my first Disciple class that miraculously filled with all the ladies who pulled me through summer, cared for me all autumn, and now joined ranks to encourage and support my holiday foray into crisis dating. We were all pitifully rusty with feminine charms and artfully selected conversation meant to attract the opposite sex, but this group of well-chosen comrades were determined to live vicariously through me and took on the challenge as though they were sixteen and dating again.

Just as every mother has her baby birthing story or the day you sent your firstborn off to school, each woman had at least one hilarious tale of dates gone wrong or one absolute rule to follow – no matter what. They were enthralled with my list of things to do and lined up to be the designated caller (once I actually had a date) who rang to interrupt the proceedings in case I needed an excuse to leave.

Most of the absolute rules no longer applied after twenty years of feminine progress, though I steadfastly held on to waiting for doors to be opened, never kissing on the first date, and still believed in nature's gift of blushing. It's disappointing to note that I eventually resorted to disembarking on my own in lieu of waiting for dates to realize they'd entered functions without me. Most everyone I would meet had abandoned the desire for conversation along with their compulsion to walk a woman to her own front door, so no worries about kissing when there wasn't even going to be a second date. Blushing…well, most guys thought blushing was some kind of hygienic malfunction best relieved with talcum or salve.

Every Wednesday morning brought new questions or suggestions as my dating welfare became the class project that preceded each week's favorite scripture. Ironically, words of wisdom always managed to appear with each new report, and the day I finally shared that "we" had an impending date met with collective excitement and nervous misgivings. We'd spent weeks talking about what-ifs and why-nots, but the reality of what I was about to do hit us all with a major dose of "what was I thinking?" I suddenly felt old and inadequate, but looked around the room and realized that I wasn't alone on this journey and didn't get to this point without ammunition. A lot was riding on this adventure and I *would not* fail.

We do not stop playing because we grow old.
We grow old because we stop playing.
- Anonymous -

One of my Mom's favorite relatives was a fascinating Great Aunt by the name of Elma. She was a free-spirited trendsetter, judging by old family photos and lore, who doted on her only grandniece the same way she'd favored her nephew. Attending the Chicago World's Fair of 1893, it's easy to suspect that she made the journey by train alone, making friends along the way and leaving many a broken heart along the shores of Lake Michigan. Evidently sowing all the wild oats she could savor, precious Elma married Uncle Miller several years later, adding one more colorful character to our lineage of eccentrics.

When I was a little girl, we used to visit the quirky couple quite often. Never having children of their own, Mom and I were oddities that rated special treatment. Their home seemed like a Victorian castle to me with all its gingerbread, overgrown hibiscus, and hoarded (necessarily breakable) treasures. Their most prized possessions filled dozens of what-nots in the formal parlor, where I was allowed to gaze but never touch. Aunt Elma passed on years before her husband, but the visiting ritual remained until Uncle Miller's mind took a turn of its own and decided that he no longer knew us.

Uncle Miller had always seemed crazy to me, so our family's expulsion came as no surprise. The last time I remember being in the great house on the little hill, he didn't even let me into the parlor. Instead, he confined me to a hard-backed chair in the kitchen and served rancid butter on ancient saltine crackers. It took years to wash the taste of that memory from my mind and still keeps me leery of fresh milk from a cow. Perhaps my aversion to misplaced hospitality would serve me well in the anticipated dating scene before me.

I speak from experience when I say that there's truth to the warning that men who've never been married before might best be avoided, especially if you're a widow used to having a relationship with a man who was used to you. I realize that years of living with the same person have a way of quickly teaching that sharing and compromise produce amazing results, but I never expected anyone getting all the way to middle age and more closely resembling one of my son's narcissistic teenage friends than any of my close peers.

Contestant Number One's profile looked promising on paper…never married, Chief of a nearby fire station, interested in sports, outdoor activities, and love of family. Unfortunately, our meeting in person revealed a completely different human being than the one described perfectly in black and white. Reluctant participants on the dating scene who merely wish to prove to firehouse buddies that a preference for beer with the guys is no indication of prowess with the ladies should fall under full disclosure on the profile questionnaire.

My head felt like exploding after two hours of listening with rapt attention and a smile on my face to stories tall enough to question and void of sports, the great outdoors, *or* love. I had to admit that his extended family of nieces and nephews sounded like interesting people I might like to meet, but I wasn't sitting across the table from them. If that funny feeling of intuition and growing indigestion in my stomach weren't enough, the minute we both stood to leave and his head didn't even reach past my nose was enough to squelch an already dubious future.

If he'd lie about his height, what else could he be hiding? Maybe an axe from the station that just happened to find its way into his trunk... I would *not* be repeating this with him again. Life is too short to waste on nonsense that I didn't even appreciate when I was young enough to care. To think that I'd spent weeks building up my nerve just for something like *this*. The girls at Disciple class were going to be very disappointed. I sure was.

My own profile listed very few, but meaningful, specifications. I was looking for a healthy six-foot or taller single male who lived their faith in God. Who knew that this rated in today's secular world as somewhere between figment of my imagination and someone from days gone by? Discouraged, but not defeated, I resigned myself to clarifying my wish list and to daily reminders that I might be waiting patiently for something that no longer existed.

Contestant Number Two evidently never heard the rental

car ad about trying harder. We agreed to meet at one of my favorite restaurants (with items I could actually order off the menu) clear on the other side of town. I was willing to do whatever it took to meet and greet the best this agency had to offer, so what were a few extra miles? Dressed to the nines in one of my stylish new suits, he recognized me immediately from my description over the phone – or maybe because I looked like the fish out of water wearing extremely uncomfortable high heels.

Dispensing with the same small talk I'd encountered on the last date, I assumed the next step would be arriving for our reservation. As I began to walk from the lobby into the restaurant, imagine my surprise when he grabbed my arm instead and steered me out the door. A half mile and several parking lots later, we arrived at an indoor mall for the chat and window-shopping marathon he'd really planned to do while we "got to know each other better."

This lasted through two exhaustive floors on those blister-causing heels, and ended at the food court where he suggested that we "go Dutch." Who knew that mentioning a desire to eat when it was already three hours past my normal dinnertime would be such an alarming issue. My stomach was growling in earnest, my head was pounding from lack of nourishment, and quite honestly, I'd run out of polite conversation two department stores ago. Baffled by his behavior and wondering if all my encounters were destined to rate in the too-weird-to-be-true category, he suddenly laid his head on crossed arms upon the table and announced that he was too tired to go on.

This was unbelievable. I spent the ride home on a mad dash to get a sandwich before closing and unloaded an earful on any canines listening about my propensity for attracting loons. I wondered aloud if there might be something in the fine print of my contract about a money-back guarantee. (There was none…I checked). With 18 more dates to go and a sickening sense that it would only get worse, Ginger agreed that I'd be further ahead to smuggle *her* into the seat beside me for next week's show rather than risk meeting any more of the "best singles in the city."

There had to be a lesson here somewhere, but for the life of me I couldn't see it. Ginger's encouraging silence and Bailey's comforting snores might have to be companionship enough. After meeting two of the city's "finest," I deemed myself fortunate to have dogs as best friends.

In the multitude of my anxieties within me,
Your comforts delight my soul.
- Psalm 94:19 -

All of the grief manuals say the same thing. You have to get through a year's worth of holidays and memorable moments before moving on. With Christmas fast approaching, I decided that a trip to Florida's sandy shores sounded much more enticing than struggling with decorations I didn't care to hang in a house full of people with only one wish of making it through the season in one piece.

None of us could imagine this holiday without Dad. His legacy *was* Christmas, and now it would never be the same. He shopped all year to create the perfect morning – which of course it never was, but in his dreams and our memories, we all thought it should be. I couldn't begin to fill his shoes and certainly didn't come equipped with his love of finding just the right gift at all the lowest sale prices within a day's drive. A week of sun and sand would have to suffice.

After all, how could anyone compete with Santa leaving a

camera under the tree with the first five frames filled with photos of him and the reindeer – all before the film even started counting? Or, how about the year we found our new house (that we didn't move in to until weeks later) unlocked on Christmas Eve…with gorgeous rugs on the freshly varnished hardwood for me, and impossible to find Power Ranger figures on the hearth for the rest of the family? Funny, how we never noticed at the time that there was nothing there for Dad.

I could never fill his shoes and had no desire to try. I packed our bags and headed south to meet my side of the family in an attempt to forget what we'd be missing and act as if we were having fun anyway. It was a difficult lesson in learning that changing the scenery doesn't change a thing if you're still living inside the same head. "Location, location, location" drilled a message into my brain as I escaped each evening to the solitude of an empty beach and too many of the same stars that I counted on the porch back home. Where was Ginger when I needed her? Just because the floor plan was different and we were eating out of cans and pizza boxes, it didn't change the fact that it was still Christmas minus the one who loved it the most.

By an unprecedented unanimous vote, we all gave up pretending and chose to leave several days shy of our week's reservation and began the long drive home. My youngest drew the short straw and headed north with me, loaded with enough batteries to power his video games and hours of music to drown out the pain. This left me with my own thoughts, which was dangerous even on a good day. Ginger and Bailey would be glad to see me return, but other than that, the future looked bleak. I couldn't shake the feeling of failure at my attempt to gain access to the single side of society but didn't know how to give up and only knew that solitude was a poor second to having someone to share it with. I would just have to "be still" and wait for miracles.

One week remained in the year I would most like to forget. A quick wash, fold, and store of vacation attire for four filled but one boring day, so I took to the trails we knew by heart and walked the dogs briskly in a futile attempt to clear the cobwebs and forge a new battle plan. I preferred early mornings just before dawn when puffs of steam rose from the backs of my little ones' warm fur and I could see my breath in the light of the street lamps. It became habit long ago to speak softly to God and carry a big stick (for any snakes in the woods) as a way to start my day. I never doubted that He heard me and thanked Him daily for sending me two adorable sounding boards who never failed to listen or unconditionally desire *my* desires.

With renewed vigor and slightly chapped lips, we returned home that morning to another mundane but well-planned day. This included a round of groceries, banking, and filling the tank, followed by a brown-bagged lunch in the car and my annual eye exam. After months of waiting by the phone for dates that disappointed or never came, I found chatting with the latest helper at the meat market more interesting than my own company. My furry friends were short on conversation, and I found myself looking forward to my exam's eye drops and questions like "can you see better here...or there?" I even found the prospect of finding someone in the waiting room willing to abandon his or her magazine and listen a worthy pursuit.

My optometrist saw me with promptness and time to spare, which immediately alerted me to the possibility of multiple cancellations – or divine intervention. After all, what or *who* else could manage those two phenomenon in the same day. With confirmation that I was still seeing 20/20, we then moved on to unbelievable topics such as sports, our children's latest academic achievements…and dating. OK, now I *knew* this was weird. We traveled in very different social circles, lived in polar opposite neighborhoods, and I couldn't even fathom a guess where the conversation was heading.

My temporary shock gave him plenty of room to embellish, and I soon realized that my attempts to get a life must've become common knowledge in town much more quickly (and embarrassingly) than I thought possible. He shared in detail his own experience with dating after divorce and highly recommended the worldwide web as the latest in technological matchmaking. He made it sound safe and easy – in a clinical sort of way, making the people and places he met sound normal and exotic at the same time. Of course, actually sharing a meal in a restaurant with someone honest and awake seemed normal and exotic at this point.

Unbeknownst to me, the doctor was quite an expert at many things besides optometry and sent me on my way with his bill and a personal recommendation for a free month's subscription to Match.com. Further investigation revealed a program touting the latest techniques and largest supply of searching singles in the nation all at the stroke of a key. This idea definitely held promise. I could access thousands of people in the comfort of my own home whenever I chose to sign on and nobody would ever know if I was wearing my robe and slippers at two in the morning *or* afternoon. After only a slight hesitation with my finger hovering above "apply here," I took a deep breath and sent my life zooming in a new direction.

A new awareness of time's passage
has scared me into action.
- Ann Wood -

I sometimes think that I was born in the wrong century. I love the written word and get goose bumps whenever trying to decipher the beautiful swirls of calligraphy found in a forgotten bin at some nondescript flea market somewhere. I also like to send (and receive) letters in the mail so I tried to reconcile the two when contemplating my latest endeavor of communication on a sterile piece of equipment void of emotion *or* swirls. The possibility of connecting with people I had otherwise no way of knowing began to overshadow my revulsion to the lack of personalization I felt missing in technology. In this case, perhaps the means could justify the ends and I filled out my computer profile with the enthusiasm and care that I felt it deserved.

The pre-determined areas of interest were somewhat restrictive, but I worked with what they gave me. I still managed to request a healthy six-foot or taller single male who lived his faith in God and emphasized the latter by *not* checking the box that indicated "spiritual, not religious." I later discovered (by trial and multiple errors) that "spiritual" in today's terms really means free-spirited with a desire to try anything, clothing optional.

I balked at the lack of choices when trying to describe myself, especially body type. I realize that even though appearance isn't supposed to matter, first impressions really do, and it became obvious that one carelessly placed check mark might mean the difference in someone responding to my profile, or not. I just didn't see myself as "thin, athletic, *or* overweight." What did that mean, anyway? Since doing away with sugar, my weight stayed the same and I no longer required multiple wardrobes depending on my latest diet scheme. Conversely, I detest the gym and definitely don't see a skeleton staring back at me in the morning mirror. After several attempts to skip that section, the computer flashed a final screen informing me to choose or abort my mission. I reluctantly chose "athletic" and decided to provide a disclaimer in the additional remarks section if I had enough room after condensing my thoughts to 100 words or less.

I filled their tiny box with words that I hoped would convey my desire for the kind of companionship I was looking for. Thoughts of marriage or lasting commitments never entered my conscious mind, but the exhilaration of finally having the opportunity to describe my "perfect" date produced a description that took even me by surprise. The person I most wanted to spend time with would enjoy my company whenever we were together and think about me whenever apart. After twenty years of marriage, I wasn't exactly sure what I wanted, but I knew with certainty what I *didn't*. Still, it surprised me that even though I thought all I wanted was anyone willing to share a seat at the theater or ball game, the basic need and desire for true Godly love still burned brightly within.

Despite misgivings for the likelihood of promising candidates emerging from such an impersonal provider, I felt certain that the tingling in my toes had more to do with falling asleep at the keyboard than any primal warnings of danger. I mashed the send button, closed the computer, and burrowed under the covers to dream the rest of the night away between my two trusty foot-warmers. I had a snug roof over my head, leftovers waiting in the fridge, and mounds of love (literally) on either side. At that foggy moment between sleep and conscious musings, I remember thinking that life didn't get much better than this.

Draw near to God and He will draw near to you.
- James 4:8 -

The process of wading through hundreds of descriptive profiles was fascinating. It's a case study of emotional typecasting, spelling and grammar skills, and a sleuthing challenge to detect honesty within the bounds of probability. Some folks reduced their sales pitch to sentences of three words or less, while others droned on for several pages about their accomplishments and conquests. People seemed to acquire a massive dose of nerve – or arrogance, whichever the case may be, during the years I was raising three kids and building a family. My description seemed tame next to their self-proclaimed lives in the fast lane. If this was any indication of the state of our nation's affairs, no wonder the jails are full and doctors of every specialty have job security.

Most everyone posted photos for consideration in an entertaining competition for the best glamour shot or senior picture taken decades ago. I never even considered including a photograph since I was the one always taking the pictures – not in them, and I didn't have a clue how to get a piece of 4 x 6 inch glossy paper through the wires from my dusty scanner and into the black box connected to the wall.

This actually turned out to be a fortunate oversight, since it drastically reduced the number of inquiries I received and most likely weeded out those more bizarre than most. I admit to looking at everybody else's headshots in my own process of elimination but more for assessment of shifty eyes and lack of smiles than a preoccupation with tall, dark, and handsome. OK, tall was definitely at the top of my list, but it was hard to tell height from a photo, unless they thought to include a yardstick for proportions or you could actually see the lifts in their shoes.

I expected to wait for days before receiving requests to "chat" but was shocked to learn within hours that there are actually droves of people in the world surfing the net for "that certain someone" and evidently never sleep. My profile was fresh on the market and mysterious with the absence of physical evidence, and the questions for more information came rolling in. My answers more often than not assured the end to any future dialog, since being a non-smoking, non-drinking mother of three teenagers and two dogs, accompanied by a strong personal relationship with Christ, seemed to scare off the illiterate and adulterous in one fell swoop. There were, however, a few willing to risk meeting for a benign cup of coffee (which I didn't drink, either) and so it began.

My strategy was simple: search for as many people who most closely appeared to share my interests, make contact as soon as possible, and repeat until my month's trial subscription expired. I quickly dispersed with anyone unable to type more than one sentence without errors and began keeping notes on a yellow legal pad for each individual, after answering one too many questions by way of the wrong inquiry's email address. I filled my calendar with a week's worth of coffee house rendezvous and supplied my church ladies and daughter all with date, time, and location information so that at least one of them could conveniently call me halfway through each appointment to make sure I hadn't met with danger or needed a plausible reason to flee.

I'm pleased to say that I didn't encounter danger that raised any hair on the back of my neck but did exit early on more than one occasion. I considered my search criteria as relatively reasonable and undemanding. I drew the line when arriving for one date only to find a self-proclaimed non-smoker puffing away at our designated table for two, and another upon learning "single" meant cavorting with multiple women while living in the same house with a wife to which he was "contemplating" divorce. So much for my theory of equating sentence structure and proficient spelling with virtue. If this was the cream of the crop, I was in for a meager harvest. It gave new meaning to what Jesus intended by his direction to the disciples to glean the harvest of their ripe fields. I definitely needed to hone my definition of "ripe."

One of my summer vacations, spent naturally on a lake in the wilds of Canada, took my brothers and me for two weeks with nothing but fish and water – and the overabundant attention of our grandparents. Taking pity on my aversion to the family rule of having to hook your own worm before dropping a line, Grandpa bought me diversion in the largest beach ball he could find. Standing no taller than four feet myself, this sphere of many colors towered above my head making it difficult to manage on land and even harder on water. Bigger isn't always better, but Grandpa's heart always wanted to do more, so this impractical giant was duly noted for the gesture it was.

Sometime between its umpteenth retrieval and knocking the neighbor's drinks to the ground, I got the brainy idea that putting this *beach* ball into the water would somehow stretch my arms around its ample girth and turn me instantly into the athletic swimmer that I was not. The minute it hit the water, gusts of wind appeared from nowhere, hurling it out with the tide. Grandma anticipated all my next moves and shouted to get back and let it go. In tears at the thought of losing my gift so swiftly, I nonetheless heeded her words of wisdom and watched it shrink smaller and smaller.

Unfortunately, my older brother somehow missed her words of wisdom and turned into an unlikely savior as he swam for my runaway treasure bound for parts unknown. Further and further he went, as the waves grew higher with the unexpected wind at his back. Everyone on shore began to panic and take up a frantic call to give up and come back to shore. He couldn't hear anything over the sound of the rushing wind and water and just kept swimming toward the horizon.

My tears battled with guilt and remorse as I watched my brother risk his life for a stupid ball. What I thought was utterly important just moments ago, turned ugly and frightful in the midst of what could now turn out so poorly. With a child's wish and a prayer came the true savior of the day when all eyes trained on the bobbing boat of my beloved Grandpa, making his way in due haste to the other man of the hour. Miraculously, both brother and ball made it into the rescue craft with the help of one of the oars and a bright orange lifesaver.

I learned two lessons that day. A gift isn't always the one you see first, and prayer always trumps fear. I would benefit from being very aware of what I currently wished for in this hunt simply for someone to sit by. Be still, my anxious heart…just be still.

With anticipated hopes and week one nearly exhausted, my search looked bleak as a pattern of failure unfolded before me. Perhaps I was looking in the wrong places, for all the wrong people, using the wrong methods. Ginger's ability to read my mood was uncanny as she herded me toward the comfort of the porch steps and another evening of gazing at the stars. It was my thought exactly. How did she do that? How did she know what I needed before I even did? Many *people* had listened before as I shared story after story of my woes and hopes, but none really heard me the way she did. None of those humans were sharing a spot on the cold bricks, watching me with rapt attention and losing an occasional drop of saliva from their oversized tongue – Ginger was.

It became impossible to feel lonely as we huddled there together, watching the night sky fill with twinkling lights and realizing that perspective is a wonderful thing. I always did have difficulty applying it to my art class drawings, but tonight the canvas was wide as the sky and clear as crystal. I decided that maybe being alone wasn't such a horrible fate and gave God the glory for whatever He had planned. Ginger concurred by nuzzling my hand for repeated petting and gifted me with a knowing smile and her sandpaper tongue. Lucky dog…she already knew what I was about to discover.

CHAPTER 7

LOVE IS PATIENT

**Memory is a way of holding on to the things you love,
the things you are, the things you never want to lose.
- Kevin Arnold -**

I can still feel the luxurious velveteen and imagine the glorious crimson hue of my dress at a long ago kindergarten Christmas program at church. With only half a dozen regularly attending, there were never enough kids participating to fill the roles of a bona fide pageant, but that year consisted of each of us memorizing a short line from the nativity story in what was supposed to be a finely tuned operation. We arranged ourselves into a somewhat lopsided circle at the front of the room looking outward at the audience of parents and reluctant siblings. Each one took turns standing front and center within the beam of our teacher's flashlight, trying not to squint from the glaring light and striving to regurgitate the words we'd performed flawlessly just moments before when no one was looking.

I had the dubious pleasure of being the last to speak, with more sentences than most, and the weight of a successful conclusion to our story on my shoulders. As if that weren't enough to bite my nails and pick at the lace on my hem, a bombshell dropped seconds before our circle was set into motion when the teacher announced that everyone would be receiving a gift from their parents for the grand conclusion of our program. Certain that this was an important message sent home that I never delivered, I anguished over the possibility that I'd be the only one left on stage, empty handed and embarrassed that I'd somehow missed the memo and singled myself out for embarrassment.

The five-minute voyage around the room seemed like days to me, as each child stumbled over their words and finally took a giant step to the left as the circle rotated in motion. I have the habit of distorting my mouth while thinking and always stick my tongue out the corner when deep in thought. Hmmm...maybe that's what Ginger is doing all those times her tongue sticks to the roof of her mouth. Thankfully, my nerves kept me from delving any deeper in my thoughts than remembering how to pick up my feet and shuffle to the next position, so my tongue stayed blessedly undetected.

However, I did wonder at the time why Mom kept waving and making frantic gestures at her face but sadly didn't realize until afterwards that it was merely an attempt to get my attention. How was I to know she merely meant to stifle the intake of air that I kept blowing into both cheeks in rhythm with the beat of my runaway heart? At the tender age of five, this unfortunately created lifelong phobias for anything remotely related to public speaking or entertainment of the masses.

Much to my family's relief my turn finally arrived, and I somehow managed to deliver my speech with the same breath of air escaping the confines of my distended cheeks. One more gulp of breath and a collective sigh from my parents later, the stage collapsed into a mass of little bodies trying not to giggle and sit still for the upcoming gift distribution. They passed around a hat filled with numbered pieces of paper from which to draw. Unable to avoid participation by clever distraction, fate (and the teacher with the flashlight) assigned me the number five.

She called each number loud and clear, with its corresponding owner making a beeline to the outstretched hand in the audience that held its corresponding package. I was happy for their fortunate bounty and wondered if I could use their zeal to disappear amidst the paper and bows thrown haphazardly around the room before my number arrived. It was too late…but what to my wondering eyes did appear, but a hand in the back with a gift, wrapped so dear.

I went from humiliation to joy in two giant steps that I'm sure didn't even hit the floor. How did my parents know? How did they keep this a secret in a household where my Dad couldn't keep anything – especially as hugely fantastic as this? Just the idea of the gift was enough, but the beautiful birthstone ring inside was the piece de resistance. It was a perfect fit, and I was sure that I'd never take it off. It's funny how a body has a way of growing out of all kinds of things, but the awestruck wonder of knowing that I was important enough to them to give such a loving gift of surprise was something I'd never outgrow.

> **Never lose an opportunity of seeing anything beautiful,**
> **for beauty is God's handwriting.**
> **- Ralph Waldo Emerson -**

After all the miserable excuses for dates I'd experienced in this modern version of "The Dating Game," manna descended from heaven. Unlike the food which the wandering tribes of Israel received (which I certainly would've been more accustomed to) mine appeared on the screen of my daily morning ritual of perusing the internet singles buffet as "HDguy57." I had no idea what the assortment of letters and numbers meant, but duly intrigued and braced with the knowledge that at least this person appeared to be a member of the opposite sex, I opened the email with great anticipation. Early indications looked good.

This man lived 90 miles south, which meant he was obviously willing to do whatever it took to meet the right woman. He shared the unfortunate circumstance of widowhood at nearly my own age and matching years of marriage. After sitting through multiple conversations listening to bitter tales of divorce and child custody, this was *definitely* whetting my appetite. His profile shared a loving account of his teenage daughter and a brief description of his church and firm belief in Jesus Christ, baptism, and regular attendance.

Wow. As if all that weren't enough, he included a photo with a casual pose against his black, shiny Harley and a smile that held warmth and just a touch of promise for the exciting unknown waiting around the next corner. Delving more deeply with eyes glued to the screen, I'm sure a double "wow" escaped my lips when it also revealed that he was actively serving in the Air Force and had a twenty-year career under his thin-waist belt.

This had me remembering my own patriotic desire for adventure and travel in high school, and I acknowledged his commitment with deep appreciation and admittedly, a bit of envy. My talks with an Army recruiter revealed, at that time, that they didn't routinely station women in exotic locales like Iceland or Antarctica, so I quickly lost interest and never pursued a military career. I'll never know if I would've even been able to conquer the push-ups required in basic training, but his photo indicated that he had, and I blushed in spite of myself.

The only thing left on my wish list was the requirement for six-foot or taller. I decided that the rest of his resume reduced this minor detail to insignificance, and I started my New Year's Day celebration with a quick reply, my phone number (which I'd never given out before) and an invitation to meet as soon as possible. HDguy57 replied within hours but revealed his shy side by postponing the phone call idea, insisting on several days of internet banter to break the ice. This merely served to whet my appetite more, with his wonderful command of the English language and attention to detail and orthography – a word he could actually spell and knew its meaning. This was impressive but not more so than his sense of humor and honesty when he admitted to not quite reaching my height requirement with his 5-foot 11-7/8-inch stature. That had me laughing out loud, and I quickly replied that my request had more to do with wanting to be able to wear heels and not have to bend over to dance, than any weird fetish with height.

The day of his anticipated phone call finally arrived, with the uncharacteristic appearance of both my boys eating pizza in the kitchen – not their rooms and Ginger and Bailey determined to occupy the same space as my nervous pacing. That would teach me not to share my excitement at having met someone worthy of Ma Bell or giving the number at the house instead of the cell phone that only worked at the end of the driveway or local shopping center parking lot.

I'd forgotten that others in the household didn't view me in any capacity other than Mom, which heretofore meant privacy was scarce and achieved only by barricading myself behind the bathroom door. It never occurred to me that my enthusiasm for a new life might clash with their skepticism and doubt for their mother's marketability. Regardless, the phone was ringing, and my heart was singing – or was that the whining of the dogs?

Have you ever noticed that people on paper (or computer screen, as the case may be) never sound the same in person? HDguy57, named "Dennis" at birth, sounded more like the deep rumble of his Harley Davidson than the only other person I could think of with that name, who happened to be a comic strip character with an ornery disposition. He was genuine, mysterious, and polite all rolled into one, and we managed to talk nearly an hour despite the obvious commotion on my end from *all* quarters. Surprisingly not daunted by the noise, he agreed to meet later that week at a point halfway for both of us at a fast food joint just off the highway. After all those miserable encounters with coffee I didn't drink Wendy's and Wednesday seemed an eternity away.

Nothing is worth more than this day.
- Goethe –

Even the day chosen for my latest encounter with destiny seemed providential, scheduled with just enough time to attend my Disciple class at church, gather much-needed support, then fly to my meeting (under the speed limit, of course) with time to spare. The girls were more eager than usual to hear my weekly social status update, having spent the last two months sharing the pitiful saga of midlife dating in awe of what they thought they were missing. I tried to tell them that *they* were the blessed ones having all the "married with children" kind of fun but my grass still managed to look greener to them, even when scalped and in desperate need of fertilizer.

I'm embarrassed to say that class that day more closely resembled the last day of school before Christmas break than our usual in-depth study of prophets long ago, and it was entirely my fault. I shared the promising bio of the man who actually seemed to be exactly whom he claimed, and all agreed that driving to the middle of nowhere didn't seem nearly as crazy as they'd first thought.

They scrutinized my wardrobe choice and insisted on a tutorial on the merits of wearing "date" jeans. Prior to my daughter's coaching, I didn't know what they were either. Much to our collective surprise, pant waists worn just under the ribcage, and sweat pants built for comfort and speed are not included in desirable attire and may account for some lack of interest on the part of our spouses and the male population in general. Who knew?

With a unanimous decision to break early for more time on the road, and the fact that none of us could concentrate anyway, a fervent prayer went up from our circle with much to avail. I was sent out the door with hugs and Ephesians 6:13-17, girded with truth by my fashion-correct jeans, my feet shod with new shoes and the gospel of peace, and shielded with the faith of my sisters in me and all of us in Christ. With the helmet of salvation and sword of the Spirit in the form of a felt fedora and large print Bible on the seat beside me, I headed south on the wings of my convertible and prayed that truth would prevail (and that email promises would finally turn out to be true).

A good beginning makes a good end.
- English proverb -

I come from a long line of folks who arrive early for *everything*. My Dad was always the first in line at any given football stadium and instilled the importance of being at the airport gate at least two hours prior to take-off years before security created the mandatory suggestion. I was confident that the extra 15 minutes I'd gained by avoiding construction would surely give me time to check for food between my teeth and pop in some mints. I also thought my prompt arrival would give me a good vantage point from which to watch my new acquaintance and gain valuable insight into his driving habits and choice of parking space. Would he back in for a quick exit, park at the

Love Never Fails

door for less walking, or perhaps choose the space next to mine because he actually paid attention to what kind of vehicle I said I'd be driving?

I did pay attention to what he said *he'd* be driving, and both of them were already patiently awaiting my arrival. He got out of his truck the minute he saw me coming, and I took the few seconds afforded me while pulling in to notice that he looked just like he sounded...genuine, mysterious, and polite. At least *he'd* been able to check his teeth and pop those mints. I threw caution to the wind, hopped out of my car with a smile, and extended my nervous hand. At least I could discern some covert knowledge from that crucial first handshake...and it was just right. It wasn't a limp fish *or* a wrestler's painful crush. He looked just like his photo, too, with a red flannel shirt neatly tucked into his Wrangler jeans.

We both seemed reluctant to break free, and I, at least, marveled at the electric current coursing through my veins. Thankfully, we skipped all the usual prattle endured in my previous meetings. Of course, that was probably because he couldn't get a word in edgewise, what with my excited chatter turned on full blast from finally meeting someone honest, tall, *and* looking just as good as his photo promised. I could only hope that his perception of my "athletic" description allowed for areas of soft and bumpy instead of toned and sleek. At least I'd caught a break with the winter weather with no humidity to add pounds to my hair.

Since previous experience taught me to expect our meeting to consist of a few minutes spent talking over a cup of coffee or the shared bottle of water that I preferred – if I was lucky, he thoroughly shocked me with an invitation to dine at an honest to goodness restaurant equipped with real silverware and cloth napkins. Now *this* I could get used to…a planner with creative ideas who thought enough about me to think outside the usual safe and boring box.

I would learn much later that I actually shocked *him* when I promptly gathered my jacket and purse and climbed into his truck, knowing not where we were going and not bothered in the least that a complete stranger sat at the wheel of my fortune. It never occurred to me to doubt his sincerity. After all, he was driving a Ford, rode a Harley, served in the Air Force – and was playing James Taylor (my favorite, which he also remembered) on the stereo. I confess that if my daughter were ever to try this herself I'd be duly appalled, but I was blissfully trusting with no radar blips of danger on my intuition screen and proceeded to buckle up and enjoy the ride.

I'm a firm believer that it's impossible to be lost while exploring new vistas and choose rather to embrace the exhilaration of not knowing exactly where I am. After leaving all familiar interstate landmarks for back roads heading north, I was convinced that by always turning left at each intersection of cotton farms, we'd eventually wind our way back to civilization. The way I figured, if we were lucky we'd end up at an exit with at least one gas station and dining establishment from which to choose. I was hoping for an option that didn't include having the two stuck together like they do at interstate truck stops, and breathed a sigh of relief with a thankful prayer when the first signs of advanced culture came into view.

Ironically, another Wendy's sat front and center at our perusal, but much to my delight, we drove right on by and settled into Applebee's instead. I was thrilled at the prospect of being able to order directly off the menu without embarrassing myself early on, with special orders for my strange eating habits that I hadn't yet shared. The last 90 minutes had already revealed my penchant for streaming thoughts aloud (and even louder when nervous), unusual love of maps, and a condensed version of my dysfunctional life, so it seemed prudent to wait before divulging more incriminating evidence that might scare him away. After all, I still sat in the middle of nowhere without wheels of my own, and more importantly, my stomach was growling.

Surprisingly, whenever I stopped to gather breath, my attentive companion revealed empathy for my saga and shared – in a much more structured and quiet way, his own story of life on the move in foreign lands, and all that had brought him to being on this bizarre journey we presently shared. Intrigued by his fortitude and casual acceptance of travel and experiences that I'd only dreamed of, I was never at a loss for questions and found myself enjoying the conversation that inevitably found its end. There were dogs to feed and children waiting for my afternoon debriefing, and I didn't think either would appreciate a delay. Perhaps it was time to reorganize priorities and move good old Mom closer to the top of the list.

Taking the freeway instead of our previous rural route, we returned to my vehicle in record time, leaving us with a few minutes to spare for another excuse to linger over refreshments. I ordered my requisite water bottle and he a Coke, as we jammed a lifetime of words into the time it takes to empty a paper cup. All those tickets for two kept bumping into the back of my brain, and I managed to propose a second date in between thanking him for a lovely afternoon and making it clear that I intended to continue meeting all the others still listed on my yellow legal pad.

At the time, it never occurred to me that my desire to continue to meet as many people as possible within the confines of my thirty-day trial would seem odd to the man *I'd* just asked out on a second date. We'd just shared the most wonderful day both of us had encountered in years, and here I was, giving the impression that I was looking for more. Thankfully, he'd wait weeks to share his honest reaction to this illogical blunder, and our next date would commence three days later.

That particular encounter would involve a rendezvous at my own front door and introduction of a strange man to two of the most important people in my life. I just hoped three days would be enough time to prepare Ginger and Bailey.

Friends are people you can be quiet with.
- Anonymous -

After my disastrous record to date (no pun intended), I couldn't help feeling apprehensive about finally meeting someone interesting who seemed interested in me. I told my daughter that even though I really wanted to see Dennis again, I was afraid that I was just too loud. I live everything out loud – life, clothes, and every thought that enters my head. Dennis was thoughtful, methodical, gentle…and quiet. I just couldn't fathom the possibility that he would want to spend time with someone noisy like me. She gave me a piece of wise advice years beyond her age, as she shared personal insight that quiet men run deep with passion. It was a little scary hearing that coming from my own daughter and unnerving to realize that her scant dating career still included more valuable on the job training than I could even imagine.

Nevertheless, she spoke with authority, and I'd learned long ago to trust her instincts. I also prayed that her experience with "passion" involved emotion and conviction only, instead of numerous other areas best left to simmer until finding God's chosen mate. I made a note to tackle that discussion on her next weekend break.

With personal doubts aside, it was time to deal with the dogs. In the short time since losing the only adult male figure he'd ever known, Bailey had managed to bite the UPS delivery truck tires, attack the lawn man's weed whacker, and bloody the nose of my financial planner at his unfortunate appearance at our door without warning. Ginger was less vehement in her guarding techniques, but it was evident that neither one was willing to concede their right to defend what they clearly saw as inherited responsibility.

They barely shared their food, much less the territory and possessions clearly marked and defended by their menacing barks and growls. These were the same animals who rolled over incessantly for belly rubs within the hidden walls of our home, but to the unsuspecting they appeared fierce and formidable. They, much like my sons, felt strongly that no addition of testosterone was necessary for the near future, and I was understandably nervous about introducing the possibility of another man's interest in my time and affection – not to mention my fearful visions of inevitable war over offering him a seat on the couch.

I used every example I could remember from my vast reading of childrearing psychology and pulled out the stops with the recitation of my dear Grandmother's wall of Amish proverbs. Ginger seemed to enjoy the lilt of the Pennsylvania Dutch, but we'd suspected long ago that Bailey much preferred Spanish, and he gave me the best eye roll possible under all that facial fur as he left the room a bored puppy.

They both acted as though I were crazy – which I suppose I was to care so much whether they'd like this new beau or not, leaving me to wonder if there'd ever be room enough on the planet for personal harmony. Judging by the crescendo of Bailey's snore and Ginger's one-eyed stare, my efforts had succeeded at least in boring them to sleep, if not achieving their cooperation to play nice and judge later.

Once in a while, right in the middle of an ordinary life,
Love gives us a Fairy Tale.
- Anonymous -

Date number two would encompass an entire day in the city, so Dennis and I planned to meet once I got the dogs walked and the boys safely off to school. Timing was everything, and I didn't want to open the door without a freshly scrubbed body and shiny set of teeth, so I arose before dawn and left myself just enough time to corral my sleeping beauties before the doorbell rang.

I think it was love at first sight for Ginger. She immediately sniffed both shoes at the door, quickly made her way up the Wranglers, and settled her nose in the palm of Dennis' hand. Bailey seemed as shocked as I did at her uncharacteristic lack of barking frenzy, and he cautiously approached this newcomer to discern what (or who) had tamed his sister's beast. Evidently finding no reason to question his motives, Bailey kindly stepped aside and didn't even protest when Ginger herded Dennis toward the coveted couch.

It took me a moment to recover, but I soon recognized the miraculous wonder of this display of unconditional trust. If they'd sensed any artificial intentions or nefarious plans, Dennis would *not* be sitting on the middle cushion with Ginger curled at his side and Bailey at his feet. Furthermore, neither one would've left room for me on the remaining cushion if they hadn't wanted to share. Wonders never cease.

Our itinerary rested on the hope that commuter traffic would disperse, parking spaces would be cheap and plentiful, the Coca-Cola Museum and Underground Atlanta hours hadn't changed, and that *I* would be able to remain silent while Dennis navigated the necessary exit lane before it was too late to turn around. I may have uttered a word or two, but everything else fell into place, and we arrived on schedule, both extremely excited about sharing the day.

I'm fascinated with history of any kind, even when it involves the popularity of a concoction that I can no longer drink. My sensitivity to sugar necessarily rules it out for me, but Dennis consumed it on a regular basis, and I was more than curious to learn more about their brilliant marketing strategy that not only revolutionized the refreshment industry, but Christmas as well. I found its storied rise to fame intriguing and especially enjoyed their complete collection of Coca-Cola Santa posters on our way to the gift shop – which surprisingly turned out to be my favorite part of the tour.

The gift shop consisted of a gigantic room on the main floor, in which they displayed an incredible assortment of products with their Coke logo emblazoned across every available surface. The room swam in red and smelled and sounded as if they were pumping sugary syrup and carbonated bubbles through the airshafts. Cramped in the aisle between the frosty mugs and key chains on the wall, we found ourselves sandwiched by shoppers on both sides. Before I could think about my claustrophobic tendencies or wonder why Dennis had suddenly become so quiet, he surprised me with a question that seemed to appear out of nowhere, but was obviously the reason why a cat seemingly got his tongue.

He wanted to know if it would be all right if he held my hand. Yes, yes, and yes! I thought maybe I'd said something wrong or talked so much that I'd scared him away, when all that time, he'd really just been working up to this…and to me "this" was huge. I love connecting with people by way of touch. I can *feel* a person's mood in the same way that someone else watches body language. This gave me a way to communicate with a quiet person without blowing him away with words. I could put pages of emotion into one little squeeze of my hand and felt the novel unfolding in his. The day suddenly exploded, with all the colors brighter, laughter lighter, and shy smiles becoming bolder with frequent use.

Hunger and a desire to walk anywhere hand in hand, led us down into the depths of the city to a clever use of space dubbed The Underground. It was really quite remarkable to see this city built beneath another city, but if not for the delightful company, I would never have stayed. It appeared from the lack of open establishments that life didn't swarm until after dark, which didn't make sense to me since it felt like a cave down there all the time anyway. I couldn't understand the draw of its popularity, but it only stood to emphasize the light of my companion in all that surrounding darkness.

We shared a pizza – well, he ate the crust while I enjoyed the toppings and then something utterly wonderful unfolded. I swear until that moment that he never actually looked me straight in the eye while talking – and this was our second date. I know many people who look up or down while gathering their thoughts. I do it too, so I hadn't thought much about it. There was a precise moment, though, as we finished that last gooey bite when our eyes collided, and I was mesmerized. They were the most beautiful shade of dark chocolate, framed by lashes unfairly worn by a man. I couldn't stop staring and for several blessed seconds he couldn't either. Fireworks exploded in my mind, the room stood still, and the only sound I heard was the wild beating of my own heart. Everything changed for me at that moment, the same as the instant I knew I'd been born again.

Joy and contentment wrapped our cozy conversation like a soft, warmed-up bun around a nice juicy foot-long, and it was hard to contain in such confining spaces. I needed air and sunshine, and at least another uninterrupted eight hours to see where this was going. Alas, the afternoon shadows were beginning to fall from the skyscrapers to the pavement, and we headed out of Dodge before the commuters made their daily dash for home.

It's amazing to discover all the topics of conversation that flow nonstop when you're with a person of God's choosing. The miles in a typical drive across bumpy concrete with thousands of other weary travelers usually seem to drag with endless boredom, but today I never wanted them to end. Evidently, Dennis felt the same way. One exit prior to our inevitable journey's end, the truck veered off and found its way to a mall, and I knew from previous discussions that he didn't even like to shop for groceries, let alone set foot inside a place designed for the sole purpose of selling clothes that he'd never wear. There could be only one reason…he was as desperate as I to extend our time together and itching for another excuse to hold hands.

We walked and talked without ever breaking contact and finally settled in front of the fountains and food to talk some more. It was refreshing to know that the person sitting across from me *did not* indicate a desire to sleep or flee and seemed content in the knowledge that I felt the same way. After months of disappointment, the answer to all my prayers sat looking at me with one gorgeous pair of eyes and a heart to match. I had no complaints about the rest of the package, either. He wasn't perfect – just perfect for me. Thank you, Lord. You sure know how to pick 'em.

> **Love doesn't make the world go 'round.**
> **Love is what makes the ride worthwhile.**
> **- Franklin P. Jones -**

It was dark by the time we finally rolled into the driveway to say goodbye. I was certain there was dinner to prepare and homework papers to sign somewhere inside, but we sat in the dark of the truck instead, inventing reasons to hold fast to each other in what little time remained. I had an irresistible urge to quench my desire to discover if his lips would taste as yummy as the promise of his chocolate eyes and leaned into the possibility just as the porch light glared on. Evidently, one of my boys had noticed our return and decided to exercise his territorial rights or perhaps just curiosity concerning Mom's delay in providing his evening meal. Regardless of his intentions, the interruption hit its mark, and I found myself blushing and suddenly bereft with the hasty parting of all body parts while we dashed to our respective sides of the vehicle. I felt like a kid caught in the candy store, except that I hadn't done anything to feel guilty about and unfortunately didn't even have the thrill of that chocolate memory to savor the rest of the night.

The moment had vanished, but not the desire. We said our goodnights and parted with a good laugh at ourselves and the promise to see each other soon. I raced through dinner and dishes and calculated that just enough time had passed for Dennis to return home. Ninety minutes flies when you're having fun, and the day's activities gave me ample diversion from the usual chop, cook, rinse, and stack of my usual nighttime routine. The boys finally wandered to their respective caves (the shuttered, cluttered, closed-door rooms they fondly referred to as bedrooms), and I pounced on the computer.

I couldn't wait to thank my date for a glorious day and waxed on about how wonderful life was now that he was in it. There's a song in there somewhere, but I'm thinking somebody already beat me to it. Anyway, several paragraphs later, without hesitation or review, I automatically signed the email "Love, Liane" and mashed the send button before realizing my hasty faux pas. Here I was again, thinking every word aloud without censure, creating a fifty-fifty chance of either sending hope down the drain or being the catalyst to happily ever after. It was too late now. I could only hope that he'd be as eager to express *his* feelings – you know, some of that deep-seeded passion my daughter assured me lay smoldering within his quiet exterior.

Every year, I eagerly await the new page-a-day calendar from one of my favorite artists, Mary Englebreit. She draws the world as if she lives inside my head and fills it with clever quotes and sayings of her own that capture exactly what I'm thinking. One of my favorites came to mind as I monitored the computer screen for signs of correspondence that part of me yearned to see while the rest of me feared to acknowledge. "Time flies whether you're having fun or not." She got that right.

Time is also full of mercy and grace, which is exactly what I received with the sudden announcement of mail on the screen. Thankfully, it was Dennis and not another ad for hair cream or warehouse tires. He wrote exquisitely about his own perspective of the day, and it fit harmoniously with my version, minus several adjectives and exclamation marks. With a tremendous urge to skip to his farewell and end this intolerable suspense I wisely chose, on second thought, to savor his analytical sonnet for the romantic gesture it was. For me, "Be still and know that I am God" translates more appropriately as, "What's your hurry? You know that My plans are always worth the wait." Yes, I know that, but sometimes He has to magnify the message, as in the arrival of those last two words at the bottom of the page…"Love, Dennis."

Only passions, great passions,
can elevate the soul to great things.
- Denis Piderot -

Thinking about Dennis and the anticipation of our first kiss consumed my thoughts more thoroughly than a last piece of apple pie, the beach at sunrise, or any one of Paul's run-on sentences in New Testament verse. I already knew the effect he had on my nervous system with acute stimulation to my sense of sight, sound, and smell. I've never cared one way or the other about well-toned abs, facial hair, or the pigment in one's eyes, but I have to admit that he was a sight for these sore ones, and I was itching to see what all the fuss was about concerning mustache hair and a sexy five-o'clock shadow. I could listen to the deep Harley rumble of his voice for hours on end, but the limitations of roll-over minutes and too many miles between him and my cell phone had me hankering for something more up close and personal.

It's been duly studied and noted in several women's magazines at my hair salon (so it must be true) how strongly women react to their sense of smell. One whiff of anything can make or break a first date, and in Dennis' case, it had me promptly emailing him after our first one about the question of cologne. His was heavenly – something like rolling Brute, Old

Spice, English Leather, and baby powder all in to one.

When asked about the details, he laughed and explained that it was just a little something he concocted with two of his favorite scents. Now they were two of *my* favorites, and I won't be divulging the recipe for mass consumption. There is, after all, only one Dennis, and I was still anticipating that first kiss. Call me crazy, but honestly I couldn't understand why he was still on the market and didn't care to advertise his best kept secret to the female population at large before doing further research involving the effects of touch and taste.

It took three days of waiting before we maneuvered our next date between his government work schedule, dog baths, and several school assignments that materialized out of thin air. By the time Friday morning arrived, I was well on my way to insane, if that means doing the same thing repeatedly and expecting a different result. I'd relived the scene in his truck the night we *almost* kissed a million times, but it never sped time any faster, and it still took 72 hours to arrive.

Two tickets to a museum viewing of Monet's Garden of oils-on-canvas lay carefully concealed in the zippered pocket of my shoulder bag. Ginger and Bailey posted sentry at the door with their gleaming coats of freshly brushed fur. I still haven't figured out how they knew who was coming, but may have given a slight clue as I blazed a trail of tiny holes on the hardwood with my new pair of stiletto heels.

I probably should've dressed for comfort on a day planned for walking, but I just couldn't see myself in tennis shoes while imagining the perfection of our first kiss. As much as the ticket companion thing had consumed my search just days ago, it paled in comparison to the anticipation of discovering whether today would be as good – or maybe even better than my vivid dreams.

The doorbell rang in mid-stride, and I somehow managed to walk – not run as I was tempted to do, and open the door looking composed and surprisingly collected.

That lasted almost half a second, with the appearance of my blue-jean knight in shining armor holding a single red rose and bestowing me with a smile that entered my body at eye-level and quickly spread to the tips of my toes. I was overwhelmed with this unexpected gesture and began babbling with nervous chatter about finding a vase and trying in vain not to spill water all over the counter and my quivering toes. Dennis came to my rescue with calm assurance and a deliberate sense of purpose as he placed the vase safely out of reach, gathered me in his arms, and laid a kiss on me that not only curled my toes, but left me breathless and limp…Oh My.

That phrase about knocking your socks off didn't come close to describing *my* sensory extravaganza. Every inch of my body was on high alert with only my automatic responses to keep me from teetering off my heels and falling into a warm puddle on the floor. Thankfully, he didn't release his grip on my arms as we finally stepped apart, and I gathered what little remained of my wits to sneak a peek into his smoldering eyes. Just as I was traveling past his chin on the way past his nose, I slammed on the brakes at the horrifying picture before me.

Evidently, that carefully chosen shade of fire engine red *did not* hold up under extreme heat. It lay in clumps throughout his moustache and smeared an oblong trail wherever my thoughts had just roamed. As he began to shake from the bottom of his belly to the laugh he could no longer contain, it dawned on me that I probably looked even worse. This was so humiliating…and exhilarating at the same time. If seeing me as Bozo the Clown didn't scare him off, then surely not even morning hair or tent-sized jammies ever would.

Ginger was no help, egging Bailey on with her head cocked sideways and a look that said, "I can't believe you just did that and he's *still* here." Dennis headed for the guest bath with plenty of paper towels and a bar of soap, while the rest of us retreated to my cache of beauty products guaranteed to remove disasters with industrial strength efficiency. I belatedly wondered if this guarantee also came with a warning label for skin loss but came away from the mirror with minimal damage and welting that the manufacturer assured their customers would disappear within hours. Perhaps traffic congestion to Midtown would be a blessing today, and I'd be fit for public viewing by the time we reached the museum. It was even more uplifting to ponder the possibility that my faithful fur-buds would cease rolling on the floor with hilarious laughter before I gathered the courage to face my date.

> **To the world you may be one person,**
> **but to one person you may be the world.**
> **- Anonymous -**

I should've known by now that a little heightened color on my face (whether naturally or chemically induced) would never deter Dennis from being the perfect gentleman on what proved to be an absolutely perfect date. Our first encounter proved that when he shared the story of one Air Force assignment abroad which placed him in close proximity to all the romantic destinations that most of us just read about in well-worn travel brochures. He was wise enough while there to honor his family's request for relaxation and bestow upon his wife a true gift of love by actually visiting said romantic destinations and enjoying himself in the process. In addition to living the thrill of Rome,

145

Paris, and Cinderella's castle, his extensive wanderings included Monet's Garden in Giverny, France. They walked the same paths and smelled the same flowers that Monet painted all those years ago, and here I was about to gaze at all those dots of color with the tour guide of my dreams.

The exhibit lay upon the third floor, so we made our way to the elevators as I shared my fear of confined spaces and traveling at the speed of light in a smelly steel box with tedious background noise. I think it was apparent by the death grip I had on his hand that I wasn't exaggerating, but as I was beginning to realize, he always has a plan and is well-equipped for whatever challenge awaits. It was comforting to know that his Air Force training not only encompassed national security but little old me.

No sooner had the doors closed and the awful loop of elevator music began, than I found myself in a breathtaking position against the back wall, fully engaged in a kiss that blew away even the perfection of our first. Somewhere in the back of my mind, I was coherent enough to wonder if we'd just made some security camera guard's day, but conscious thought was fleeting, and I decided to float on the moment instead. I would never think of elevator travel in the same way again, nor would I refuse to follow this man to the ends of the earth. I could get used to this.

The day was wildly successful – including the master's works, though it was hard to exceed expectations after the elevator ride. We were spending another one of those days we didn't want to end and found ourselves surrounded by modern sidewalk art (I was unaware that such a thing existed) sitting on one of the sofas placed in the center of the room for contemplative viewing. Thank goodness for the signs that identified it as such, for it was easy to assume it was just part of the exhibit. Anyway, it offered a comfortable place to snuggle and hold hands while the flamboyant art surrounded us with cover for our lack of interest in the "art" that we were supposedly there to be enthralled in.

I was more interested in paying attention to Dennis than any old world or modern art master could offer and admittedly ignored anyone or anything else around us. Hence, the extreme jolt of surprise when roused by the security cop with his scary-looking stick as he pointed to his watch and informed us that the museum had closed 10 minutes ago. It would've been embarrassing if touring solo, but we just giggled (well, Dennis doesn't giggle, exactly) and hurried out the door through which our guard held firmly open. I would've felt bad about keeping him from his dinner, except for the tiny smile I saw lurking behind his practiced smirk. Tough guys have soft hearts...or so my daughter tells me.

CHAPTER 8

LOVE REJOICES IN RIGHT

Often, the best ideas start out as dreams.
- Home Companion -

My unusual methods for attracting men – and the unexpected men I seem to attract, is legendary. At the tender age of five, I was already dressing with flair in a leopard coat with matching purse that inspired my first nickname and guaranteed a daily chase during recess by all the boys I loved to hate. I was first on the block to garner a kiss while playing husband and wife in a personal illustration of the American playground song "k-i-s-s-i-n-g" with our new Canadian neighbor across the street. My mother attempted to nip *that* in the bud by threatening to delay dating until the age of thirty…fat chance. Third grade delivered my first love note in the form of a coded message passed across the aisle during a math test. "Bid Glove Bayou" cleverly appeared with the instructions to cross out all b's, d's, g's and a's.

At that point, I thought, "I Love You" simply meant holding hands with the cutest boy in class and taught me early on the advantages of long curly hair and a custom wardrobe. Sure, it wasn't long after that I cut my flowing locks in a futile attempt to acquire an easier do, and my hand-sewn clothes were more out of necessity to dress my funky proportions than any remarkable fashion sense. Nevertheless, I'd tasted momentary success and tucked away its valuable lessons for future use.

Decades later, I still don't do anything in half measures and certainly don't march to the beat of the drum in most everyone else's band. After experiencing love at first sight (which admittedly happened on our second date), I was more than willing to abandon my trusty yellow legal pad and commit myself to one man. This caused much consternation on the part of those most closely connected to my woes and wild tales and even a few groans from the next batch of promising contenders whom I'd lined up for the following week and just canceled. My family looked on with reserved interest, content to watch the show unfold while wary of the possibility that life as they knew it might really be about to change. Friends reminded me about my self-proclaimed edict for independence and a singular desire to merely filling the seat beside me. The would-be suitors online insisted that I must be a flighty dame with a penchant for trolling without bait and dejectedly cast me into their delete files.

Dennis and I knew differently, and we enthusiastically began our whirlwind romance into absolute bliss. My calendar was wide open. With one child living on campus and the other two contentedly ensconced behind closed doors whenever home, my life was an open book waiting to fill its pages. Ginger reminded me that she had first dibs on several chapters per day but with her obvious enchantment with the same man, I was able to negotiate a contract that pleased all parties concerned.

Comforted by maintaining a starring role, she gave me artistic license to proceed as long as her bowl was full, all furniture remained at her disposal, and that I would invite her new amour as soon and as often as possible. Life was good. With Ginger's blessing, I was sure she'd put in a good word for me and that all paths would straighten with divine inspiration as long as she was along for the stroll.

Dennis had accumulated over a month's leave since arriving at his latest base assignment, and his present job description involved working odd hours for commanders in Europe. Normally, this six-hour time difference might seem more of a deterrent than description for the perfect job, but arriving by 4:00 or 5:00 in the morning and departing no later than 2:00 pm each day left a lot of daylight hours for leisure and certainly time for us. We were a match made in heaven – really.

Normal is nothing more than a setting on your washing machine.
- Janet Prince -

There was nothing "normal" about our courtship, but it really didn't differ from your average fairy tale if you simply take into account that we crammed as many 18-hour days in a row as possible into the span of a few short weeks. Once I'd finally found that certain someone who really did "enjoy my company when we were together, and think about me whenever apart," I was determined to handle this magnificent gift with due haste and awe. It didn't take a brain surgeon to recognize this opportunity for living, and I swung my calendar of events into motion with a tight grip on my partner's hand and a wad of tickets in the other.

My calendar now sported lots of colorful notations for classics performed at the symphony, romantic piano concerts, Alan Jackson with his band of fiddles and guitars, and a rousing rendition of "I'm Proud to Be an American" by Lee Greenwood singing ten-feet from our spot on the lawn. There seemed to be a musical theme to my list of "most wanted" though the subject matter followed an eccentric and extraordinary path. To Dennis' credit, he only fell asleep once during the operatic solo at one of the symphony numbers, and that was only because he'd slipped his dress shoes off to rest his aching feet and got a little *too* comfortable.

He seemed willing to do anything to please me – even don a suit and tie, venture into overpriced parking garages after dark, and do a fancy hug and sway anytime "our" song came on the radio. This was probably even more mortifying for him when executed on the mall escalator or in front of the kids, but his efforts were endearing, and I fell more deeply in love every day.

My part in this romantic epic was easy in comparison, but I had an unfair advantage. I was willing to try anything once (I'm having a mortifying flashback of running into the snow machine while attempting the beginner's ski slope), and I've always had a secret desire to wear leather. You know…the kind with all the silver studs and fringe that sways whether you're walking or not. Ginger and I were soul mates on this subject though I prefer to *wear* my leather rather than shred and consume it. I'm guessing that her initial ardor for Dennis had as much to do with his genuine cowhide scent as it did with her obsession with his beautiful brown eyes – ditto.

During my limited experience with men, I've learned that they aren't outwardly exuberant with emotions of the heart and that it takes careful discernment to determine whether they share and care to return a woman's feelings or they're just being polite. I was thrilled to put this theory into practice the day Dennis invited me over to ride his Harley.

Keep in mind that it took decades before Harley dealers even allowed potential customers to *sit* on their bikes, let alone test drive before buying, so this was a big deal. It ranks up there pretty close to a proposal of marriage, so I prepared for the day with much reverence and glee, dressed in date jeans, my designer leather jacket, and as close as I had to black leather boots and gloves. I decided to wait on the fringe and studs until after this inaugural ride, on the slim chance that I'd scream the whole way or develop some sort of prickly rash from the speed.

The odds of either were highly unlikely with my penchant for breathtaking inspiration, and I donned his borrowed do-rag dotted with little pigs, strapped on a spare helmet, then swung my leg over the back of the sissy bar as if it were a ritual I'd done a million times before. Trust and obey in all things Godly and pertaining to bike safety. Good advice, as I listened to my pilot's instructions to hold on tight and enjoy the ride.

I would soon learn that no self-respecting Harley Babe calls her jacket a coat, refers to the little pigs as nothing but H.O.G.S – as in Harley Owners Group, and you "ride a bike," not drive a motorcycle. Riding "two-up" is another way to say I'm a comfortable backrest, and every biker respects the unwritten code that all helmets and gear left on a bike while entering restaurants or rallies are "hands off." I loved everything about this new underground persona and quickly requested that our second ride's destination head straight for the nearest bike shop to purchase my first set of chaps. I was official now, and I felt like a free-spirited cowgirl every time I suited up. I could definitely understand why Ginger enjoyed all those wind-in-the-fur golf cart rides. Maybe I should get her and Bailey some goggles and talk to Dennis about adding a sidecar...or maybe not.

Of all the music that reached farthest into heaven,
it is the beating of a loving heart.
- Henry Ward Beecher -

With little more than a month under our dating belts, the ultimate test of romantic fortitude would soon be upon us. Valentine's Day has always been a source of bittersweet expectations for me, thus the necessity for cautious planning for all holidays involving food or the color red. Dennis already knew not to bring a box of chocolates, but I confess to staring at the wall more than once while daydreaming of lipstick and that single red rose. A dozen more of each would certainly place this chosen day back on my list of favorites, and I couldn't wait to see what might unfold.

My surprise for *him* involved the perfect outfit, a new pair of heels (of course), and another pair of tickets to a couples dance at church. I would top it off with a cuddly stuffed animal procured at the Build-A-Bear Workshop, complete with red straw hat, American flag, and a recorded message of "I Love You, Dennis" when you squeezed her little paw.

The cat or bear, in this case, was out of the bag, once the kids got wind of this tidbit of information when I accidentally left my gift out for public viewing and their curiosity prompted some nosy paw pushing. Oh, well…if Ginger and Bailey's relinquishing the couch to "our" boyfriend hadn't already tipped them off, I guess this was as good a way as any to announce the depth of my feelings. The whole idea of their mother as anything other than chief cook and bottle washer was hard for them to imagine, and thoughts of romance bordered on the absurd. At least that meant they wouldn't be hanging around the living room when Dennis arrived. I told myself to be thankful for small mercies.

Who needs a box of candy when your date looks good enough to eat? I wouldn't have cared if he arrived in sneakers and jeans, but there he was, dressed to the nines in a suit and shiny shoes that I immediately imagined on the dance floor in a cozy hug and sway. Just as I formed the thought that life couldn't get any better than this, he pulled his arm from around his back to present a tiny little box wrapped in red foil and topped with a bow. It looked suspiciously like jewelry, and I belatedly wondered if I should've bought him some expensive chrome instead of the furry friend waiting on the couch.

Despite my nervous fumbling, I finally managed to unwrap the package with paper intact (you never know when red foil might come in handy) and lifted the lid to a gorgeous blue star opal. Dennis explained how the blue stone comes alive when tilted toward the light, creating a perfect star in its middle, and that he was giving me this gift as a promise for our future together. As a child of God, I know how perfectly I come alive when tilted toward Jesus' light, so this ring around my finger would surely shine night or day.

In all the years of navigating boys into men, I never had the pleasure of enjoying the ritual of wearing a boyfriend's class ring, I.D. bracelet, or even the oversized football jacket that made it onto some of the luckiest girls' backs. I always thought I'd missed something by not wearing someone else's property and wondered why nobody ever wanted to mark his territory on me. How awesome to know that it was all just a plan to save the best for last. I loved this man with everything in me and watched him place the symbol of his on my second finger from the right, knowing with all certainty that it wouldn't be long until another ring found its way to the opposite hand, three fingers to the left.

> **The greatest part of our happiness**
> **depends on our disposition**
> **not our circumstances.**
> **- Martha Washington -**

Another month passed quickly, with trips between houses that surely carved grooves in the pavement and produced many a night of reluctant parting. On the rare occasions when we weren't together, our nightly cell phone marathons put a permanent crick in my neck while curled against the steering wheel in an attempt to pull in better reception at the end of various parking lots. The police cruisers knew by now not to question the crazy woman at the end of row "P" and chose instead to meander past my open window with their familiar wave and knowing smile.

While the thrill of discovery and trying new things never grew old, the reality of our circumstances did. I prayed for patience, but knew with all my heart that I was ready to join forces with this military man harboring multiple misgivings. He was used to a calm, analytical pursuit of happiness, while I dash headlong into the briar bushes of life. We were quite a pair. Both wanting the same result but frustrating the other beyond reason with each other's confounding characteristics. Dennis confided that he was looking for a sign – something big that would offer clear and concise direction – so I prayed for a sign.

I should've known that God would answer in a very big way, something way beyond my ability to conjure in my wildest dreams. Something that might involve packing boxes, passports, and several time zones…something like a move to Germany. A recent job posting at the base materialized out of nowhere (well, *I* knew from whence it came) for which Dennis was duly qualified, promptly placing him in the commander's queue. He wondered what I thought about him applying for the position and added (before my stomach plummeted from the idea that he might leave the country without me) that if I were interested, he'd kind of like to take me with him.

I contemplated the notion for about a millisecond, planted a big kiss squarely on his mouth, and produced pen and paper to begin a list of things to do "just in case." He smiled and shook his head in bemusement, leaving me with the fleeting thought that I'd seen that look just this morning on Ginger's face. How does she *know* these things? I really needed to pay more attention every time she and Bailey huddled behind the couch with whispers and guilty looks, when it wasn't due to carpet surprises.

One thing led to another, and I began to find myself at carefully selected venues in which the topic of conversation always found its way to whether or not the parties involved would be willing to give their blessing on our marriage. Keep in mind that up to this point we'd talked all the way *around* the subject of marriage, but not exactly when, where, or if I even *wanted* to get married. In all fairness, I wear my emotions like a bright Hawaiian shirt and electric pink jeans, but since I'd never heard a precise question or given an affirmative answer, this still left me somewhat frustrated that everyone in my family had heard the question except me.

The boys acquiesced with varying degrees of begrudging permission. My daughter gloated about being right, suggesting that she'd gladly accept thanks for championing Dennis' cause in the beginning of our courtship with dinner or a movie out. I can only imagine the conversation that transpired with my darling little puppies, but it probably involved talk of fenced backyards, neighborhood felines, and the promise of unlimited salmon treats. My sort-of soon-to-be fiancé seemed confident in his pursuit of our future, but one obstacle (if you don't count me) remained.

Dennis is all about honor to God and Country, with a heavy dose of old-fashioned respect for a father's wishes. In my case, this meant coordinating a lunch date with my parents halfway between several states to secure their blessing. To bolster the outcome, the location would include minimal travel off the interstate, a restaurant buffet with ample choices, and at a time that didn't interfere with Dad's TV sporting schedule. The Internet provided the first two, and propitious planning placed the date of his presentation safely between the Super Bowl and March Madness.

If Dennis was hoping to surprise with his topic of conversation, I'm afraid he was sorely disappointed. I've never been shy about sharing the good in my life, so my folks were well aware by this point what I *hoped* was coming their way, and Dad prepared accordingly. He loved to tease, and I should've known that this occasion would be too tempting for him to resist.

In my formative years, I had the debatable pleasure of enduring several forms of loving attention that didn't quite reach cruel and unusual punishment, but at times, came close to the realm of embarrassing for a little girl already struggling with weight and haphazard hair. My Dad covered everything from "Beanie" to covered bridges and Christmas cows.

You'd have to be my age or older to appreciate the moniker "Beanie" that some of my relatives unfortunately still call me today. The reference comes from an old television cartoon about a little boy who wore a felt hat equipped with its own propeller, and his faithful dinosaur "Cecil." Beanie and Cecil evidently captured my attention to the point that I begged for the show's advertised hat, and in my youthful ignorance, I made the mistake of gladly wearing my beanie for all to see. My Dad just couldn't resist that one and bestowed the nickname that never went away.

A normal person might think that Sunday afternoon drives in the country would provide endless opportunities for rich family bonding, unless they'd ever met my family. Being the youngest and only girl of three, I rated the seat up front between Mom and Dad – mostly to keep the peace with my brothers safely out of arm's reach. This would ordinarily mean less teasing, except that the biggest kid of all still sat behind the steering wheel and delighted in finding the most remote stretch of woods available, turning down its deserted gravel lane, and inevitably finding an abandoned – and sometimes rotting, covered bridge in the middle of nowhere.

This predicament always took me by surprise, as the car would drift to the middle of the bridge and come to a complete stop with its sputtering engine and dinging dashboard. My eyes would expand to round saucers in my wee little head, pooling with tears, as Dad would announce that we must be out of gas. I was terrified and rewarded him with the same pathetic reaction each time he did it. Mom would give him "the look" after taking pity on my stifled sobs, and the engine would mysteriously roar back to life with a shift into gear and muffled laughter from the backseat.

The cows entered my life years later, on my first Christmas home after moving out on my own. I'd purchased a finely carved crèche from a co-worker who generously offered to sell this museum-quality purchase at garage sale prices, and a new collector was born. Dad disappeared to the basement moments after critical study of each piece, only to emerge later with a stable and corral fit for "The King." My set included baby Jesus, Mary and Joseph, the Wise Men, a shepherd and his flock, one donkey, and a cow. I placed each carving reverently in the places I always imagined they'd be, allowing the sheep to graze beside the manger, and locking the other animals safely behind the fence. I figured there was a lot going on in the stable, and they didn't need to be worrying about a wandering cow.

That one thought mumbled aloud would instigate another excuse for Dad to poke fun at my peculiar imagination and created a running mystery for the next thirty years about, "who left the corral door open, and where the cow was now?" Oh, what I'd give to feel my cheeks rise in color once again, with one last gentle jab at my offbeat personality's expense.

Still seated at the crowded buffet, the waitress finally cleared all our dishes, and the subject arose at last. I was hoping for a quick cut to the chase and a rousing welcome to Dennis into our family, but of course that would be too easy – and certainly wouldn't satisfy my ornery father. His days of wearing a Civil Engineer's pocket protector upon his shirt's breast were long past, but the pocket itself remained, from which he proceeded to pull a single sheet of paper. He unfolded the missive with great fanfare, cleared his throat in dramatic fashion, and announced the heading of "pros and cons" to the question of handing his only daughter over to the man anxiously waiting across the table.

He was boldly prepared to go where Dennis probably was not. Being an only child with a child who *was* an only child, his family thrived on quiet order and reserve. My dad was one of seven mischievous children and carried a smile (and that ornery gleam) in his eye even while sleeping. Dad was enjoying this way too much, but I was confident that Dennis would rise to the challenge and realize the rules of engagement (no pun intended) in time to play along.

After all, the first time he ever met my folks, Dad proceeded to inform him that I was a Republican, just in case Dennis might harbor any "liberal" tendencies. I never had the heart to tell Dad that I'd voted for a democratic governor – twice, and that contrary to popular family tradition, I had that independent thing going on in all areas of my life. I figured that if Dennis really wanted to join with this eccentric collection of family, he might as well get used to "Life with Father."

The first order of Dad's business was to read a very long list of reasons why we *should* get married, suspiciously including all of the things I'd been saying during phone calls that I didn't even know he knew existed. Never underestimate a father's ability to listen in on conversations best left to mother and daughter when you think no one else is listening. At least my eyes were filling with tears of laughter this time. I was still Daddy's little girl, but he had my ultimate happiness at heart and managed to save me from extreme embarrassment by finally moving on.

I have to admit to some trepidation while waiting for the other shoe to drop from the "con" list. Other than overcoming the logistics of a possible move overseas, school changes, overall emotional upheaval, and two dogs who didn't know how to fly, I couldn't think of a single reason to keep us from merging. Hindsight would reveal a substantial list of things I wish we'd thought of sooner, but I was definitely running on adrenaline and blessedly blinded by love and a hankering to get this show on the road.

The suspense was maddening. I may have just imagined it, but there even seemed to be a distant drum roll behind Dad's back as he paused for effect, and *finally* proceeded. I was expecting more and hoping for less. What I got was short and very sweet. In answer to all the reasons why he wouldn't give his blessing; he had none. Dennis was a sure winner and always had been. They were thrilled at the prospect of our union and wished us all the best. They knew we'd need better than best to get through the impending merger but they were behind us all the way. Only one obstacle remained. I just had to figure out what would get this wonderful man to pop the question to *me*.

Grow old along with me!
The best is yet to be...
- Browning –

I didn't have to wait long. With clear blue skies and just enough lingering winter chill to warrant the need for wearing all of my chic leather; it was a perfect day in paradise for my Harley man to act. Forever in awe of new adventure and the chance to hop on the bike and hold on, I was oblivious to the flight plan and never cared where we were going or how long we'd be gone. With my arms securely wrapped around my future, the details didn't really matter. If not for the occasional sore back and bottom, I'd ride the Harley until the gas gave out and then hop on again with my fringe a-flyin'.

There was brief mention that today held a quick stop at the Harley dealership for routine maintenance before our usual meandering about the landscape, so I packed extra money for cruising the clearance rack, as well as our peanut butter and jelly. Halfway there, doom fell upon us. There we were, minding our own business – Dennis with the road and I with him, when a rock flew out of nowhere, smashing the headlight into a million pieces. This wasn't good.

It was painful (and impressive) to watch him gather all the dangling pieces and shards on the road as his face turned red from stifling the words that I'm sure he wanted to expel but was too polite to utter. Careful, calm, and collected met lawless, loud, and livid. The war raged within as he climbed back on and rode carefully toward our destination. For once in my life, I decided to remain quiet and prayed instead. It was a wise choice, with the blessing of just the right parts in stock and a recent cancellation that allowed time for the repairs.

I thought all was well. The angry flush was receding from

his face and several interesting pieces of chrome lay upon the sale table that appeared to be on his wish list. Shopping always serves as a pleasant distraction for *me*, so I assumed we were on the same wavelength. Never assume anything, especially if it involves the opposite sex and brain waves. I was heading to the psychedelic spandex in my size, when all of a sudden he grabbed my hand and began a mad dash out the front door and around the side of the building. What did I do *now*? I was sure that I hadn't said anything stupid about the mishap and even more certain that I'd uttered only words of encouragement at the parts counter.

We came to a stuttering halt around the side of the building and stood there for several seconds while gazing into each other's eyes. I waited in anticipatory silence until my back began to itch against the scratchy concrete wall, and my hands that held his firmly began to sweat. He must've known that I was surely going to burst from curiosity and word frustration and took pity on my sorry self with words to live by. This wasn't about broken headlights or interrupted plans. This was about us. This was a proposal…an honest-to-goodness, melt my limbs, absolutely romantic offer to spend the rest of my life with the missing piece of my soul…accompanied by a gorgeous diamond engagement ring that showed the world that this was for keeps. He finally asked me – and I said "YES!"

> **There is no more lovely,**
> **friendly, and charming relationship,**
> **communion, or company**
> **than a good marriage.**
> **- Martin Luther -**

I had exactly one month to plan a wedding, pack my entire household, finalize a decision for the boys' educational futures, and possibly obtain immunization shots, updated passports, and matching airline kennels for a move overseas. It's a good thing love never fails. My yellow legal pad quickly became office central and organized the event of the century – at least within my lifetime.

Since everything else hinged on the wedding – and it surely rated first on my list of things to do, I tackled its organization with gusto. I wore my Mom's gown the first time around and wanted to preserve its beautiful satin and sentimental appeal for my daughter just in case she ever wanted tradition continued. This called for a trip to the bridal shop (it's a tough job, but someone had to do it), and wading through all the styles meant for the young and giddy. It was a little uncomfortable at my age, stepping in front of the three-way mirror within public viewing, especially when the audience was there for all those first-time brides, but at least their comments were unsolicited and honest. We all fell in love with the dress that I, naturally, tried on last, and although it was practically perfect in every way, I still had to leave it for minor adjustments – and I suspect, the opportunity to exact from this blushing bride, all possible rush fees.

The cake was easy. I couldn't eat its sugary goodness anyway, so I ordered what I thought smelled the best and picked out a style that would accommodate the red-white-and-blue ribbon with which I wanted them to decorate each layer. I was marrying the military man of my dreams and didn't intend to pass up this opportunity for flags, pomp, and romantic circumstance. Dennis would be wearing his "dress blues"…it's hard to resist a man in uniform, and I'd found these yummy patriotic mint wrappers that positively had to grace the tables.

I also managed to discover the perfect cake topper hidden behind the most popular selections on an outing meant for finding all the silk flowers that Mom would be transforming into a timeless bouquet of red and white roses with cascades of blue-something's that passed for a reasonable substitute for nature's bounty. The plastic concoction showcased a bride dragging her reluctant groom toward an imaginary altar with unbridled joy. It made me laugh, which was a definite sign for its suitability. It also got my cogs turning toward the crafty personalization that was sure to follow.

I envisioned miniature do-rags on the happy couple in diminutive patriotic designs with just the right Harley decal that I'd been saving for an occasion such as this. All those dollars and drawing circles at art school would finally team-up with my pack-ratting skills and overflowing bins of unrelated notions in a fitting tribute to this eclectic dream.

Many may argue the merits of my unconventional choices of the past, but I honestly don't try to make the same mistake twice. My insistence for frugality at my last wedding reception rewarded my Mother with a severe case of poison oak when she used contagious ivy found at the side of the road for table decorations. The effect was lovely and her long-sleeved dress hid the catastrophic results, but I really wanted *this* mother-of-the-bride experience to radiate from love and not another fiery rash. A quaint Victorian party house was booked, complete with catering staff who relished the idea of buntings on the veranda and listening to the "Air Force March" on their honky-tonk piano as they watched the bride and groom marching down the aisle.

Since this wedding would represent the ultimate answer to prayer with a storybook ending, I had a lot to be thankful for with an abundance of words spilling out of my head onto the pages of my swollen yellow pad. My vows had to be special…a way to announce to the world how I felt about God, this second chance at happiness, and the wonderful man He'd given me to share it with. I scoured the Bible for scripture that fit my mood and finally settled on thoughts written in Matthew, Romans, Joshua, and Song of Solomon – with a smattering from several contemporary sources, and even a few thoughts of my own. Getting them down on paper was the simple part. Memorizing was another story…

> If we believe, we will receive whatever we ask for in prayer.
> I thank God for answering my prayers
> with the blessing of your love.
> And how ironic that I found love, when all I was looking for was life.
> You are my best friend, my Godsend, my hero, my light.
> You are the love of my life,
> and the missing piece of my soul.
> I shall cling to what is good
> and will cherish every moment God keeps us together.
> Place me like a seal over your heart
> and carry me with you always.
> For just as I love God
> with all my heart and all my soul and all my strength,
> so I shall love you.
> Forever and Ever, Amen.

Every chance for solitude within the next few weeks found me silently reciting these words in a desperate attempt at rote memorization. Years of mindless consumption hadn't done me any favors to the portion of my brain that easily grasps recall and recitation. Nevertheless, determined to conquer my fear of public speaking and crowds in one fell swoop, I girded myself with leather and studs, making good use of all bike excursions and the blanket of cover that loud pipes provide in the rushing air. I didn't want Dennis to overhear my vows prior to the ceremony, but even if a few words did escape the quiet of my brain, unless they accompanied a frenzied tap on his shoulder, he just thought I was musing aloud at passing motorists or stray dogs.

Speaking of dogs, I would be remiss without the mention of my faithful friends on the home front, who contributed countless hours to every aspect of this endeavor. I would describe their involvement as unconditional love, except for the fact that they were quite clear in their conditions. You scratch my belly and I'll scratch yours...or something like that. They knew life with Dennis would involve *a lot* of scratching, so they were willing to endure listening quietly while I stumbled through line after line, filled with confidence that my pathetic human brain would somehow acquire canine capabilities just in time. I took their look of interest as a sign of encouragement. Surely, the fact that their eyes were *open* was an indication of their support even if my voice *had* turned into repetitive "blah-blah-blah" hours ago. Ginger never failed to provide moral support with her inevitable hug and a kiss, though I wonder if that nose in my face was really just an attempt to silence me in disguise.

Those who look for beauty, find it.
- Anonymous -

It took four months to reach this day, and though I admit that a normal collection of 120 in a row doesn't seem like much, I still wonder why it took Dennis so long. Four *days* had *me* believing in miracles and jumping feet first into this inevitable conclusion. The morning of our nuptials dawned excessively bright with a promise for new beginnings and a clear blue sky. First order of business was walking my best friends in a futile attempt to smooth things over concerning their lack of invitation to the wedding.

Ginger still appeared miffed that her search for a dog-designed bridesmaid's gown in her signature shade of pink still remained unsuccessful and all explanations about county health regulations and seating capacities went into one cocked ear and out the other. Bailey just moped with his head stuck halfway under the bed, but Ginger followed me everywhere like a little kid asking the same question repeatedly, hoping that at some point I would tire of the hassle and give in. She could stare and smolder with the best of them, and I was sorely tempted to surrender by sneaking them in with the hanging bag of my wedding gown. If not for the obvious need for last minute wrinkle and hair removal, she might have won me over. I'd just have to find someone else to zip up my dress and give me a once-over before herding me out the door.

With a quick look at my trusty yellow pad, it appeared that bathing was next, followed by a manicure, pedicure, and a quick stop next door to satisfy my aversion to delegating responsibility by checking on the cake. I might've been able to forgo the cake in an attempt at breaking free of old habits, but my nail salon experience had me a little uneasy. The appointment that I made weeks ago mysteriously disappeared from their schedule, and the woman who usually did my nails appeared with a bulky Ace bandage on her good hand and several bruises on the other. I admit that compassion for her pain fell a distant second to my panic, as I struggled to interpret her animated explanation in a disjointed combination of several Asian languages and broken English. This *was not* how I'd planned to spend my morning.

I hoped for calm reassurance at the bakery that all was well and carefully delivered. What I found was the shocking sight of yet another misplaced order and conspicuously absent patriotically decorated cake. It seemed unlikely that a red-white-and-blue request could go unnoticed, but evidently, that's what you get when the person taking your order goes on vacation and forgets to explain to the nightshift why there's a bag of ribbon stapled to the receipt in the back of the drawer. If my head could explode without messing up my hair and painted nails, I think I would've attempted the procedure right there between the bagels and cheese.

God saved the day, as usual, by keeping my body intact and sending a thirty-year bakery veteran to fill in on the morning shift that very day. She whipped up a reasonable facsimile to my wishes from several cakes baked for other reasons and used her well-honed skills to transform near disaster into a masterpiece whether my recent behavior warranted it or not. While attaching the last piece of ribbon on her way to the catering van, she waved me out the door with a warm greeting for best wishes and reminded me to focus on the road ahead and not the potholes behind me. Angels come in all sizes, and they sometimes wear white aprons with icing on the pocket.

> **You don't marry someone you can live with,**
> **you marry the person who you cannot live without.**
> **- Carrie P. Snow -**

Overall, it was nearly impossible to let little things like nails and a cake that might not arrive in time to feed my hungry guests spoil this auspicious day. I'd been here before in the dreams of my childhood, and my vision was too precious to surrender to present-day stress. My dreaming always began with a tattered old suitcase in the closet above the stairs that contained the most wonderful array of costumes and props. It was an odd assortment of cast-offs meant to be used at Halloween, but I knew that any day's journey through the rubber wolf mask and feet would ultimately give way to the frothy gowns from Mom's sorority dates with my Dad-to-be. It was worth the risk of touching the creepy creature with the funny smell for the discovery of treasure that always lay beneath.

By the time I lugged the choices for each day's creation down the steep incline of makeshift shelves the afternoon light would filter into the room at just the right angle, and looking at myself in the mirror was almost ethereal – at least to a hopeless romantic with gangly legs and a toothy smile. I would stand suspended in silence, looking at the odd assortment of ill-fitting excess, but seeing the woman in the white fairy tale that I hoped someday I would become. Someday was truly here…and I didn't even have to lug my own suitcase.

The scene at the rented Victorian was everything my vision had hoped it would be. Its grounds swarmed with activity, as the caterer steered scrumptious-looking food trays to the kitchen, and Dennis directed the rest of us into designated parking spots and loaded each one with a piece of luggage and polite orders for the upcoming schedule. Dress rehearsal would commence at 1200 hours (a way to tell time that I was still getting used to) and would someone please find the minister? I was ushered into the bride's changing room, an area which was decorated to almost look like it didn't share the women's restroom, but it made maneuvering yards of satin, petticoats, and pantyhose within the confines of the glorified stall a hazardous feat.

After getting through my morning of dizzying mishaps, my carefully constructed schedule was belatedly beginning to unfold with somewhat satisfying precision. I sat barricaded behind the bathroom door while eating my packed picnic lunch, though I wonder still how I was able to ingest anything more than bread and water while my stomach played Ping-Pong with my brain's attempt to recall the vows I only hoped I had dedicated to memory. I could hear the muffled voices in the room beyond beginning to increase in volume and smiled at the thought that every empty chair would soon hold a friend or family member with all eyes trained on...me.

Not once in all the times I gazed into that childhood mirror did it occur to me that the act of walking down an aisle would also be a moment in which I subjected myself to the singular scrutiny of people who knew everything about me and still called me friend (or didn't kick me out of the family tree). This was scary stuff, and having the experience of my first marriage firmly under my belt should've worked the kinks out of my jitters by now. I wondered – for a split second – if this ceremony business was worth the risk. After all, I could easily trip over my train, forget my vows, or ruin the new family photo album with tear-streaked mascara. The punch could find its way to the front of my dress, or all of the relatives I'd be meeting for the first time might demand a sudden recall.

This was it – the point of no return. Dad was calling through the old oak door that it was time, and I pictured what lie at the end of my rainbow rather than running a gauntlet of conjured fears. With a tear in his eye and my hand held firmly on his arm, we strolled in joyful lockstep to "The Wedding March" on a piano sorely out of tune. Everyone stood with wide smiles outshone by only the radiant beam of my own, and I managed to float to the front for the symbolic exchange from father to new son. My trembling fingers stilled at once, as we joined hands, and I lost myself within the gaze of my beloved.

The ceremony was a lovely concoction of traditional vows and unique creativity that allowed for one unforgettable change.

It was always of utmost significance to us that we place the importance of our newfound love securely between the bookends of life that each of us had brought to this union. Twenty years times two and four beautiful children created the foundation for a philosophy centered on life. Loss would always be a part of us, but this ceremony was all about choosing to live forward. It took some gentle persuasion, but in the end, even the minister was convinced that our swap from "death do us part" to "until the angels close our eyes" was a more uplifting testament to heaven's intention of holy matrimony.

Dennis chose Proverbs 31 as the centerpiece of his vows that seemed to flow without any indication that he shared my handicap for memorization. Humbled by his confidence in my character and thrilled to be the one he chose as Mrs. to his Mr., I almost forgot to be nervous about my turn to speak as I envisioned my new name on all our matching towels and a mailing address still to be determined. Prompted by a squeeze to my hands and a nod from the minister, I miraculously produced a flawless delivery of words from my heart and shared a knowing look of satisfaction with my military man. I can do all things through Christ who strengthens me. Thank God, He also sent me Dennis to hold me up while I was doing it.

Yet another lovely surprise followed us down the aisle as our pianist from church banged out a rousing chorus of the "Air Force March," and we stole our first unedited kiss in the hallway while we waited for our guests to assemble on the front porch. It's military tradition for the bride and groom to walk beneath swords of an impeccably dressed honor guard once the couple is married. Since we weren't holding the ceremony on base, I'd acquired the use of a junior ROTC unit filled with young high school cadets in dress blues and shining armor. It was the last page in this red-white-and blue fairytale beginning, complete with the last man standing giving me a firm tap on the bottom with his sword. My cheeks flamed in surprise but probably no more reddened than the young man with the shy smile who sheathed his gleaming culprit upon command.

After a little dancing, lots of hugs, and more time away from kissing than Dennis cared to spend, we finally headed south toward our honeymoon of sun, surf, and solitude. With my vow firmly planted to cherish each day God keeps us together, this was certainly a wonderful way to begin. I awoke the first morning of our official wedded bliss, aware of the miraculous blessing of finding love again and this warm, wonderful man at my side. We shared a knowing smile and then wished each other affectionate greetings we still use to begin each day. "Good morning, Mrs. Rowe. Good morning, Mr. Rowe."

Our honeymoon was delicious, with the perfect combination of schoolgirl romance and the wisdom of multiple years of trial and error. We shopped and lay beneath a striped umbrella to satisfy *my* desires and spent the day hurtling around a racetrack at 200 miles per hour to satisfy *his*. Quite a combination, but it only serves to prove that compromise is the spice of a very contented life.

Someday when we're old and gray – halfway there, I'm sorry to say – and whiling away on a porch full of rockers, surrounded by spectacular sunsets and secluded woods, we'll have some pretty spicy memories to share. Not the least of which would be me in a bikini and the afternoon that I rode shotgun screaming all the way around Daytona Speedway in a miraculous feat of not hitting the wall. I'm a firm believer in trying (almost) everything once before passing judgment. This was definitely on the list of "I can't believe I did that" – and don't need to try again.

In order to synchronize a work schedule, avoid Spring Break, and cash in on all possible travel discounts, the week we chose for this blissful getaway fell a full month shy of the end of the boys' school year. The United States Air Force now recognized me as a duly wed dependent, but all of our meticulous planning had unfortunately omitted the logistics of newlyweds who would have to spend the next thirty days in separate houses numerous counties apart. What a nightmare. Ginger and Bailey still slept beside me, so they didn't mind. I, on the other hand, sort of had my heart set on spending the next several decades with someone who didn't sleep sideways…and sported much less hair.

I couldn't believe that after finding "the missing piece of my soul," I had agreed to this bizarre arrangement. We'd already received notice during this wearisome wait that someone else would be filling the vacancy in Germany, so that nixed our plans to travel foreign lands. Disappointed, but not daunted, I promised myself to get on with life *together* as soon as possible and made quick work of the pack and move before anything else materialized to keep us apart.

I had vowed to follow this man to the ends of the earth, even if that meant the flatlands of middle Georgia. I would carve out an exciting existence with my newfound love despite the difficulties of finding time alone amidst the confusion of kids, canines, and a military career. I told myself that I was fully equipped to create solutions for solitude and did what I always do whenever stressed: relax, redecorate, and if all else fails…remodel.

**Clean out a corner of your mind
and creativity will instantly fill it.**
- Dee Hock -

Whenever asked who or what I might like to be that I never was, my answer is simple. I figure that I already am who I want to be; otherwise, I'd make adjustments, right? For me, the dream is all about where I always wanted to live and what it would look like if I ever got there. Fortunately, Mr. Rowe and I shared enough of the same vision to make an otherwise irrational undertaking a pleasant one as we joyfully extended our honeymoon bliss on an adventure guaranteed to test our vows and sanity.

The journey began with a sales pitch for mountain property by a friend, and cubicle mate, who was just getting started in the wonderful world of part-time real estate. She was privy to our goal of retirement in a little cabin in the woods and knew a friend of a friend who had three acres of paradise she was certain we'd love. With the promise of mountain views and local cuisine to tempt us even further, we followed her north the next weekend to cooler climes and the possibility of dreams coming true.

After an hour of wading through tall grass in fear of finding indigenous snakes, I was convinced this couldn't possibly be our dreamy destination. *My* vision consisted of wide vistas with a small manicured lawn and minor conveniences such as plumbing, electricity, and the ability to make a phone call. Paved roads would be nice, too, but seemed to be in short supply. I was beginning to realize the true meaning of nature in the raw. "Untouched beauty" was just another name for expensive since my desire for rural living was more rustic and pricey than I thought.

The rest of the scouting party found me leaning against the

side of our truck, excavating enough mud from the tread on my tennis shoes to fill at least some of the ravine that I'd just managed to scale on my way back to civilization. Mr. Rowe is a very perceptive man. He knew that I agreed wholeheartedly with the concept of a mountainous retirement but understood the reality of being able to take the girl out of the city as long as the city amenities came with her. He also knew my desire to relocate did not outweigh my appreciation for proper shoe care and therefore anticipated a quick stop at the mall on the way home for my inevitable search for new climbing shoes. I just hoped they came in something other than camouflage drab.

This was going to be a process of elimination. We fell in love with the area, just not those three acres. We responded to the call of the wild in every gust of wind whistling through centuries-old trees with a yearning that sent us northward over the next several months in a systematic search for the perfect property. A local realtor filled us with tales of history and mountain folklore in an admirable attempt to distract us from that inconvenient list of missing amenities. It was possible to find a gorgeous view, adorable log cabin, gurgling stream, and two-car garage within the tri-state area of our search – just not in one listing. It may have existed, but it certainly didn't seem to be for sale.

After exhausting the MLS listings and several tanks in his gas-guzzling four-wheel drive, our realtor ended the search with a home on four acres, a lovely view, and detached garage. This sounds perfect on paper, but most of the cabins we'd looked at were built for weekend rentals, and this was no exception. My mind whirled with doubts as we mounted each staircase of its three levels, and I moaned under my breath at the sight of plywood kitchen cabinets with plastic brown bear knobs and the botched basement bathroom with pull-chain light fixtures and crooked commode.

I could think of a million reasons why this was *not* the place of our dreams and actually listed dozens – on you guessed it – my yellow legal pad. It was missing most of the crucial requirements for our description of perfect, but its majestic view and smell of natural pine (inside and out) kept luring us on an endless loop of fitting a square peg into that proverbial round hole. Black hole would be more like it as I began to ponder the possibility of turning what was obviously not "House Beautiful" into the home of our dreams. I could see the virgin forest through floor-to-ceiling windows, a complete kitchen overhaul, all new cabinets, refinished floors, a wall removed here, another blown out there…in short, gut it and just about start over.

Thankfully, Mr. Rowe was at the wheel when I called the realtor on our late night drive home to ask for demolition estimates in preparation for a possible offer to buy. Otherwise, I suspect he might've been tempted to squeeze sense into my delusional decorating mind. I'm sure he'd mentioned his aversion to remodeling, or at least change in general, in logical and repeated detail numerous times before, but I honestly didn't realize – until it was too late – the potential for catastrophic results whenever mixing contractors with their love of other people's money.

CHAPTER 9

LOVE HOPES ALL THINGS

**It is the creative potential itself in human beings
that is the image of God.**

- Mary Daly -

I get a pit in my stomach every time I pass a church marquee with the slogan, "If you want to hear God laugh, tell Him *your* plans." I can imagine all too clearly how He rolled on the floor with hysterical laughter each day during this latest foray into my addiction with disassembly. Even on the back of the bike, I'm always looking at all the houses passing by thinking about adding bushes and trees to their landscaping and wishing for a polite way to suggest changing the porch furniture or adding five different gallons of paint to enhance their ornate trim. My brain is always thinking about ways to re-make, re-do, and tear down what others deem perfect to begin with.

It would take years for my benevolent Mr. Rowe to understand this peculiar habit, one that I suspect he'll never get used to. Ginger had long since given up trying to figure out why our chairs kept moving from one side of a room to another, and she didn't seem to mind the opportunity to matte down another square of carpet while embracing the adventure of guessing a fresh route through the maze. She developed an automatic response of putting her paw down at any notion I ever developed to recover her favorite pillow or monkey with food bowl placement or design. I guess I should be grateful that she didn't spill the beans about this peculiarity whenever discussing me with Dennis during our courtship, but treats always trumped truth on her list of personal priorities.

Once this project began, I quickly organized a folder of ideas. The bulging package soon became a 3-ring binder with plastic zippered pockets that bulged even more. It held all the business cards and a collection of magazine photos that would ultimately become the master plan for our idyllic retirement retreat. I went headlong into the remodeling, determined to include everything we'd always wanted if we ever got the chance, thinking that if this was where we planned to live for the rest of our lives I was going for broke...a phrase that soon acquired a much too personal meaning.

The first clue to my "perfect plan" achieving oxymoron status should've been our choice of timing. Summer has a way of turning into fall, which quickly turns into early winter at higher elevations. The papers were signed two weeks before Christmas; we spent vacation days between holidays lining up a contractor, and demolition began in January. I'm not sure why I thought it was a good idea to start the process by tearing off one side of the roof so we could create a master suite upstairs, especially when most days barely reached above freezing, and the utility bill had my name on it. The flaw in my logic indicated the distinct possibility that our contractor either ignored or never got the memo about turning down the heat. I suspect the former.

Views were much better from the top floor, and I naïvely trusted the best guess of the weatherman as he predicted a tiny window of clear skies and no white precipitation for the next seven days. The gigantic industrial-sized dumpster was in place, the crew had arrived with long underwear, crowbars, and lunch, and Mr. Rowe had agreed to give me all the rope I needed to either hang myself or swing safely to the other side – of what, I didn't know. Let the demolition begin.

Nothing happens, and nothing happens, and then...
EVERYTHING HAPPENS!
- Fay Weldon -

The creator of "Angie's List" is a genius. I am not. I'm just an unfortunate sap with a trusting soul who began deconstruction prior to the debut of her internet sensation and discovered, by noteworthy experience, that being on a city's Chamber of Commerce list does not indicate a glowing endorsement for customer service or reputation. I found out the hard way that being on their list simply means that a business paid their annual fee of twenty bucks or so. I also learned to be extremely cautious if the entrepreneur in question has a magnetic sign posted to his vehicle's door, a license tag wired to the frame with no screw in sight, or a fish emblem slapped on their rear bumper. Magnets are useful for swift removal from one registered vehicle to the next, tags are for people who obey the law, and even the Bible warns that love is not boastful, pray in seclusion, and fast so that others don't know it by the look on your face. I would soon discover that our contractor's version of Christianity was a perfect example for how *not* to live my own faith.

I supplied this man with a personal copy of my detailed binder, an account at the local hardware store, and our present mailing address, confident that his nods of acceptance during our initial meeting at the site indicated that he understood and embraced my vision. He put on a good show the first few weeks, keeping us apprised of progress with numerous phone calls and packets of photos meant to lull us into blind appreciation for his abundant skill in all areas. He assured us that he could do it all – and had the photographs, if not the references to prove it.

I guess it should've occurred to me that it doesn't require

179

excessive skill to demolish a home and throw its contents into a pile on the front lawn, but he had us convinced that he knew what he was doing and, at least for now, he was right on schedule. Besides, the photos revealed several interesting plant roots and emerging bulbs that had me temporarily distracted.

That weekly photo packet gradually became a ritual for my canine cohorts and me. Going through the photos gave me a sense of ownership for the home we owned, even though strangers tinkered daily with the house I had yet to live in. It also gave everyone else proof that the folly existed. Ginger and Bailey quickly caught "cabin fever" and began counting the days in between. With a great show of exuberant noise and vertical jumping, they somehow managed to rouse themselves from napping every Monday to make the trek to the mailbox. The mailman learned not to delay for small talk at the beginning of the week and chose instead to pitch the manila envelope to the back of our box and move on before our trio arrived. I suppose he may simply have exercised professional courtesy by never asking what lay within those envelopes that caused such euphoria, but I suspect his curiosity's restraint had more to do with overwhelming relief at the sight of "contract pending" on our front lawn.

The coffee table became imagination station, being just the right height for viewing. If I sat down and pushed the table away from the couch with just enough room for the puppies to fit on either side, we all got a peek at the latest prints spread out in numerical order. I quickly learned to save myself the headache of reorganization by placing the backyard shots along the edge of the table first. This made it much less tempting for Ginger to pounce and reshuffle in her unbridled attempts to get a better look.

While *I* was making plans for mass planting and bush removal in the spring, my friends had *their* eyes on the lower forty (feet, that is). Just off the back porch, the "lawn" dropped off the side of our little plot of mountain in a cascade of blackberry bushes and random patches of unclaimed earth. I could see their cogs turning with plans for the rugged trails that would soon become their own private passage through undiscovered territory. There would be no more sissy sidewalks or fenced in runs for them. Freedom, here we come!

> **The single biggest problem with communication**
> **is the illusion that it has taken place.**
> **- George Bernard Shaw -**

I have yet to figure out why it is that estimates and schedules apply only to a builder's current project until they acquire their *next* project. In our case, about halfway through things went careening on a downhill slide once the painter applied the wrong color stain to the basement which turned every inch of the beautiful pine walls, trim, and ceiling into a dark and very depressing nightmare. It's hard to judge the magnitude of a situation over the phone, but the fear in the contractor's voice prompted an unscheduled weekend turn and burn to assess the damage, and I cried my first set of tears.

I don't think turpentine is meant for mammoth paint removal with a roller, but that's what we got, and it really did appear lighter, if not free of life-threatening toxic fumes. The builder assured me all those ugly streaks would disappear over time – and that it was normal to wear white surgical masks during remodels of this size. I should've asked how many years that particular rule applied.

I'm always looking for solutions, be it in my health, life, or general welfare. This comes from reading, anecdotal sharing, and seminars designed to "change your life in three days or less." One of the kernels of their collective wisdom seemed to be a common denominator of reducing stress, especially by never combining major life-changing events or decision-making in the space of one year.

Well, I'd outdone myself this time by somehow managing to cram the death of a loved one, life-threatening surgery, two moves, a new marriage, remodeling, and the sale of two homes at once into this timeframe...and I wasn't done yet. Senior Master Sergeant Rowe would be terminating his agreement with the Air Force after a stellar career of 21 years, 4 months, 29 days and the miscellaneous hours that would lead to his most honorable discharge, mere days before our scheduled move to the mountains.

I'd been warning the contractor for months that this was the plan and had endured too much time standing my ground for all the fancy touches he'd deemed "frivolous" to back down now on the completion date. The moving company was frustrated with my litany of excuses to postpone and gave me the ultimatum to pick a date by the end of the month or find someone else. I left the contractor the same message and braced for his reaction and inevitable reply.

As I lay in wait for his call, I had plenty of time to think and pull inspiration from what I know best. When my children were quite small, one of my favorite ways to calm the little dynamos on a rainy afternoon was to suggest an appointment at the "beauty parlor." This required agility, creativity, and a tin full of hair pins, combs, and spray. They shared a small, narrow bathroom at the time, whose length accommodated the four of us as long as we lined up single file and didn't launch into impromptu flight simulation with outstretched arms or a flying leap off the toilet seat.

I always got to be the lucky guinea pig and cheerfully surrendered my crop of bedspring curls to their whims. As a harried mom with dinner and three loads of laundry waiting, I'd give anything for a few precious moments of quiet – and did. The simple pleasure of having my hair brushed between gleeful tugs on my mass of tangles was worth all the neighbor's stares at rock star hairstyles or just a jumble of rainbow-colored barrettes (if my littlest guy was head beautician for the day).

I reminded myself that all those "frivolous fancies" were just as important as the colorful contents of that beauty tin from long ago. If I could master the art of collaborating with three small, creative geniuses under the age of seven and deal with a deadline of wrapping up our fun in time for dinner, then surely I could handle any bluster from a man who might have a temporary grasp on my checkbook. I could do this. I prepared for any excuse he might conjure in his wildest dreams. Too bad *his* dreams became *our* nightmare.

Patience is the best remedy for every trouble.
- Titus Maccius Plautus -

Hearing fear over the phone was becoming an annoying habit. Unfortunately, the contractor's return call also included outbursts that suggested his imminent nervous breakdown. This didn't sound good. I was understandably frustrated when I left him my message concerning our move, but I didn't remember any sharp language that would incite this kind of response. Five minutes into the call, he was coherent enough to utter the word "flooded," and I promptly sank to the floor.

How could a cabin on the side of a mountain – with no view

of water within miles, be "flooded?" Last time I heard, the final coat of varnish was drying on the floors, the dumpster was on its way out the drive, and the final certificate for occupancy awaited county approval. The answer to the million-dollar question (as in all things) was in the Bible, with its profound statement that the love of money is the root of all evil.

In our contractor's quest to fill his coffers with a stash of our cash, he'd overstated his competency with plumbing in an attempt to install our new fixtures without the benefit of user manuals or any legal state accreditation. Evidently, there's a scientific formula for choosing the size of a toilet's braided hose that connects it to the hole in the wall where the spider web of PVC piping creates the magic of fingertip flushing. Water pressure per square inch equals the thickness of hose required, but unfortunately for us, he didn't take into account that pumping water three stories up might require the jumbo size.

He also made the mistake of trusting his over-inflated opinion of his own expertise, leaving the job on a Friday afternoon and not returning to the scene until several days later. Sometime within that fateful 48 hours, water gushed from the exploded hose of the upstairs bathroom, thoroughly flooding that level and gradually seeping down the walls to the first floor, where it finally pooled in the panels of the basement ceiling.

Several rooms of freshly refinished hardwood now lay in a mangled pile of warped and mildew-ridden lumber on the lawn that just recently began to green with the spring rains and sunshine. The walls appeared to be drying out but their odd bulges and curves from their drenching seemed to indicate future difficulty in hanging level picture frames or shutting doors without a firm push against the wall. Four months of sweat, equity, and tears had evaporated quicker than the moisture still clinging to the rotting boards, and hopes for a timely move and greatly anticipated farewell to the ever-present thorn in my side dwindled with my patience.

In a burst of inspiration, I recalled his claim of "licensed and insured" on the side of his truck and placed a call to the friendly neighborhood agent marked on the rusting sign. Surely, this situation was exactly the reason for which companies carry protection...unless you're dealing with someone devoid of reason. Our contractor seemed to prefer the *appearance* of professional integrity on paper only and chose not to file claims for fear he'd lose the ability to say with a straight face, "of course I carry insurance." That's like being a card-carrying NRA member who doesn't own a gun. What's the point?

I wanted to scream – or at least throw something (or someone) down the mountain. I'd trusted him and his fish emblem on the bumper, mistakenly taking all those conversations when he name-dropped Jesus as a sign of truth and honor. I had a worthless piece of paper in my files and gaping holes in the floors where my moving crew would soon be rolling their dollies. No self-respecting firms were falling out of the sky to finish the botched job, and the government-sponsored evacuation from our present location would commence on schedule, no matter what.

I wish I wasn't so familiar with "no matter what," but I now know that it entails a lot of coercion, redrawn plans, and outright begging. The home of our dreams would unfortunately become the house that we settled for, but I'm thankful for small mercies and breathed a sigh of relief on the day we arrived with two cars, a motorcycle, and hyperventilating dogs, and found the driveway free of dumpsters and the contractor's cheesy promotional sign chucked into the back of his truck.

Ginger and Bailey are such good examples of character. Barking and guttural growling began the moment we turned into the drive as we caught a glimpse of our contractor trying to squeeze his clipboard through the crack in the side window where two wet noses already claimed space. He kept badgering me to sign off on his punch list, as a way to rid himself permanently from all liability and future confrontation. As much as I would've liked to roll the window down far enough for teeth to meet skin – and sign *anything* just to be rid of him – a blessed voice of caution whispered to at least wait until discovering what he was in such a hurry to dismiss.

He kept us outside as long as possible, finally suggesting that we finish the tour inside sans furry companions, seeing as how he'd just spent hours of toil replacing the flooring and highly recommended that they never set foot inside. He hated to see his efforts wasted, don't you know. What a joke. My dogs had more integrity in their right front toenails, which by the way, I fully intended to allow on every square inch for which we'd paid twice (thanks to him).

Mr. "I'm-in-a-hurry" mysteriously faded into the background after all five of us entered the front door at nearly the same time. Instead of savoring that initial "wow" moment of gleaming pine and shiny windows with vista views, we nearly fainted from the smell of ammonia and the shock of seeing every square inch of flooring covered by yards of brown butcher paper and duct tape. He mumbled more nonsense about not wanting his exhaustive hours of sanding and varnish to go to waste until after our move was complete and how grateful I should be for his thoughtful consideration. His actions warned me long ago to doubt his every word, and I literally found it hard to swallow. Besides, I failed to see the logic of removing the paper and tape *after* the refrigerator would wheel into place.

My Mom insisted long ago that I must have a flashing neon sign attached to my forehead that turns on every time I find myself in the company of folks who find pleasure in testing my gullibility and fortitude. If I had a nickel for all the times she'd asked me if my light was on, I would easily have financed this entire project with coin to spare. I could imagine my light glowing brighter and brighter, moving from room to room, as the punch list became a sea of yellow highlighter and angry red notations.

There was a gaping crevice of several inches between my carefully selected tile border and custom-ordered garden tub that he insisted was normal. He was of the opinion that one tube of caulk and a roll of duct tape would solve everything, and he didn't seem to notice every time we tripped over his "custom" floor registers as we dodged the stream of said caulk that oozed in a river down the hall.

This same man told me that he'd never heard of shower doors and installed the line to the basement space heater oblivious of gas company regulations. Thankfully, Mr. Rowe averted *that* disaster by insisting on professional inspections prior to letting our wannabe expert flip the switch. Just as suspected, his propensity for faulty installations produced a notation on the subsequent report stating, "Possible explosion prevented." What a pity that exploding headaches aren't prevented just as easily.

A mistake is simply another way of doing things.
- Katharine Graham -

Sometimes it's just better to retreat, regroup, and usher the source of irritation out the door. The movers would arrive whether I was ready or not, and I still thought my logic was sound concerning the removal of all that ugly brown paper before heavy objects adhered it permanently to the floor. Once we finally had the place to ourselves, we began the task of systematically ripping each piece from its anchor of tape against the wall but soon joined the dogs in a frenzied game of grab and go when we saw what lay beneath.

It looked like someone had opened the windows, turned on a gigantic fan to pull every piece of construction dirt and dust to mix with debris from outside, while applying a thick and sloppy coat of varnish to the roughly sanded floors. Add a day or two of suffocation from the blanket of butcher paper, and imagine all of the above smashed into a gritty mess. I looked at the bright side – we would no longer need to worry about *anything* the movers might do to jeopardize our hefty investment. Our contractor had taken care of that all by himself.

The peace and quiet of life in the 'Gateway to the Smokies' was going to be short-lived…interrupted by the crazy notion that we really ought to be getting what we paid for. Every stick of furniture on two floors now lay upon itself from end to end on the screened porches as we cleared the local hardware shelves of their tarps and plastic in a futile attempt to cover the objects of our affection we'd unwisely unpacked just days before. Any notion I might've entertained about an idyllic life in retirement took a giant leap with the faith I was going to need to adjust to this latest assault on our lazy days of summer.

The basement became our only source of escape with its carpeted floors still sporting a protective path of paper that saved it from the fate of above and a blessing in disguise in the form of the folding mattress in our good old green tweed couch. If not for the frigid temperatures from a faulty climate-controlled air duct system and the sound of dropping spiders on their nocturnal sky jumps to the moat of paper surrounding our bed, I might even recall this episode with comical clarity instead of the eye twitch that still begins with every pound of a hammer or whirr of a saw.

I longed for the day when all I could hear was a soft snore from the hammock and the distant calls from the wild woods that brought us here in the first place. I needed to be still and remember that God was God, whether I was on top of this mountain or headed down another valley. The floors would dry, the furniture would find its way back home, and I would sleep without the pain of the folding metal brace against my back once more. Ginger and Bailey would take to their sanctuary *beneath* the bed instead of the covers, and all would be well.

Happiness is a choice that requires effort at times.
- Aeschylus -

From the moment I met Dennis we've always had a plan – never a dull moment and always looking ahead with passionate zeal for the perfect life. Moving to the mountains was a deliberate decision to place ourselves within a stone's throw of three states full of trout streams, a biker's paradise of curving highways, and a climate that promised at least 10 degrees below stifling city heat – and maybe even a smattering of snow. I was well aware that paradise is also the home of creepy crawlers and in our case, the occasional roaming bear.

New neighbors came calling with baskets of bread and the latest tale of hungry critters upsetting the bushel of birdseed from the back of their truck parked just yards away. I would've thought they were pulling the leg of us "city folks," if not for the telltale tracks in the mud and the droppings much too large for even Bailey. Besides, they were more than eager to share their proof in the packet of Polaroids that exposed the junior black bear bandits on their midnight run through the forest. I couldn't help thinking that their mama couldn't be far behind.

I called upon my trusty security team of two and gave them carte blanche with the acreage we now called home. Five years of training in the wilds of suburban streets had Ginger and Bailey itching for action, and I figured their vicious barking could work as well on bears as it had the frightened deliverymen or an occasional door-to-door salesman too persistent for his own good. By keeping the snake population at bay, they would also secure my steadfast appreciation and a lifetime supply of baked bones.

They expanded their trails to include a blanket of protection far beyond *my* comfort zone and spent dusk to dawn in a constant vigil of in and out – then in and out again. I reminded myself to be more careful of what I wished and took advantage of their next after-dinner naptime to formulate a new plan. This wasn't my idea of relaxation, no matter how many wild animals they scared away. There had to be a way of giving them the freedom to race out the door at the first sign of danger (birds chirping, squirrels climbing the nearest tree), while still keeping the screened porch hermetically sealed. Ginger claimed the brains and Bailey the brawn. Perhaps I could use both to solve this problem.

Who would've thought that a simple screened door handle and a pair of precocious dogs could pull off – pardon the pun – the answer. Per my instructions, Mr. Rowe attached the handle to the bottom right corner on the outside of the swinging door and adjusted the tension to give just enough time for both doggies to re-enter before catching tails in a painful pinch. As usual, Ginger held the advantage with no tail to begin with but she always went first anyway, so that was a moot point. I got down on all fours and showed them how to open the door with my version of a paw, with Ginger grasping the concept the first time, despite my human handicap.

She made several obliging attempts to open the door with Bailey watching, and it finally dawned on him that if he used his own extremely long paw instead of Ginger's short one, they'd gain access to the water bowl much quicker. Racing *out* the door had never been a problem – they just barreled through at lightning speed and catapulted off the deck steps and down the mountain in their quest for adventure. Now they had the means to hurl themselves back inside with similar finesse and basked in my praise of their Herculean efforts.

The grounds were secure and my days as a doorman were over. Multi-tasking was never my strong suit, so the prospect of finally planning entire days in a row filled with nothing but the things we'd retired for in the first place was intoxicating. Could it be that we'd found the calm *after* the storm at long last? The thought left me wondering how long I could hold my breath so as not to foil the feeling…not long enough.

Gaze on [Jesus];
Glance on problems.
- Sarah Young -

I think that people are a lot like a collection of butterflies. We seem to float from one crisis or grand achievement to another, just as the Monarch or simple moth flits from flower to fragrant bush. Each specimen has unique markings and acquired tastes that define its individualism, yet rarely travels alone. The older I get, the more people I meet as I do my own floating in search of sweet nectar. With every new conversation comes the realization that we all have weird uncles or choices we'd rather delete, and I'm not the only one who got to my forties and wondered where I went wrong with my children or why I can't ride the rollercoasters anymore without losing my lunch.

There are plenty of butterfly bushes to choose from, so avoiding hazardous rides is easy. Coming to terms with children is not. I was so busy basking in the joy of newfound love and moving miles away from past pain and civilization that I just assumed the rest of the family was as deliriously happy as I was. It never occurred to me that they wouldn't embrace the lack of corner coffee shops or malls and that a two-hour excursion for home cooked meals and free laundry was more than they bargained for in this new state of matrimonial bliss.

I'm a strong advocate for lowering the age of majority to sixteen, since that seems to be the time at which hormones collide with wheels, and parents now lose their authority to a government that we've allowed to take over responsibility for everything except their finances. We had four under the age of twenty who believed they knew best and that we knew nothing. One chose procreation and then marriage to a charming young man with multiple addictions. Two remained in college and flew under the radar with minimal contact between check installments, and our youngest decided that life would be better lived with anyone other than me and ultimately moved out at the tender age of seventeen. To quote a lyric from Mr. Banks in "Mary Poppins" – "in short, you have a ghastly mess."

The one bright spot in all this turmoil was the birth of our precious baby granddaughter. She's a testament to all that is good in a world that sometimes seems out of control and not making much sense. God's creation of ten perfect fingers and toes with downy hair and rosebud lips was manna from heaven. I had no claim to her bloodline but considered myself her Grandma from the moment I held her just moments after she arrived. I didn't feel like the vision I'd always had of a plump old woman in polyester and apron strings who sat for hours reading to their grandchild on the back porch, but I hoped that this tiny bundle of joy would someday embrace her "Marley," leather, lunacy, and all.

Many days during that chaos, Mr. Rowe and I felt a lot like the yummy filling of an Oreo cookie, sandwiched between the responsibilities of being parents and honoring the fragility of our own. In the midst of his Mother's lung cancer and the volatile destruction of our daughter's tenuous marriage, I sent Dennis on a heart-wrenching mission of mercy. Fulfilling his Mother's wish to see her first and only great-grandchild, he packed up baby, daughter, and tons of resolve to make a trek through the air across several states and one time zone.

I remained behind to move one son into the dorm and retrieve an odd assortment of family cast-offs to begin our daughter's temporary housing in the guest room to commence immediately upon their return. My visions of idyllic paradise faded quicker than the white lines in my rearview mirror as I wondered – for the millionth time – how life had gotten so complicated. Would it be too much to ask for one crisis at a time?

Sometimes it's better not to ask. During the mad dash from city to darling doggies waiting impatiently for my return with the key to their freedom, I suddenly found myself smack dab in the middle of a ferocious electrical storm that had unfortunately chosen to follow the only road heading my way. The raindrops grew larger, and traffic slowed to a crawl as I approached a tangle of cars pulling to both sides of the interstate in a frantic dash for cover. I mumbled under my breath about their lack of fortitude and jumped when the cell phone rang at the same time the latest flash of lightning crashed precariously close to my side of the car.

Perhaps this would be a good time to re-think my hasty judgment of all those road mates seeking protection and safety. I pressed on and put my trust in the Lord. Prayers got shorter and noticeably louder with every flash and crash, but I took comfort in the illumination of the roadway through the otherwise blinding storm.

Ordinarily I don't answer the phone while I'm driving, but a quick glance at the screen revealed the name of the son whom I'd just delivered to the dorm, and he seldom called about anything. With thoughts racing about whatever emergency would rate this kind of attention, I pried one hand away from the steering wheel long enough to take the call. Evidently, the emergency was me.

He was calling to warn about the path of impending doom large enough to warrant the notice of every media outlet that even he subscribed to and to pass along the dire alert for life-threatening weather traveling an identical path as my own. He was hoping to hear that I was already home and heading to the basement for cover, but he heard the shrill anxiety in my voice and the telltale smack of wipers against the pouring rain and knew that his crazy Mother was in it up to her ears this time – not quite literally…yet.

This would rate as one of the most harrowing adventures I'd ever had with my eyes open and one that left indelible lessons that I would rather have learned under less traumatic circumstances. Foremost would undoubtedly be God's admonition to seek Him first and move slowly enough each day to catch all the subtle hints He bestows upon those of us who possess enough savvy to know the hints exist in the first place. A summer sky that darkens to pitch black hours before the sun goes down certainly qualifies, as well as torrents of rain that move in continuous sheets as if poured from a bottomless bucket. Add to that the unpredictability of nature's power plant in the sky, and the trail of breadcrumbs seems impossible for even me to miss. Note to self: eyes are the window to the soul on purpose. The fact that God saw fit to bestow me with two only serves to magnify their importance.

A trip that normally took two hours had easily doubled, so seeing four brown eyes and eight leaping limbs never looked so good. Normally, I would've made a feeble attempt to make Ginger and Bailey sit at attention while I at least got my feet inside the door. I was so glad to be standing on dry ground in the presence of infallible friends and home sweet home that I dropped to my knees in surrender to the bruising assault that would surely turn me black and blue by morning.

I didn't even take the time to empty the car of its floor-to-ceiling cargo. I was weary of responsibilities, and the only decision I wanted to make now was tea or water and which rocker to sink into on the back porch. Ginger seemed to sense my limitations and curled into a ball across both bare feet. Bailey helped himself to the unrestricted outdoors via the custom door, with a flying leap into the backyard. I envied his strength and ability to focus on one thing at a time.

His present focus was a self-proclaimed ritual that involved two of his favorite things – barking and being the center of attention. From the first twilight since moving in, he would move into position at the top of our hill and proceed to bark persistently in a clockwise motion until the sound of returned echoes would signal readjustment to another zone. The pattern was always the same. First, all barks projected eastward, then south, toward the west, followed by a call to the north.

Mr. Rowe always thought it sounded like a primitive form of online chatting, much like the beat of Indian drums with the sophistication of smoke signal communication. I don't presume to know what was said each night, but if you listened very closely, it was obvious that Bailey and his tribe did. In any case, after each ten-minute rite, Bailey would let himself in with a satisfied smile and a spring in his step as he mounted the bedroom stairs for well-deserved sleep. On this particular night, Ginger and I weren't far behind.

> **Every blade of grass has its angel**
> **that bends over it and whispers,**
> **"Grow, grow."**
> **- The Talmud -**

I hadn't had babies in the house for decades, yet here I was, packing away all breakable objects and filling the outlets with safety plugs. We'd offered food and shelter for the next six weeks, but the rest was up to our daughter. Our home would provide a sanctuary away from the turbulence of a broken marriage and shattered dreams, but tough love was in order for the rest. We would soon see if parental wisdom could vie with youthful omnipotence and still allow any of us to remain standing. I kept inhaling to counteract my anxiety, but Ginger's worried stare was proof that I was clearly out of control. How foolish to think I was ever in.

Maybe a quick stroll down the drive to retrieve the mail would reestablish a normal breathing pattern and give the dogs a legitimate reason to bark. After all, they hadn't surveyed the land for at least thirty minutes, and one could never be sure that danger wasn't lurking unless initiating elaborate reconnaissance. Hmm...perhaps I should've broken the news gently that their efforts would be more effective if Bailey could somehow contain his wagging tail while trying to appear ferocious with his fearsome facade. No matter. We all knew that danger wouldn't lurk until the sun went down anyway, and we still had several hours of daylight remaining.

Mundane mail is a good thing. Stacks of junk mail and catalogs are excellent material to fill the recycle bin and keep the empty water bottles from rolling around the trunk on our weekly trek to the landfill. I rarely emerged from this daily task with more than a bill or two, as the bulk of each day's treasure hit the bin before ever leaving the garage. Alas, routine occasionally suffers defeat and can leave a body rather breathless.

This was going to be one of those days, when a quick shuffle through the stack revealed an official-looking envelope from the county constable. I was well aware of the duties this particular governmental office performed, having an unfortunate abundance of experience with small claims court through the pitfalls of land lording a host of rental properties in a past life. I laughed at its timing...a teenage mother and infant were on their way, our garage would soon be full of other people's stuff, and now I held in my hands a notarized summons outlining the lawsuit from our contractor – listing outstanding payment for items that I was pretty certain we'd already paid months ago. I felt the invasion of our privacy and integrity through every bone in my body. Lord, help me (again).

Mr. Rowe is the one who always makes the nightly rounds to make sure that all doors and windows remain securely locked.

For this reason, I never bother to venture to the basement unless we're both going down to "play" at our respective hobbies. With him out of town, I never would've bothered going down the extra staircase or subject myself to the endless wait through rural dial-up on the computer if not for this poor excuse for a letter. I needed to examine our records and put to rest the gnawing angst over this latest assault – and do it before sundown on Friday. Our contractor may be many things, but his compliance with the Sabbath was commendable and perhaps the only thing honorable about him. I knew I could count on the fact that once the sun dropped behind the mountain on this particular Friday, he'd be AWOL and unresponsive for days.

It's a good thing that Ginger and Bailey followed me down the steps like lambs with their mama. If not for them, the shock of gushing and ricocheting water with every slosh of footsteps on the soaking carpet might easily have done me in. Another toilet, another flood…would this nightmare never end?! It shouldn't have surprised me to see another braided hose flapping in the breeze as water shot out of the uncontained plumbing at maximum pressure, spewing water at a rate that now measured several inches at its source, with rapidly expanding damage from the bathroom to the rest of the rooms. I took one look and did exactly what men think women do in times like these – I totally freaked out.

The next few minutes are a bit of a blur, but I seem to recall running from the basement to the kitchen, screaming for help, and trying not to stumble across the backs of my frantic dogs. We made that journey up and down several times, until I finally realized that no one was coming to my rescue and I needed to get a grip. Within that pause, I recalled vague words of wisdom from my husband to cut the water at its source. OK, I could do that. My shoes squished anyway, so I waded in and finally figured out which way to turn the knob after squirting myself in the face several times before thoroughly soaking the rest of my body.

You can tease all you want about plumbers, but I think their expertise is grossly underrated. I promptly called the one who fixed our previous flood disaster and roused him from an ill-timed vacation nap with my hysterical plea for help. With the knowledge of help on the way, I then called the contractor and got voice mail, strongly suspecting he didn't answer because he thought I was calling about the lawsuit. If only. Then I called Dennis in Oklahoma and left *another* message. What was this – a conspiracy, or just an elaborate scheme to test my fortitude? The former would indicate the devil and the latter my reliance on God. It always turns out better when choosing door number two.

Before the comfort of any returned calls, I managed to obtain the services of a flood damage company who worked round the clock for fees that I didn't bother to ask. At this point, that was the least of my worries. I moved what little I could to higher elevations, but the piano and several other heirlooms sat in the path of devastation, so the sooner we moved them out and got the carpets ripped away from the walls, the better. They brought in several industrial-sized fans that resembled the turbine engines on a jet and sounded like runway six at the local airport. I was informed that we'd have the thunderous noise at least three days or until all moisture was extracted and dried out. We had *a lot* of moisture, and the baby would arrive in two days. Perhaps she'd think the turbines were some sort of lullaby for giants.

CHAPTER 10

LOVE DOES NOT INSIST ON ITS OWN WAY

**If you want to feel rich,
just count the things you have that money can't buy.
- Proverb –**

I grew up with an original Barbie and Ken. My Ken boasted felt hair, and Barbie's curves appeared biologically impossible but perfect for haute couture of the time. Political correctness and, in my opinion, a sad decline in what's considered elegant or attractive, has watered down the mystique of dress-up and dreams that the dolls were invented for in the first place. Their wardrobe included the requisite swimsuits, black evening gown with gloves, and a coveted majorette's costume store-bought and delivered for one of my birthdays, but the bulk of my treasured memories came from an old Singer sewing machine and my Mom's loving hands.

I had outfits for every occasion, suspiciously identical to the quilt scraps that combined to cover my bed, with an occasional one-of-a-kind creation like the designer-worthy leopard dirndl skirt with matching cape. Never at a loss for imagination (or energy, for that matter) my Mom outdid herself the Christmas of "The Wedding."

The Wedding was a complete collection of bride, groom, bridesmaid, groomsman, and the flower girl, plus trousseau for the honeymoon and a cool new convertible sized for two dolls and a small suitcase in its lift-up trunk. It was heaven on earth for a little girl in love with her imaginary friends, and a sure nightmare for my exhausted parents when all I desired that morning was undivided attention to admire each new outfit as the wedding party changed clothes. Thank God for Aunt Mabel.

She was my beloved Grandpa's maiden sister, the sibling who elected to stay home and take care of their mama instead of starting a family of her own. She came to our house every Christmas I can remember to share a holiday meal and evidently enjoy the aftermath of our annual morning of wrapping paper chaos. I've never forgotten our fashion show, and still see her look of joy and rapture – if I look hard enough, as she ooh'd and ahh'd over each new outfit during the hours-long presentation. She became my instant hero for her unconditional devotion to little (not so old) me and her ability to make me feel like I was her favorite – the one person she'd rather be with than anyone else in the whole world. I took her example to heart and finally knew – all these years later, why a person would do such a thing.

Music is only love looking for words.
- Lawrence Durrell -

In the muddle that yoked our lives throughout that summer of uncertainty, one precious memory survives as proof that love does not insist on its own way. If I'd had *my* way, the earth would remain a constant 72 degrees with no humidity, cloudless skies, and I'd have a head full of long, straight hair. Lord knows that I frizz at the hint of rain, Georgia summers are hotter than a griddle on breakfast morning, and I generally only get what's good for me anyhow.

We soon fell into a routine of strangers passing in the night – or very early morning, as the case may be, with our visiting nomads. Mr. Rowe became chauffeur, confidant, and all-knowing expert of parking garage etiquette and meter maid goodwill on his weekly jaunts to a county court system four hours south and light years away from anything resembling our own marital bliss. The concept of divorce was foreign in itself, but our daughter's harrowing adventure through domestic violence, and the unforeseen consequences of drug abuse was an educational experience we'd all just as soon forget. I'm afraid that this dad and grandpa got the shorter end of that stick through *his* occupational hazard, though on nights when our grandbaby cried herself to sleep for want of her mother, my task might've been the most difficult of all.

My grown children would be the first to say that their mother is eccentric, though they'd have to admit that life with me was never dull, and that more often than not, they fell asleep each night with full bellies, a chapter of "Mr. Popper's Penguins," and a daily dose of homegrown adventure. Comforters became "magic clouds" at story time and "The Twelve Days of Christmas" turned into a morning favorite on our way to school, complete with my one-armed performance of twelve drums all the way to a partridge in its pear tree. It may have been years since my glory days of mothering productivity, but I wasn't inept and refused to let a minor thing like lack of sleep and 20-hour days with an exuberant infant slow me down.

My tiny charge was born in perpetual motion – even while sleeping – and could scoot the length of our cabin in six seconds flat. With Ginger and Bailey having already claimed that turf weeks ago, we had a problem. How do you explain to dogs that the noisy creature dropped at their doorstep in the middle of the night was not a chew toy or begging to be licked? She couldn't bark, her toys were off limits, and she didn't yet understand the concept of quiet time or regularly-scheduled afternoon naps. My back ached from keeping her above the combat zone, and she was tired of watching the world go by from the perch of her buckled up high chair. What would Aunt Mabel do?

Like a one-armed paperhanger, inspiration dawned, as I drug the portable crib out of the guest room with my left arm, while straddling baby on my ample right hip. The door jams took a brutal beating and doggies scattered from all the clatter, but we made it to the kitchen in one piece and I made quick work of creating center stage. It's amazing what you can do with a stew pot, wooden spoons, and a stereo full of Jim Brickman. He's my favorite "romantic piano sensation," and to prove it I have every CD he's ever made.

Ginger and Bailey grew up on his love songs and lullabies, so they didn't realize the show was about to begin until the volume pumped way above normal and the dancing began. We'll use that term loosely, but with spoon in hand for my microphone and apron swaying as I circled the crib, we definitely had a show going on. The dogs fell into step behind me with resounding joy, as our miniature audience of one bounced to her own rhythmic beat of the spoons and howling croons. Every refrain of "Baby, It Must Be You" accentuated our purpose of making this moment all about the little one at the center of our universe. It was Divine.

It's truly amazing what a six-week deadline, house rules, and unceasing prayer will produce. Within the short and the long of those forty-two days, our daughter now possessed a job, small apartment, and daycare in the town at the bottom of the hill, and we reclaimed the use of our garage and the quiet retirement that we thought would elude us forever. The hours of commitment to their cause held a grateful mixture of satisfaction, frustration, and joy, as we watched their tiny family embark on a promising future. Our granddaughter wouldn't remember, and our daughter would probably choose to forget, but God smiled on our contribution and said it was good.

No excuses remained to put off living any longer. It may have been past the season for running trout, but the Harley was full of gas and no longer hemmed in by boxes filled with someone else's dreams. An entire room in the basement lay fully stocked with tiny paint bottles, brushes, and glue for years of artful ideas that ruminated in fear of spoiling. Ginger and Bailey had their jungle trail firmly trampled by now and skillfully scented for territorial jurisdiction. We no longer set the alarm – and let our body's circadian rhythm find its own gentle hum. We were living what most people only talk about doing someday. What a pity that I wasn't able to bottle the feeling to use on the days for the *rest* of our lives.

Life begins at the end of your comfort zone.
- Bumper Sticker -

In the span of a year, we lost loving chunks of our hearts to the ravages of lung cancer and heart disease. Dennis' mom succumbed to the effects of a fifty-year smoking career just days before her great-granddaughter celebrated her first birthday. On a typical winter day for Oklahoma – several inches of ice covering several inches of snow with winds to plummet the already freezing temperatures to well below zero – a small band of devoted loved ones braved the closed roadways to whisper a fond farewell to a woman we would warmly miss. She would leave an aching hole the size of their southerly neighbor Texas in the hearts of her husband and only son and have me wondering why I hardly got the chance to know her before she was gone.

We wouldn't even get through another season before my Father passed to join her. Nicotine and tobacco played a deadly role in his body also, but his heart was the culprit that would finally refuse him – and that was really saying something. His insatiable desire for life kept his ticker ticking years beyond the medical community's predictions – in addition to Mom's iron grip on his diet, and belief that one should always eat dessert first. He put the rest of us to shame for complaining about minor aches and pains when his whole body rebelled against him and he stubbornly refused to listen. A consummate athlete and competitor in all things, he just changed the rules when his body lagged and never quit until he reached that final finish line. He always chose life. Despite my inability to master any of the sports he loved so dearly, in that philosophy at least, I'm definitely his daughter through and through.

An accumulation of hoarded sky miles vanished in mere months as they yielded to sorely needed visits to our Mom and Dad now going solo in opposite corners of the earth. An airport shuttle driver from the city and a kennel assistant with two first names became intimate friends, as we spent more time out than in. Ginger retaliated to our absence with dramatic silent treatments, laying in the farthest corner of any room I occupied upon our return, and leaving toilet paper confetti to welcome us home and remind me of her irritation.

It didn't matter that I'd found her and Bailey their own private retreat in the mountains in which to spend their forced holidays and that they'd charmed their way into the heart of their kennel master for her undivided attention and free roam of the farm. They never looked back whenever leaving, but I could always count on a cold-nosed shoulder upon my return. No one can actually *make* another person feel guilty, but Ginger could twist me into a pretzel with one eye closed and attitude oozing from every sway of her dismissive hips.

I know that God will never give me more than I can handle, though sometimes I wonder why my shoulders have to grow to the size of a linebacker to carry the load. The lingering sting of canine resentment followed me all the way through the airport on our latest journey to console Mr. Rowe's dad. The only thing worse than Oklahoma in winter is Oklahoma in its sweltering heat of summer, but electricity keeps the oil rigs and air conditioners humming on constant high, so who am I to complain? There is also nothing in the way of their desert tundra to hinder the use of cell phone communication and that, more than anything, would threaten my composure's demise.

I've learned since to make it a rule never to answer voicemail when outside the radius of effective problem solving. The fact that my physician was calling to inform me of an abnormal mammogram and an urgent plea to obtain an immediate ultrasound did me little good when I was days from home, and even further from the simplicity of approved insurance providers. I was *supposed* to be the one supporting the fragile composure of a loved one through grief, not the recipient of possible impending doom.

It was bad enough being at the mercy of a constantly charged battery, but now I had to wait through this pre-planned visit and endless hours more to know if an alien invasion of cancer had somehow infiltrated my body's boundaries. I needed to get home. I wanted to know, one way or the other. I, I, I…it was time to focus on Him instead…and enlist the help of some faithful friends (once they'd sufficiently made me suffer for leaving them again).

In the multitude of my anxieties within me,
Your comforts delight my soul.
- Psalm 94:19 -

During my brief stint at art school, my favorite of days involved the use of charcoal and a model with flaming red hair. She always arrived late, wrapped in the warmth of an ankle-length fur and clicking down the hall in stilettos a shade brighter than her flowing tresses. She was an artist's dream. Her classic features were symmetrically placed in a face that drew inspiration from either side of the room, making it the only place I've ever seen that really didn't have a bad seat in the house. We could've spent hours in study of her face alone, but this was Anatomy 101. Therefore, with charcoal raised and easels at the ready, she would always take her seat in the middle of the room and shed her coat with a dramatic shrug of her shoulders.

I never quite got over the awe of watching that coat slip to the floor and reveal the perfect example of what God must've intended with Eve. Every limb and curve knit to perfection, and although I never heard her speak or do more than sit serenely for each eagerly anticipated hour, her vision remains as my shining example of what *I* believe to be the feminine ideal.

With that vision of elusive perfection in the back of my mind it was hard not to imagine the worst while we waited…and waited…for the hospital's hurry-up and wait schedule. Finally, I underwent the ultrasound that revealed a mass on my left breast that would have to come out. Without the benefit of biopsy, I would go to sleep for surgery not knowing if cancer would take my breast or just leave me scarred. Either way, there was no longer any chance that I would ever reach that elusive feminine ideal – however unrealistic it probably was in the first place. For all I knew, that model could've had difficulty counting to ten and balancing her checkbook. Still, this situation had me terrified and working on a major pity party, so it was time to bring in the big guns (no reference to my chest, I assure you).

Walking to clear my head is always good. Taking someone along to remind me that my problems are not the center of the universe is a job for Ginger and Bailey. They reduce everything to the smallest denominator…I exist to serve *them*. They always seemed to feel that massive restitution was due for shirking my duties after each extended absence – and thus, as I bounced and staggered at the end of both leashes on my way down the mountain, it felt good to participate in someone else's normal. Meeting the needs of my narcissistic sympathizers seemed the least I could do in exchange for their undivided attention that I knew lay at the end of our trail. After all, they were multi-tasking wonder dogs, able to leap tall buildings in their sleep, while raising one eye at a time in response to current lamentations.

Having just entered my second half-century, and not quite ready to relinquish any body parts, I spewed generous pieces of my mind skyward as I railed at God about fear of the unknown and the injustice of having eaten foods resembling cardboard and dirt in exchange for the news now jeopardizing that incredibly "healthy" lifestyle. Ginger thwarted my diatribe with a stern glance backward and reminded me that everyone – including me – would adjust accordingly.

Several months prior, I'd found a small lump atop *her* left hip that took us to the vet and down her own path of self-discovery. It now excluded that area from back rubs or brushing, but other than a pronunciation of her swaying hips, her life was pretty much the same. We were told to leave it be as long as it didn't get squishy and start moving around. It didn't impair her ability to swipe treats from the edge of the counter or take the stairs three at a time, so lack of a definitive diagnosis didn't seem to matter. I wasn't nearly as able to dismiss my own complaint with as much resolute confidence. I marveled at her nonchalance and wondered why it should be any different for me.

Curling against each other with an added hip bump would not require a certain bra size or perfect proportions from either one of us. I could wait on her and Bailey with one breast or two. I could just hear her saying, "What's the big deal, anyway? After all, a nap is always a good thing, whether taken in the OR...or right here on our own back porch."

Out of the same mouth proceed blessing and cursing.
- James 3:10 -

Despite his gruff bedside manner and several unsolicited remarks about my inevitable aging, my breast surgeon left me with a very tiny scar and pathology's assurance that I remained cancer free. Relief is an understatement and embedded itself among my favorite thanksgiving prayers, along with gratitude, peaceful understanding, and everlasting love. I would keep the shape I'd grown accustomed to and never think of my body or invincibility the same way again. I also became an overnight advocate of monthly self-exams, adding a host of colors to my diet's former dull brown that boasted wellness and vigor, fully determined to live each day like I was dying – which the experts assured me I wasn't. For me, that included loving my husband, two dogs, a Harley, and a host of others that I hold dear.

It *didn't* include a new investment firm purchasing the mountain across the valley that encompassed our beautiful view, the systematic razing of its towering trees, and a constant parade of dump trucks and earth-moving equipment on our heretofore lazy deserted road. Our paradise had fallen to the lure of economic progress, and I vowed that it would be time to move when I counted fifteen consecutive construction vehicles passing our home in the span of one day.

Solomon warned that it was better not to vow than to vow and not pay. He might be the wisest man who ever lived, but I'm guessing that he probably promised at least one of his 700 wives something that he didn't deliver and that's from whence this particular bit of wisdom comes. My lesson began with the appearance of 22 dump trucks in one morning. They sped past our walking foursome and led me right into the inevitable conclusion of listing our home that very day.

Timing and amassing a small fortune through real estate are two things it seems I will never acquire or possess. Our realtors produced a lovely artistic video tour of our home that premiered on the web in all of its 360 degrees of grandeur on pretty much the same day as the rest of the country decided to enter into a great housing decline. Values plummeted 30% (or more) overnight at a time when mountain property ranked in the top three worst investments, ranking just slightly below Florida and Las Vegas. Retirement getaways and entertainment meccas had suddenly lost their luster in saturated markets full of folks just like me.

This is the reason why I no longer dabble in the stock market and try to avoid schemes to "get rich quick" that will be undoubtedly guaranteed not to work (for me). I'd watched my "Happy House," the one to which I moved after my first husband's untimely death, languish on the market for years before letting it go for tens of thousands less than my comfort zone. Add to that the discovery that its crawl space was teeming with mold from Georgia's wettest spring on record and you can easily understand my pessimistic outlook on any future real estate success. I love to buy. It's just a safe bet that I'll always end up selling for less.

Imagine then the trepidation of Mr. Rowe at this recent turn of events. He was just as sick about losing our view and privacy as me, but he'd left the military to achieve a stationary assignment, and here I was again moving us into uncertainty as a result of a few disparaging thoughts spoken aloud. There'd be no sympathy for him from canine quarters either. They were used to my outlandish notions and figured new digs meant more of everything for them. My guilt for uprooting them – again – would produce my excessive time, attention, and treats…perhaps a new motorcycle peace offering could find its way onto the back of the moving van just as easily.

> **Success is about living the gift,**
> **not impressing the neighbors.**
> **- Kristen Billerbeck -**

Months went by without a nibble, exhausting my emotional and physical reserves with the daily grind of sweeping the floors, hiding the clutter, and making sure that Ginger hadn't decided on a whim to deconstruct cardboard boxes left too low on the shelf. The initial excitement of believing the realtors' assurance that our home "wouldn't last long" faded along with their crooked lawn sign, and it was time to try something different. I decided to retain my daily ritual of making the bed and hiding breakfast remains in the dishwasher – just in case, and advised the realtor to never appear unannounced while we left in search of our next undisturbed plot of paradise.

Travel is always better on the back of a bike, so off we went after a quick trip to the kennel, packing a change of clothes, and remembering to bring a map with lots of thin lines meandering off the well-beaten paths of "planned asset development." The places we went looking seldom allowed for phone service, let alone clean restrooms, so it came as no surprise at the end of one such excursion that we stopped to picnic at the foot of the hills and noticed multiple blinking mail prompts, all emanating from one source. You might know the first opportunity to show the house *ever* would occur on a Sunday afternoon, out of cell range and two states beyond a quick trip home to turn on the lights, set the mood music, and evacuate the dogs.

In our realtor's zeal to say he finally had a showing, he ignored all warnings to the contrary and proceeded without caution into guard dog domain. By the time we finally returned home, the dogs were hoarse, no rug or pillow remained unscathed, and the window blinds hung skewed and tattered from every window on the first floor. It wasn't difficult to guess how far the realtor and his clients had ventured access by simply following the tracks of devastation within. Once the dogs awoke from afternoon naps and realized unauthorized human threat was imminent, not a thing was spared between front and back doors on the wraparound porch.

It took days to sand out the scratch marks from windows and walls, but if you tilted the wooden blinds just right, no one was the wiser. I could hardly blame Ginger and Bailey for doing what guard dogs are supposed to do when the guy I was paying good money to listen and do didn't. No wonder Ginger thought she was the queen of everything and that Bailey was king of everything else.

Make the most of yourself...
For that is all there is of you.
- Ralph Waldo Emerson -

Teaching the satisfaction of receiving a paycheck for a job well done was a gift that my parents bestowed upon all of us kids at an early age. I've worked hard all these years for good reason and no doubt that's why it disturbs me so to see good money thrown at incompetent receivers. The first paying job I ever had was babysitter for two small boys who lived across the street. Their parents were a pair of chic airline employees with a social life that kept me in steady summer employment that helped fund my first full-fledged remodeling project. Ten-year-old career options were limited at best, so I never considered negotiating my fifty-cent per hour wage. Nevertheless, even my desire for a bedroom makeover had its limits.

My threshold peaked at dirty diapers, runny noses, and little boys in general. Just because I had older brothers didn't make me an expert on male anatomy, and I knew even less about the care and feeding of little people who required considerably more than my extended family of dolls. Even knowing that a summer full of guaranteed Saturday night business would boost my cash flow, it just wasn't worth the smell of toxic waste on the go. The night they left me with two sick children and a sink full of dirty dishes, I accepted the fact that I just wasn't built for compassionate nursing of anything but my own wounds and left the position of sitting with babies to the rest of the world.

Fast-forward five years. This time I was a teenager looking for ways to amass cash in the middle of oil embargos, economic recession, and cornfields as far as the eye could see. Again, my options were limited, especially at the mercy of the limited availability of my parents' wheels. One of mom's well-meaning friends thought she had the perfect solution, and before I could summon the courage to say no, I found myself sitting squarely on the edge of her sofa with a 10-hour shift in front of her severely autistic son.

I have no clue what would lead anyone to assume that a girl with better than average grades and no social calendar somehow qualifies for special needs expertise, but here I was. With an enormous burden of responsibility and a bone-deep fear of the unknown, I realized early on that even though this boy appeared slow on the surface, he communicated in a foreign but no doubt superior language all his own. I really didn't need to do more than help him through normal bodily functions and make sure that the house didn't burn down. He took care of the rest and entertained us with both plenty of noise and a box of crayons. I was exhausted by day's end, accepting my check with a new appreciation for wonders of the brain and extreme confidence that I'd never do this again. Poor Mr. Rowe…Heaven help him if he ever needed a nurse and I was all he had.

Nothing beats the feeling that you're actually doing what God's called you to do. Add to that the reassurance that He's given you someone to do it with and that's even better. Mr. Rowe always wanted to combine his love of motorcycles with a burning desire to tell others about his journey with Jesus, and I just wanted to be the Misses to his Mister. I wasn't crazy about becoming a member of anything besides a church, but he convinced me that joining a local chapter of Christian motorcyclists would satisfy his urgent call and my love of storytelling and leather.

I can't say that I ever got used to the organized labor of somebody else's idea of what Jesus would do in large crowds of burly men and women with cigarettes and kegs of beer, but we bypassed their usual group initiation of coffee making and memorized lines from day one and proceeded to do His bidding our own way.

It wasn't unusual to walk for hours through throngs of swaying bodies at rallies or shows without striking up a single conversation. But just let us head to the nearest gas pump where

Mr. Rowe would help me off with my helmet or walk hand-in-hand through an aisle of Twinkies and chips, and we'd inevitably run into someone who'd been watching…and waiting all day to ask what it was that made us so different. It never occurred to us that we *were* different, but it's hard to hide the Divine love that had brought us together in the first place, and I guess that's the secret ingredient that's missing in most seekers' lives.

We dabbled in some of our local chapter's group activities and even tried a state-sponsored weekend that touted educational opportunities guaranteed to increase membership and bring lost souls into the fold. I came away with a few new t-shirts, some helpful hospitality tips, and admittedly (with my own struggle with nutritional addiction) some doubt for the effectiveness of leadership enamored by unlimited food bars. Even so, many of the speakers were truly inspiring and we returned home with a profound desire to kick our own commitment up a notch, and finally placed our non-refundable reservation for the nationwide version of what we'd just encountered into the mail. I still questioned my role in this uncomfortable passion, but Mr. Rowe was convinced that it was the way to go…and I was going with him, one way or another.

Our newfound commitment put us in much the same position as it does when donating to public charities that sell its unsuspecting benefactors' names. It puts you on a list that works on the same principal as subscribing to one catalog and mysteriously receiving a deluge of others for things you didn't even know existed. In our case, we were fresh volunteers with a Harley and a flexible retirement schedule that placed us in the bull's eye of many a ministry's management. There were endless opportunities with teams for prayer, prison, hospitality, and get-down-on-your-knees-and-wash-the-feet-of-others   kind   of service.

Mr. Rowe's talents and willingness to serve put him at the head of the line for upcoming leadership positions and garnered an invitation to our first – and only private biker barbeque, where we would actually meet a few of the people behind the microphones and magazine articles that produced his interest in the first place. We thought our future was clear – ride for the Son and see where it took us. Be willing to be still and be part of something much bigger than both of us. We were certainly aware that God's ways aren't our ways and thankfully never saw the next detour coming.

> **Success in marriage depends on being able,**
> **when you get over being in love,**
> **to really love...**
> **- Eleanor Roosevelt -**

Working under the assumption that we knew where we were going and that it would soon take us away from the dogs for days – if not weeks at a time, we filled the next several weeks with as much normalcy as possible to throw them off the track. For example, how many Rowe's does it take to change a bed? Answer: four. One to lift the mattress, another to tuck the sheets, and two furry behinds strategically placed halfway beneath the bed and between the first two participants' legs so that completing each military corner becomes a monumental task. It would make much more sense to tackle this project alone, but I tried never to refuse "help" when it was offered. Besides, it's hard to explain the difference to Ginger and Bailey between inviting the scrunch of all four of us onto the minimal square footage of the couch and then discouraging this kind of well-intentioned behavior. Hindsight told me that I should've gone solo, since that one act of kindness would forever change…well…everything.

One minute, we were laughing and pretending to mind their intervention. The next, Mr. Rowe was clutching his back in what became the turning point in a never-ending struggle with severe chronic pain. A body can only take so much. For me, it was a refrigerator. For Mr. Rowe, his kryptonite was more a combination of lifting and shifting one too many ammo crates, U-Haul loads, and quite possibly the dozen or so bushes I imagined happier on one side of the lawn instead of the other.

His body had finally cried "Uncle," as all subsequent x-rays and scans produced graphic proof that nothing lasts forever. The doctor declared his back a "total mess" and marveled at how the spine of a 50-year-old could resemble that of someone a quarter century older. We really needed to find medical professionals with better bedside manners or at least ones who'd be willing to present the truth in smaller doses and much less descriptive terms.

Anyone with an unfortunate familiarity with back issues knows the drill. Test after test, followed by more tests. Then the doctor offers painkilling drugs, mind-numbing shots, and the prospect of surgery with no more than 50/50 chances that you'll fall somewhere between healing completely or running the risk of never walking again. All of these choices and decisions occur during a time of excruciating pain for the patient and life-altering responsibilities for the giver of care. Normally, prudent advice would be never to make decisions under such circumstances, but the absence of good judgment is what got us into this to begin with, so why start now.

Most of Mr. Rowe's best moments occurred flat on his back

on the living room floor with both legs looped over the top of the ottoman. It was the only position that afforded split seconds of relief in his waking moments and one that thrilled his hairy nurses beyond belief. They smelled his distress and surely meant well as they proceeded to cover his face with sloppy kisses and the lingering odor of unspeakable treats. If not for the sticky heat and humidity of that endless summer, it would've been comfort to the soul to be plastered with such devotion. Alas, I spent more time shooing them away than rewarding them for their efforts, but at least I have them to thank for getting me down on my knees (where I should've been in the first place).

Living with my wholesome approach to life had surprisingly infiltrated the well-fortified walls of Mr. Rowe's meat and potato mentality, creating a dilemma for one so rooted in rote. The thought of surgery was out of the question, as well as pins and needles, and the addictive prospect of pain management's tiny little pills caused a shiver to course down both our spines. He'd heard all my stories before about miraculous recoveries due to obscure herbs and exotic exercise and the overnight healing of my sickly son, compliments of a science that twists and turns the body into a steady climb back into normal shape. At a time when the thought of climbing anywhere – let alone onto an examination table – brought cold sweats, the motivation of pain would transcend all previous prejudice and bring him to the door of Dr. Brandon, mountain medicine man, chiropractor extraordinaire.

He wasn't the most famous, and thankfully, not the most expensive, but he was definitely a part of the Master's Plan. Fresh from an interview with a colleague in the city known for expertise in spinal decompression, he corroborated the success our sister-in-law touted of the same procedure just months before. Normally, we'd take family advice with a grain of salt, but her new golf and tennis scores spoke for themselves and Dr. Brandon was forgoing our fees just so we could see another. This had to be a Divine appointment.

Even miracles take a little time.
- Ralph Waldo Emerson -

Vertebral Axial Decompression, or Vax-D for short, became our only focus for the unknown future. Five days a week, Mr. Rowe literally rolled out of bed so I could put his shoes and socks on for a 3-hour daily trek down and back up the mountain. He would strap on a glorified harness that attached to the machine that stretched his spine so that life-nurturing fluids could once more fill a series of tiny spaces fallen upon themselves like a stack of cards. I sat in the waiting room chair beside him, watching the process for six weeks straight, wondering each day if this torture rack would be worth it.

It eventually got to the point, for fear of inflicting more pain, where I abandoned the thought of touching my husband for reasons other than guiding him in and out of the car, handing over soap and towel, or lacing his shoes. The doctor kept telling us to be patient with a disclaimer that all bodies are different and reminding us that he could only do so much with the pitiful remains of a spine like this. Imagine bones grinding one upon another without the benefit of lubrication or padding, multiply that by four discs (so far), and you get the gist of it.

Improvement came in agonizing baby steps with celebrations for things like buttoning his own shirt or sitting at the table through an entire dessert. Life was tedious torture, while Mr. Rowe concentrated on breathing through his next step, and I assumed all the chores he used to do on top of everything

I should've done months ago. I tried to whittle the list when he wasn't looking…it was just too painful to see his manicured lawn going to seed while the car became a stranger to soap and screamed with its brother Harley for an oil change.

I had no doubts about the foundation of our marriage, but our nerves stretched as thin as our paycheck, and the dogs had had enough. Every day that we left at 8:00 a.m. and returned by 2:00 p.m., the volume of their whining seemed to increase. Barks with attitude have a way of piercing temporal lobes, setting teeth on edge, and for the first time in my life, had me wishing for an empty nest as well. In a futile attempt to barter assistance, I begged the kids to reclaim their pets at a time when I really needed their help. It never came, and I was terrified that life as we knew it would never change. Oh, it did. It surely did.

Strength is a matter of a made up mind.
- John Beecher -

One of the best ideas I've ever had was situating our master suite on the entire upper floor of the cabin. It was like living in the clouds, with a breathtaking view and fresh mountain breeze blowing from all directions. A symphony of crickets and croaking frogs lulled us to sleep on the nights when the rain on the tin roof didn't soothe us, and it was the best sleep we ever had…especially if the nocturnal wanderings of deer and bear managed to remain undetected and not rouse Bailey (and subsequently the rest of us) from deep sleep.

It was on a night such as this that I awoke to a loud groan, crack, and thud, and knew from the warm bodies that I nearly tripped over while bounding out of bed that it wasn't the dogs. I rounded the corner into the bathroom to find Mr. Rowe passed out cold on the floor. Shock does weird things to the brain and makes me loud and loony. I flew to his side, jammed my half-dressed body between him and the wall, and started shaking his shoulder with one hand while I propped up his head in the other. That one came up wet with blood, so I ceased the shaking and switched to high-pitched yammering at his unresponsive repose.

I suppose that my recollection of time was unreliable at best, but the pool of blood was expanding, and the beads of sweat on my forehead were beginning to run like rivers by the time he came to. It could've been several seconds, or the hours that it felt like, but "Thank you Jesus!" his eyes finally fluttered open as he politely requested that I cease and desist whatever it was that I was doing mere inches above his face. The man must've thought I was crazy, but really, who was the one lying flat on his back unconscious, out of bed, in the middle of the night?

Once I determined that a crack to his ear was the only cause for blood, I administered some painful first aid, and spent a good five minutes watching him slowly roll over like a beetle on its back, until he was able to crawl onto all fours and finally accept assistance for a slow shuffle back into bed. Patience is a virtue that I didn't possess at the moment as I peppered him with questions as to what in the world had happened. He remembered having to use the bathroom, and stubborn man that he was, didn't want to wake me for help. With an exasperated glare that surely indicated my thoughts on *that* subject, I remained uncharacteristically silent and waited like Paul Harvey for the rest of the story.

As close as he could tell, he only made it halfway there before the pain in his back sent him over the edge of consciousness and evidently tumbling between the vanity and the wall. The logical conclusion from the direction in which he began walking and where he finally ended up would suggest finding him in a crumpled heap, continuing in the same direction from which he started. Nevertheless, his body lay perfectly placed with both legs settled straight as boards with arms at his sides, his toes pointing in a completely different direction and body arranged exactly square within the narrow space where he'd ultimately fallen.

There was no possibility for hitting his left ear, falling without hitting the wall to his right, and being able to arrive flat on his back with toes pointing in the opposite direction, unless aided by supernatural forces. While I was freaking out and he appeared lifeless, he remembered feeling cool to the touch, completely out of pain, and oblivious to my presence. It had to be another God thing – and probably the only explanation that was capable of escaping my wrath. The Angels were with him that night, and we were both thankful… for very different reasons.

Though no one can go back and make a brand new start,
***anyone* can start from now and make a brand new ending.**
- Carl Bard -

It only takes one horrific moment to alter the course of events in a cycle that seems otherwise impossible to change. My stubborn obsession with recouping any former real estate blunders in the sale of one beloved retirement home suddenly became irrelevant when compared to the priceless value of health. I reduced our selling price by tens of thousands, bracing for what I hoped would be a feverish onslaught of interested buyers.

Our house hunting, previously limited to mountainous regions, gave way to a much larger circumference that now included finding a home just minutes away from Vax-D and medical care in general. The God thing was on a roll, and it wasn't long before news traveled about the fortunate deal that had arisen out of our own misfortunes and we quickly adapted to a new schedule. Six hours on the road, pick up the dogs, jam everybody in the car, and sit in the neighbor's driveway until another showing ran its course. It was sad and uncomfortable on several levels, but we can do all things through Christ who strengthens us with an extra dose of gumption and tanks of gas to keep the A/C on full blast as we watched someone else become the keeper of our castle.

The day we finally received an offer on our cabin, I took to the highway with our realtor and a pocket-sized list of prospects at the southernmost tip of where we were willing to go. Finding a one-floor, maintenance-free home and lawn to match didn't seem like a lot to ask for, but I knew what Dennis needed and what I would put up with and the extremely disappointing list hit the back seat by mid-morning.

Since finding myself the other half of a broken body, I'd been spending rare moments of leisure in pursuit of a worldwide web safari all my own. On the slight chance that I'd stumble upon the answer myself, I'd been systematically visiting locations on our way home from treatments for the last month or so. One neighborhood, in particular, caught our attention, even though Mr. Rowe could only peruse the homes from the comfort of his car seat and rely on my interior descriptions with blind trust. I steered the realtor off his predetermined sales pitch and right into the driveway of the Neo-Craftsman that would ultimately become our new home.

We closed the deal on our cabin on one morning, cleaned, moved out, and moved into our new retreat the next day. That's the way to do it if you can. Blessed with a cleaning lady and moving crew who might not sport a complete set of teeth between them, we valued their precious reliability and knew with all certainty they would be impossible to replace. They made me a firm believer in never judging a book by its cover. Their lives were glowing testimonies of doing exactly what they were supposed to be doing. Our own life now was very different from the one we'd planned, but with the help of all friends listed above (and even higher) we were starting with a clean palette and several new walls for me to paint. None of them even required removal...yet.

CHAPTER 11

LOVE ENDURES ALL THINGS

Be joyful in hope, patient in affliction, faithful in prayer.
- Romans 12:12 -

It took eighteen months before anything of earth shattering significance would befall us again. The repetitious monotony of daily Vax-D's gave way to weekly, every other, then once-a-month maintenance, and days were beginning to feel a little more like normal. Well, only normal if you count the purchase and sale of three more Harleys, complete redesign inside and out of a brand new home, and watching the weeds grow in the overabundance of empty lots in our subdivision as the housing market collapsed completely, and we all became too familiar with the words short sale, foreclosure, and forced eviction.

I've lost money, jobs, and occasional pieces of my mind, but never a home. I can't even imagine how that feels, not having a place to hang your hat and know that water will run cold out of the faucet and hot in the shower spray. The thought of not having a permanent room at our own inn is very humbling...which makes me wonder how I could have ever gotten to the following point of no return.

We chose our home because of its diminutive size, ease of care, and a cul-de-sac location with access to neighborhood pavement and county road just steps beyond the backdoor. The level, deserted stretch of road in the rear was perfect for its solitude and ease of use that Mr. Rowe's rehab required – and our out-of-shape dogs preferred. Life in the city had turned us all a little soft in the middle with Bailey gaining more than most.

I think he and I shared the unfortunate inclination to turn to food when all else fails to soothe our depression's demons, and leaving the food bowl constantly full certainly didn't help. I inadvertently mistook his unhappy cries for help as hunger pangs and literally fed the fuel for the cause of his unforeseen departure.

For weeks at a time, we shared the melancholy blues that couldn't be shaken with normal fresh air and the distraction of redecoration or a game of fetch. I was too preoccupied in my own malaise to consider the pertinence of my daughter's suggestions that Bailey probably suffered from known causes to be determined by the vet. Any extra money – *and* my emotional well ran dry months and a move ago, so thoughts of expensive surgery or drugs for the dog were not a high priority. Other than this irksome advice, no one was knocking down our door to wipe up the frequent indoor potty problems, or multiple midnight and pre-dawn "runs." Even Ginger made herself scarce whenever accidents arose, though we suspected – for quite some time actually – that more often than not she was probably the instigator, if not perpetrator, of most of our problems.

This notion and the day that I found myself on all fours with a bucket of soapy water and a roll of paper towels to wipe the rear of "Mr. Messy," finally pushed me over the edge. I could hardly take care of myself, let alone the recuperation of my husband's back, with one dog who acted as if she wanted to eliminate the competition and another who suffered silently with his own sores. It broke my heart to even entertain the thought of separation from this faithful friend of nine years, but I began to explore heretofore-unspeakable options when the tears wouldn't cease and my fingers were chewed to the bone. Bailey knew that change was coming, and it took both of our breath away.

My daughter met us in a parking lot that I avoid to this day. Faced with the reality of either taking Bailey for her own or knowing that his fate would lie with the local shelter, she took him home. I cried for days while grieving his loss and coming to terms with my failure to provide, while Ginger went into shock when it finally sunk in that she had me and the house all to herself.

They say that time heals all wounds, but it took months and the onslaught of a life-threatening disease to build bridges for reconciliation. Bailey and his new mama bonded instantly, so in the end, it was worth it. I think all of us thought me heartless at the time, but God knows that I must've had an enormous one to be able to break repeatedly and still have enough to put back together time after time.

When the well's dry, we know the worth of water.
- Benjamin Franklin -

The rest of that winter seemed to drag with regret, and I gladly looked forward to the promise of a spring like those I remembered. Growing up in my household, April Fool's was always a day looked forward to with great anticipation. My Mother's notorious ability to create fun out of nothing turned this holiday into one of her specialties. On April 1st, it was highly likely to find plastic worms in a lunchbox or fuzzy spiders in a dresser drawer. She pulled her all-time favorite stunt on my Dad when they were newlyweds, by tucking a piece of waxed paper between slices of ham and cheese. She single-handedly proved the theory that love is blind and evidently without taste buds. Dad ate the sandwich without blinking and gushed over her culinary skills while swallowing every bite.

My attempts to follow her example were feeble at best – just ask any of my children and prepare for eye rolls and groans. Despite this obvious handicap, I found myself preparing for yet another new April, wondering how best to loosen the saltshaker lid just enough so my husband would get an extra jolt to his oatmeal.

Ever since the scare with my lumpectomy, I'd been very diligent with my breast self-exams at the first of each month. It was something I did without much thought and admittedly performed with a casual nonchalance that belied its importance. Distracted by a saltshaker and good-natured fun, I suddenly found my frivolity doused with a frigid dose of reality as my fingers stumbled upon "the lump."

Life stood still. I remember that moment with horrible clarity, as if someone was forcing me to drink terror from a bottle that my paralyzed fingers couldn't seem to surrender. Perhaps this was just another one of Mom's jokes. Well, no...she was two states away and definitely not standing in my bathroom. Facing the mirror and pondering ridiculous notions such as doing my monthly routine backwards to see if it would disappear or wishing on a "pinky swear" that I'd been mistaken, I lowered my arms and eventually managed to quit shaking. It was time to process my options. I could do the exam with my left hand and hope for a different result, tell Mr. Rowe and hope that he wouldn't bolt...or maybe emit a stupendous scream just to clear the air.

I was leaning toward door number three when reason prevailed, and with an ample dose of prayer, I reminded myself that I'd noticed lumps before and that chances were good that everything was going to be all right. Still, this spot felt decidedly different, with a shape and size that I suspected mimicked

"THE" lumps that other survivors always warn us not to dismiss. I confess that this little glob of mysterious matter had me scared to death. I decided to tell Mr. Rowe, consult a doctor, and continue to pray...not necessarily in that order.

By this time, Ginger had stood watching me long enough to know that something was wrong, and she didn't like the vibes from my body language at all. She knew this was going to take more than a hug and a kiss to make better. This, in her case, was more like nuzzling her way under my arm and licking it clean.

In usual fashion, I told her in detail what had just transpired as if she was the surgeon and I the patient. She cocked her head and pinned her ears flat as if to say that she was armed and ready. Petting her relieved some of our stress, but at a much deeper level, I think we both knew that this adventure just might beat all. We shook our heads and expelled deep sighs in unison, then made a grand exit together, seeking the missing thread in our steadfast tri-cord of solidarity...Mr. Rowe, Ginger, and me.

There cannot be a crisis next week.
My schedule is already full.
- Henry Kissinger -

I don't believe in coincidence, so it didn't surprise me that I'd previously scheduled my annual physical for that very day. It seems odd now that I look back on it, but I never even mentioned the lump to my doctor during the exam as he pronounced me fit and healthy in every other way. My lab results didn't indicate any demons coursing through my veins, and I knew that a mammogram was the next order of business across the hall anyway. I suppose I still held out hope that I'd imagined the threat and that they'd send me home with a lollipop and a smile. As long as I didn't say it, the threat wasn't real. Since dreams seemed to be the order of the day, I might as well request a free exam while I was at it.

Imagine my surprise when I *did* mention it to the mammogram technician and her team sprung into battle mode, treating me with scrutiny beyond anything I'd ever experienced in their office before. It was like pushing the code blue button in an ER. Up until this time, I was just another pair of breasts slogging through the insurance paperwork, getting my yearly-required checkup, and sending me out the door with a normal chart and a gold star. Frankly, I think "normal" underrates and I long for the days when I checked out redundantly boring.

The mammogram confirmed my suspicions, and I was quickly ushered through a big ugly door for an ultrasound, stat. Well, that was just great. I'd already waited an hour to get this far, my head was aching, and I had to go to the bathroom. Of course, that was out of the question because they wanted to push their oversized mouse on my chest against as much fluid as possible. Where was Ginger when I needed her? I could use her as an excuse and we could *both* escape around the side of the building for some relief.

I wanted to be anywhere but lying on that cold metal table, so I told myself to relax and asked the nurse if my husband could join me. Relaxation and cancer scares don't mix, so seeing him enter the room was like getting a present from heaven. God sends angels in all forms, and I happen to live with one. His warm hands kept me from leaping off the table, and his gentle smile reminded me that I had never been alone.

The radiologist performed his task with efficiency and completely devoid of emotion. He told me that in *his* opinion, I could wait another six months and repeat the tests if I so desired. Without further explanation of what all the black and white shapes meant on the screen, he promptly left the room. Part of me wanted to agree with his lack of urgency. The other part was still screaming that something was terribly wrong, and I wanted answers.

Thank the Lord for the kindness of his capable assistant. She took one look at the screen and vehemently advised me that if it were *her* decision, she would call for a biopsy appointment as soon as possible. Trust and obey are words to live by. I had the appointment scheduled before leaving her side.

Even if there's nothing to laugh about, laugh on credit.
- Anonymous -

The biopsies were taken about a week later in an environment much warmer than the last encounter but with the entire requisite smells, ugly green walls, and cold metal table. There were two areas on my chest that needed checking. The first pinch of a needle quickly removed a simple cyst. I breathed an enormous sigh of relief and thanked Jesus. Have I mentioned that I sing "Jesus Loves Me" whenever I endure dental work or appointments such as these? I was just singing through the fourth silent rendition of "I am weak but He is strong" when the nurse asked the doctor (without thinking that I'm listening to their every word) why is it that all she sees is blood. I don't think the protocol includes sharing that kind of information since the doctor sent an obvious eye glare her way, promptly bandaged my chest, and then told me to get dressed and go home. With a polite warning not to call *them*, they would call *me*.

A few days later, I got that call. This time it was from a man with a very bored and detached voice, who began rattling off the biopsy results in medical jargon that was quickly going in one of my ears and out the other. It was somewhere between two mile-long words with lots of extra syllables that I caught the word "carcinoma." I politely asked him to repeat the diagnosis.

It still amazes me how I could summon courtesy from a brain that was otherwise frozen. He delivered the verdict in letters: DCIS. I looked around the kitchen for a scrap of paper and frantically began writing it all down on the back of the grocery list. He must have repeated the definition of Ductal Carcinoma In Situ enough times that I finally got it written legibly. I vaguely remember him telling me that I might want to get in touch with a breast surgeon and then something about having a nice day and goodbye.

Sometime between pulling the knife out of my chest and remembering to breathe, I walked out to the porch where Mr. Rowe was trying not to look like he'd surmised the message, and repeated to him what I'd written on the crumpled piece of paper. While shaking my head in disbelief, I eased myself into a rocker and began the methodical motion of back and forth. The birds were singing, the butterflies were floating from one blossom to another, and my heart was still beating to the same rhythm. The whole world looked and sounded the same, but I no longer was.

I couldn't seem to move from the protection of the porch. Mr. Rowe, however, disappeared to the computer to mount a massive assault. Knowledge is power, and my husband's middle name is Thorough. We came to discover that out of all the kinds of breast cancer a person can have, DCIS is the "best" kind. I gag every time I hear someone say that about any life-threatening disease. How can there be a best or worst kind of any foreign substance growing in a person's body with the intent to kill? That has to be one of the things that the medical community says when they don't know what else to say. The truth can be painful, but at least it's honest. I can deal with pain; fear of the unknown robs the room of its oxygen.

At this point, time began to resemble the slow motion in one of those bad Hollywood "B" movies that drag on but you keep watching in hopes that it'll get better. Every appointment seemed to fall seven days apart. We lived our lives on a weekly basis and no longer moment-to-moment. Dogs live everything in the moment, so it was with great difficulty that Ginger coped during the following weeks. She must've sensed that my lack of enthusiasm with belly rubbing, forgetting to offer up the treat jar, and long spans of unblinking staring meant more than my usual lapse of memory or unusual human behavior.

These days all she knew was that most of our time lately was either spent on the phone, sitting at the computer with our heads buried in research, or that we were spending hours away from home – and more importantly – without her. Animal experts say that dogs have no comprehension of time, but I wholeheartedly believe that Ginger knew exactly what was going on – and was keeping a running tally of slights she'd deal with later.

> **How things look on the outside of us**
> **depends on how things are on the inside of us.**
> **- Confucius -**

It took God six days to create the heavens and the earth and on the seventh day, He rested. Soon my life began to revolve around sevens without the benefit of His perfect example. For the next six weeks, every Thursday meant a new doctor, test, or result. Every six days in between were spent waiting for the next seventh day. I thought to myself, if God could do all that in a week then surely I could at least get through mine without complaining. No wonder patience is a virtue, and I've never dealt well with numbers.

I saw the breast surgeon on one of those anticipated Thursdays, and ushered in the day with an immediate MRI to make sure that the previous tests hadn't missed anything. Now, I'm not a brain *or* breast surgeon, but it seemed to me that they could've saved a lot of time, money, and several pieces of my mind if they'd just done that in the first place. This waste was doing nothing to boost my confidence in traditional medicine and was bound to generate more appointments causing subsequent grief from my unchaperoned loved one at home. If reducing my stress was really the most important advice my doctor could give me, this was a pitiful example.

The new study revealed several more suspicious-looking areas in my other breast; so they herded me downstairs for more biopsies to a place the administrators liked to call their "lower floor." In reality, the lower floor was just a full basement beneath a house turned into a breast center, which in a former life had actually been someone's home before the local hospital turned everything commercial. It appeared that someone had tried to decorate the sterile environment with quirky touches of home in a well-intentioned attempt at softening the blow of why we patients were there. Unfortunately, the iron bars on all their basement windows made me feel more like I was sitting in prison, and I found myself thanking God for ranch floor plans.

**Aerodynamically, the bumblebee shouldn't be able to fly,
but the bumblebee doesn't know that,
so it goes on flying anyway.
- Mary Kay Ash –**

Endless days of waiting finally brought us to several options, which, in all honesty, were more than I expected I'd have. By God's grace and because of my diligence in early detection, I still had three choices. One, I could have another lumpectomy with multiple radiation treatments and years of chemo follow-up drugs; two, undergo a mastectomy; or three, do nothing and hope for the best.

My mid-life crisis happened in my early forties with the culmination of chronic depression, obesity, daily migraines, and a floundering faith. After reaching out to God, I finally recognized being at the bottom of my darkest well and began the long trek upward with a new Bible and the complete eradication of sugar, caffeine, and all artificial ingredients from my diet. Through various trials and many errors, I also swore off cow dairy and gluten since then with a shift in my universe to everything organic. It would not be an understatement to say that I was physically ill at the thought of radiation or chemotherapy drugs coming anywhere near my body. In my case, Option 1 was never an option.

Option 3 hit elimination before it saw the light of day. Despite suggestions from a host of "experts" who were certain I could "just wait and see," I doubted any of them would wait to see what happened to lumps of unspecified matter that didn't belong in their breasts either.

That left Option 2: the mastectomy. Even the word sounds creepy. In an earnest effort to know more, Mr. Rowe mounted another technological assault as I reluctantly began the task of reading everything I never wanted to know about removing breasts. I was surprised to learn that there are actually five different procedures with varying degrees of tissue removal from which to choose. I'm not a fan of buffet dining – too much getting up and down from the table – and this kind of smorgasbord definitely put a bad taste in my mouth.

Nevertheless, for all the research that we compiled, all the nights I couldn't sleep, and all the prayers uttered in desperation, the idea of the mastectomy began to take root and grow like a gnarled old tree.

Another word for creativity is courage.
- George Prince -

As a young girl, it was a rite of passage up north to work through the order of Blue Birds and Camp Fire Girls, before moving on to advanced tap and ballet. My Mother's esteemed history, with her own storied rise through the ranks and colorful beads on every inch of her coveted vest, proved a hard act to follow. Each bead represented a task or achievement found in the well-worn pages of her 1936 edition of *Book of the Camp Fire Girls*. I had every intention of following in her footsteps with dreams of matching vests and my own earmarked pages of illustrious accomplishments. Everything proceeded as planned until we began a series of field trips that unfortunately included a journey to the county jail.

The vintage cinderblock building wasn't equipped with any of the luxurious amenities that inmates seem to enjoy today. The overwhelming stench of urine and sweat mixed with the leers and obscene comments hurled through the bars, just inches from our very young faces, seared an image in my brain that keeps me from willfully breaking the law to this day. I couldn't leave the building fast enough and begged to quit the group all together even faster. With warnings from my parents that quitting was an act of finality that I should enact with careful thought and no misgivings, I nonetheless submitted my resignation with glee.

As a nine-year-old, I had no basis for comprehending the consequences of leaving the circle of social prominence, but it didn't take long to learn what it feels like to be an outsider and I soon found myself wishing for a way back in – especially when the *next* Camp Fire trip involved music and miniature men. Regret is a sour pill to swallow with a dose of fallen pride. All these years later I tasted that pill again, knowing that all the things I'd chosen to cram down my throat in years past could never be taken back, and my fate with cancer was sealed many mouthfuls ago. I'd never have a beaded vest or my Mother's creamy skin, but I'd learned the hard way how to use careful thought with no misgivings for a wiser outcome.

My flesh and my heart fail;
But God is the strength of my heart
and my portion forever.
- Psalm 73:26 -

It seemed like a good idea at the time to gather advice from my female family members and a small circle of friends, since nothing I read from the medical "experts" had put me at ease and I'm a firm believer in alternative medicine and ideas. Perhaps my methods were less than scientific, but the power I sought from knowledge had more to do with my heart than my head. Some shared advice reluctantly, while others were quick to act with fervent urgency. Ultimately, their feelings sifted into two camps, with vastly differing beliefs from the group of women under the age of thirty and those well over seventy.

The ones under thirty were appalled at the idea of losing a breast. Their perspective was all about the future...babies or boyfriends and looking like a Barbie doll. They couldn't imagine living in a world without a normal-looking body image and believed that the miracles of modern science must surely be the answer to everything. They looked to the future and held fast to the viewpoint that any risk involving the use of radiation or chemotherapy was worth doing in exchange for keeping their breasts.

The women over seventy had been there and done that, and they didn't see the need in keeping something that had outlived its usefulness. As a mother who had breastfed her babies who were now part of the Y-Generation, I could relate more to this line of thinking, but I had to admit that the younger crowd had my vote with self-esteem. Every time I heard someone tell me "you'll never miss them," I experienced a violent physical reaction with the thought that it was easy for them to say, when they didn't have anything to lose. I've heard before that you don't miss what you don't have, but I *did* have breasts and admit that I enjoyed them.

I was right in the middle of the age sampling and just about equally divided in my own wavering opinions. I thought to myself, Ginger never even had the chance to give birth or nurse her young, so she had no thoughts on the subject and would view me the same whether I had bumps on my chest or not. Thankfully, my loving husband felt the same way.

My heavenly Father was no less compassionate or understanding. He's patient with me long after I give up on myself and is always there to nudge me forward when I think that standing still is an easier option. It was tempting to think "why me," but "why *not* me" felt more comfortable as He gently eased me into the harsh reality of my circumstances. My prayers were like a caterpillar inching their way from one stage to another, always following nature's inevitable conclusion. There are times to question and times to plead for mercy. I did both and more, but in the end, the butterfly-to-be in me accepted God's challenge to trust Him to know best.

Life is all about Plan B.
- Anonymous -

Days of riding the golf cart with the wind in my hair and trusty Ginger by my side evoked a compelling desire to get on the Harley and battle the elements instead of the war in my head. I contained my hair with a do-rag and helmet and wrapped myself around Mr. Rowe instead of the dog, but the result I sought was the same. We rode west toward the sunset in hopes of waking to a new day and clear thinking, choosing an unlikely destination in the form of a Civil War battlefield turned National Park. It seemed fitting to share hallowed ground in a place of conflicting emotions, as I found myself contemplating *their* mortality instead of my own.

Another face-off with the breast surgeon would occur ironically on the day of our sixth wedding anniversary, just days away. At a time when I should've been celebrating my loving pledge that united me with the man of my dreams, I would instead be committing my life into the hands of a woman whose only agreement with me would be to cut me open with no guarantees. As we wandered through the various fields of battle, I wondered how many plans for anticipated weddings, birthdays, and travel had fallen at the end of a rifle, or the mutilation of a cannon's mini ball.

All those souls fighting for ideals and the freedom to live, as they desired, reminded me of my own struggle with the cancer that grew within me and threatened an advance on my own future. In the end, our united nation would survive, though won with precious blood and sacrifice. I clung to the image of Christ doing that same thing for me and swung back onto the bike for a thoughtful ride home.

Every cancer patient's journey is different, and

unfortunately, no one can make your treatment decisions for you. With a prayer for strength and courage, I chose to undergo a "simple, complete, bilateral mastectomy" with no follow-up radiation or chemo drugs. I could agree with "complete," but I thought "simple" was a description far beyond cruel. The doctor felt that my choice might be a bit overzealous, considering DCIS is stage 0 in a 0-4 cancer range. Nevertheless, the position of the cancer would most likely eliminate my entire right breast during surgery, and hours in front of the mirror couldn't dispel the notion that I would somehow be lopsided if we didn't make a clean sweep. I clung to the hope that my healthy ways would be enough to turn on the good genes and strangle the bad, and that this decision would save my life for more years than the experts felt I had coming. *My* expert said to trust in Him, so I did.

It sounds so matter-of-fact now that I'm living with the decision, but it was never a choice that I made lightly. My palms sweat and my heart races every time I allow myself to think about how I used to look and how drastically one decision has affected the rest of my life. The key word for me was "life." I didn't want to hang on to anything that would come back to haunt me if the cancer had already spread and just not grown to the point of detection. History has proven that I'm the 1 out of 100 who gets the short straw; so I erred on the side of caution and moved in the only direction meant for me.

> **If you don't start out the day with a smile,**
> **it's not too late to start practicing for tomorrow.**
> **- Unknown -**

Nearly two months after first encountering "the lump," I found myself in the shower of a hotel room just across the street from the hospital on the morning of surgery. I urged Mr. Rowe to go grab a bite of breakfast before the upcoming ordeal, as it seemed appropriate to be saying goodbye to my breasts in private. With all the ravages of war, famine, and disease, it seems odd that I would mourn the loss of something that wouldn't be essential to my existence. Still, they'd nursed my babies and filled out my clothing in a way that spoke femininity in no other way possible. My head knew that I was more than the flesh I was about to dispose of, but my heart struggled between survival and status quo. Ready or not, I left the old behind and counted on that New Creation promise to carry me through.

Surgery would involve the removal of both breasts and the placement of skin expanders underneath my chest muscle for the next several months to stretch my pathetically thin skin to make room for the permanent implants. The plastic surgeon made it sound like a very logical and nearly painless process that would give me the illusion of womanhood. I'm convinced that a male was the one who invented mammograms and this "nearly painless process" called breast reconstruction. There is no other logical explanation for developing procedures such as these unless you'd never actually experienced them yourself.

Two surgeons and six hours later, I awoke in recovery to the wide smile of my husband and the news that all had gone well and that the cancer hadn't spread into my lymph nodes. "Thank you, Jesus," I whispered to myself. The DCIS, which medical science touts as "good cancer" because it's contained within the cell structure, had begun to grow and invade during the eight-week wait between diagnosis and surgery, but the early detection was crucial and the doctor was pleased with my results. I gratefully arrived home the next day with the prognosis of a 97% chance that breast cancer would never reappear – which was good news since I didn't have breasts anymore.

If you pray for rain,
be prepared to deal with some mud.
- Unknown -

I prepared in every way I knew for the shock of viewing my altered flesh, but never imagined the magnitude of the other challenges we'd face in the coming days. Despite dire misgivings, I adhered to the doctor's advice for pain management the first two weeks, spending the *next* 14 days detoxifying and praying forgiveness for errant thoughts against said doctor. My body rebelled against his drug "therapy" and produced too many of the side effects, save hair loss, that chemotherapy and radiation predicted. I'd whacked my breasts off to avoid the ravages of their manmade poisons, but here I was anyway, tossing my cookies with an exploding migraine that squeezed the breath from my tender chest with every spasm.

The skin expanders were surely a tool of the devil. Made of thick, heavy plastic, they'd been stitched to the wall of my freshly scraped ribcage and covered by my chest muscle that stretched as if a short rubber band tightened with thumbscrews under each arm. Ouch! I admit to wondering about the comfort of the rigid expanders in a basket of samples in the doctor's office prior to surgery, but never in my wildest dreams envisioned this kind of pain. Every nerve in the vicinity crisscrossed the line of extensive stitches like a roadmap, wreaking havoc on all five senses for months to come.

Summer has never been my favorite season. It's hot, humid, and had now become the time of year that seemed to breed discontent within the bodies of the Rowe household. I didn't think we could ever out-stress the trauma of the back episode but here we were, back on a weekly train to torture. Every Monday we spent half the day driving south and back to pump as much saltwater as I could stand into each bump – insisting that more was better, like a clueless cook who jacks up the oven temperature thinking it'll cook faster.

When my youngest was probably four or soon-to-be five, he accompanied me and his other two siblings on the way to school each morning. I was determined to walk off fifty pounds, and he had a crush on the crossing guard so with my baggy sweats and his bright green Big Wheel, we embraced the fall chill with gleeful abandon. He announced one day, with pride and bravado, that he was "faster than a speeding mackerel," and though neither of us knew what in the world he meant, the memory stuck with me. I imagined myself riding on the back of that fearless mackerel, swimming upstream with a smile on my face, tainted a sickly shade of green.

I was determined to survive the cancer *and* this self-induced torture in as few days as possible, no matter the warnings to proceed with caution and slow down. The doctor assured me he'd be just as happy to complete this project in months or years, but *he* wasn't the one with foreign objects stitched to his person, and I really didn't care to memorize his mundane magazine selection in the waiting room. It was too late to change my mind about anything except frequency, volume, and attitude. I decided to press on with stubborn determination, go through the pain to get it over with as soon as possible, and smile through clenched teeth as though I meant it.

I don't deny that my judgment left a lot to be desired. It's a wonder that my chauffeur didn't quit days sooner, but thankfully his love (and a blind eye) were able to accommodate even my most absurd requests. Thus our 7-day ritual continued, the battle divided into quarters... desire, inner turmoil, endurance, and then the long drive home. After folding me into the passenger seat and pulling the safety belt as far from my body as two pillows would allow, Mr. Rowe drove as smoothly and quickly as possible through a maze of potholes and cracks that seemed to appear overnight in a race to return me home before passing out. It took the next five days to slowly recover, and just when I started to feel like I might be able to walk upright again, we'd head south for an encore...week after wretched week.

It was nerve-wracking for all of us. Mr. Rowe cursed the cancer every time he endured my muffled screams from the pain of gently lowering me into bed at night, then repeating the process as he slowly pulled me out each morning. Ginger wanted to comfort me with multiple tongue-lickings but never was able to stomach the smell of blood. She didn't understand that the horrible groans and cries of pain escaping Mommy's mouth were merely the audible reactions to every movement in her body.

Who knew that the chest muscle connects the brain to eating, walking, sitting, standing, talking...even *thinking*? I felt like a prisoner in my own body that was rejecting itself with every painful move. None of the research had done this section of the nightmare justice. Perhaps that was just as well since what you don't know won't hurt you, and it would've thrown a wrench into an already daunting decision-making process.

Ginger remained downwind but never far from my side. She learned quickly not to jump, jostle, or lay too closely to one third of my body. She played quietly, slept during my naptime, and patiently waited for snacks. She was the poster child for canine charm school. What a relief to observe her and be reminded that God made dogs to show us how miraculous it is to embrace simple pleasures. Just getting out of bed without screaming or assistance, walking to the mailbox, then going a little further next time to the neighbor's mailbox was an accomplishment. Ginger was there every step of the way. She never tugged on the leash, stubbornly hung on, and always looked back to make sure I was following. That sure does sound a lot like Jesus.

It took several hours on the day that the bandages came off before I summoned the courage to look. With Ginger guarding sentry just outside the door, I locked myself in the bathroom and slowly unwound the gauze and pitched it into the trash. Oh, what pleasure I took in symbolically discarding the past. Too bad the future wouldn't be that simple.

Aside from the pain, I really didn't feel much different and could've been persuaded to believe that my 36-D's would still be there. Alas, that was not the case. I stared at the mess on my chest and laughed somewhat hysterically at the Bride of Frankenstein bumps that stared back. With no nipples and only a hint of a rise, it was a disturbing fact that I was now less than I had been with a soul-deep desire to become much, much more.

In a very convincing sales pitch, the doctor had sung the praises of plastic surgery, promising to reconstruct my breasts to match whatever size I previously had – or even bigger. I had allowed myself to envision the possibility of living larger and even had a set of nipple tattoos picked out. It was fascinating what they could do with skin origami and a bit of ink, but now that I was through the worst, I began to question the surgeon's claims and reconsider my original wishes. Chronic pain has a way of putting things in perspective, and I wondered – not for the first time – if good things really could come in smaller packages.

**It is impossible to get better
and look good at the same time.**
- Julia Cameron -

I already embraced the concept of beauty in miniature, having enjoyed the hobby of small-scale dollhouses with my parents for years. When that obsession grew to the point where I no longer had space to "house" these tiny gems, I began to collect boxes, preferably those with signature Mary Englebreit artwork, in all sorts of diminutive shapes and sizes that spoke to my creative soul. I'm convinced that someday I'll use them as the perfect wrapping for all those perfect gifts I've yet to give, so they sit on the bottom shelf of a half-forgotten buffet and multiply every time I allow myself the perusal of discount paper aisles. Never satisfied with one of each, I have duplicate snowman suitcases, dozens of tiny jewelry squares, and 3-box nesters for every holiday known to man. Boxes shaped as books pose as the real thing right next to a precious paper-covered treasure chest that used to hold a bar of scented soap.

It took eons to eradicate the smell of honeysuckle, but my goal to use the miniature-domed chest as the perfect presentation for yummy chunks of Christmas chocolate was ample incentive to finally separate from one of my boxes in this hoarded collection. Ginger watched with nonchalant interest every time I aired the box after countless rounds of Febreeze and took great pleasure in "helping" Mr. Rowe when it finally came time to unwrap his gift of goodies. The chocolate disappeared during the distraction of a well-placed pig ear, and we all sighed with satisfaction for a gift well planned and received. In spite of good intentions, the box returned to its former home in lieu of new surroundings in the garage or man cave, and my collection remained blessedly intact.

The box sat untouched for months after as snow gave way to spring and April ushered in the catastrophic consequences of the cancer and reconstruction hell. Collections other than research papers and insurance claims became insignificant in the scheme of things. If not for Ginger, it would've remained dusty and unimportant, forgotten on the shelf of things representing the way things used to be. Leave it to her to bring clarity to a decision process that I insisted on prolonging, using her uncanny ability to search and destroy that which I hold most dear.

She knew about the room to which I used to disappear whenever I longed to create or sit quietly amongst the comfort of cherished collections, walls of art, and bookshelves full of illustrations and words that spoke volumes to me. She also knew that's where the chocolate box lived in all its former glory. Meeting me at the room's threshold after returning home from one of my last pumper treatments, she looked me straight in the eye and promptly made a beeline for the opposite end of the house.

Glancing past her retreating dash, I gasped at the obliterated destruction before me. The empty spot on the shelf, and a lingering trace of chocolate led to the obvious conclusion of my tyrant's rant. A few shreds of colorful paper surrounded a pitiful-looking glob of cardboard, well doused by dog saliva, and her vigorous attempt to make a powerful statement. She had had enough. It was well past time to get on with life. She needed me, I needed her, and Mr. Rowe needed clean carpets and domestic bliss among the female faction of the family.

Ginger's ways are usually unsolicited but seldom without wisdom, or at least well-intentioned worth. The tattered box would find its way to the trash and leave a space to either fill with new treasures or carefully rearrange what I already possessed. My body was no different. I finally succumbed to the realization that no amount of needles or pain was worth trying to fill those dreadful expanders to some arbitrarily acceptable size. God made me to His exact specifications, so I quit trying to change the blueprint. We scheduled surgery number two for the removal of the expanders and placement of the permanent implants and I braced myself for another round. After all, I shared with Ginger, "How much worse could it be?" I would soon realize my misfortunate choice of words and later be wishing them permanently stricken from the English language.

CHAPTER 12

LOVE DOES NOT REJOICE AT WRONG

**Awareness of [Jesus'] amazing Love
will help you stay in orbit around the Son.**

- Sarah Young -

With every cross country move I've made it has also been a necessity to find a new church home. My journey with Jesus mirrored the crazy contortions of life, with unexpected requirements hidden in the pockets of mayhem and joy as each fresh beginning unfolded. My aversion to society and placing myself in the spotlight of anything seem unlikely qualifications for a recurring public speaking role, but that's precisely the position in which I've found myself, however briefly or reluctantly, in my last three congregations.

In my inaugural visit to the podium, it was the intoxicating vigor of my newfound faith and undoubtedly my proclivity to say loudly – out loud – what my mind is thinking, that put me in the preacher's sights when it came time to advertise his upcoming Bible study bonanza. I gave up trying to memorize the few paragraphs that easily came to mind and made it through several seconds of terror with shaking knees, a death clutch on the polished wood of the podium, and my hopelessly crumpled notes.

I shared the joy of finally being able to understand all the stories on the movie screen that Charlton Heston had brought to life in his portrayal of Moses, and how I loved the feel of a Bible's special paper, especially now that I had my very own. Someone kindly assisted me off the stage before my knees could collapse, and I found my way to the family's pew by instinct and their smell of fear. Threat of parental embarrassment to teenagers produces quite an aroma.

Several days later, I received a call from a woman whom I met briefly while welcoming her to the neighborhood during the delivery of her copy of the new directory. I had recently volunteered to update all address and phone numbers of our very own rich and famous whom I now found myself living in close proximity. It was my job to update and then deliver every resident a copy-bound version. I thought this would place names on the faces of neighbors who would otherwise remain unknown. Rarely did I venture past their front doors. In her case, she'd welcomed me into the foyer and offered a juicy account of how they'd scored the coveted sale of that year's Southern Living dream home. I came away with a feeling of insignificance on my way to our own humble abode and a burning desire to update the kitchen linens.

Once she identified her address, I knew immediately to whom I was speaking but couldn't make the connection of why she'd be calling *me*, until she mentioned Charlton Heston. It seems that she was one of many who'd had the dubious pleasure of catching my fledgling debut at church, and in wracking sobs, she unloaded her heavy burden of indecision and sin that my willingness to speak had unleashed. She thanked me profusely for the profound effect my simple words had made in her heart, and I gave all the glory to God and whispered a quiet goodbye.

My second encounter involved a less intimidating environment with the comforts of Christmas and a cast of numerous others all helping to hang the annual greens. New and unknown, I had answered a church bulletin's call for an upcoming day-by-day advent booklet that planned to publish just in time for the Season of Hope. They accepted my submission with much praise *and* the friendly warning that they'd be asking the authors to read some of their more "interesting" stories in conjunction with each week's advent candle lightings...in front of God and everybody.

At the time of writing, it was very easy to compose a rousing account of what my appointed day's scripture meant to me. I have limitless examples of how my life changed because of Jesus. If I'd thought to ask or consider the consequences of sharing *everything* to a room full of people who didn't even know my name, I guess I still would've written about blessings that I just can't contain – only in a slightly edited version.

When the phone call came from the next pastor asking me to be involved in a four-part series entitled "What Really Matters," I guessed that word of my battle with breast cancer had somehow reached his ears through the Sunday School grapevine. After shaking hands at the end of each service, I presumed that he recognized my face but knew next to nothing else about me. As he began to describe the format upon which he wanted each of us to expound, he was quite candid about the fact that he actually knew very little about any of us, except that our names had crossed his mind and seared his heart as God's chosen spokesmen for the project.

One person would deliver his or her testimony each week, with 15 minutes to say in his or her own words – without his preview or censure, what he or she thought really matters in his or her own life. Along with a young teen, new father, and a gentleman with wise seniority, I could fill the gap for all other categories that might include mother, widowed wife, and/or near death experiences.

Since my faith includes the mantra of "trust and obey," I

agreed to his challenge before asking for details that would surely send me running into the belly of the nearest fish. God's sense of humor cast me, as the opening act in this upcoming trial that would bare my errors for all to see on the very eve of what I hoped would be my final encounter with breast reconstruction. The procedure to remove and replace the cause for untold irritation would not be the centerpiece of my speech, but its anticipated outcome far outweighed any anxiety over standing at the front of a massive room filled with folks who still thought I was just visiting.

How does one go about sharing intimate portions of her life with heart-wrenching (and sometimes embarrassing) detail? The only way out is through, and by the time I was finished everyone in the room knew more about me than they probably wanted to, but the intimate details of my encounters with Christ had the room stunned and attentive. Unaccustomed to such glaring honesty, even the pastor faltered, skipping the following plan to sing, and moved directly into his sermon. Thankfully, the choir took no offense and relished the chance to practice one more week on this week's song.

**Life isn't written in stone.
It's about editing and revising
until we become the person
we dreamed of being.
- Faith Sullivan -**

Buoyed with well wishes and a feeling of peace at having accomplished a frightful goal, I found my circumstances the next morning a bit less intimidating than I'd imagined. Clothed in my pale green hospital gown and a pair of warm tube socks, they laid me on my back on a rollaway gurney and set the brakes while we waited for the doctor. I checked to make sure nothing was showing, even though I didn't have much worth seeing anymore, readjusted the uncomfortable ties on my straitjacket while Mr. Rowe plumped the pillows, and made notes in our battle folder about the delay.

Having been through this routine with the same staff before, I laughed at their tired old jokes and watched the nurses' staff exchange knowing glances at my chart when they realized I was back for more. I'd garnered memorable status in the cattle call of patients the last time around when multiple sticks from all nurse and anesthesia personnel on the floor were unable to find a cooperative vein that would accept their protocol of drugs. Once the body has surrendered lymph nodes, that location and its surrounding tissue becomes off-limits for future tampering. That line of thinking makes perfect sense, but for my history of hard sticks it does create a problem.

They eventually resorted to jamming their needles and tubes out of the side of my neck, where evidently there runs a very large and important vein. This time around, they skipped the formalities and just set me up for another neck go round but couldn't seem to find the sweet spot like before. As a result, I had to lay on my side with one arm raised and propped with the pillows Mr. Rowe had just perfectly positioned beneath my head. I didn't even have the benefit of seeing whoever was floating in and out of my tiny cubicle, since the pump of drugs could only flow with me facing the wall, my back to all visitors, and laying in a contorted position that looked much like the aluminum foil antenna on my Dad's old black and white TV.

My plastic surgeon finally arrived, leaving us to wonder why patients get a bill for being late, but physicians float unnoticed. With the OR schedule dangerously flirting with the omission of that day's lunch hour; they whisked me down the hall while administering their final shot of drugs that knocked me out simultaneously with the whoosh of the automatic doors. That was fine with me. Being oblivious to all the blood and guts that surely entertains the operating room – aside from waking up – is the best part of any surgery.

> **Do not go where the path may lead.**
> **Go instead where there is no path**
> **and leave a trail.**
> **- Ralph Waldo Emerson -**

I have a three-drawer cabinet full of hanging folders that house yet another of my vast collections of things that other people probably don't think are worth keeping. This one contains dozens of scrapbook papers in all colors of the rainbow, forgotten bits of ribbon and trim, and all the magazine clippings of other people's art and photos that I like to repurpose in the creation of my own encouragement greeting card line. One of my absolute favorite photos came from a Thanksgiving issue of a publication no longer in press, but the image remains firmly planted in my things to remember.

The scene is very simple. There are three young golden retrievers sitting side-by-side in the kitchen with bottoms and tails intertwined, and the view taken from behind as if you're seeing what they see. Their focus is riveted on a hot, juicy turkey that appears to have come fresh from the oven and placed on the counter buffet as it awaits the rush of hungry guests to the table. I can't see their faces, but I smile every time I think about how they must be drooling with anticipation and marvel at their restraint. There's a really good reason why I don't have a similar photo of Ginger.

I also think about the turkey, and how if it could talk, it would tell the tale of pride at looking so scrumptious, then shrinking a bit with embarrassment when it realizes that all eyes are on the prize in the middle of the room. Whenever I awake from anesthesia, I feel a bit like that turkey, with unfamiliar voices hovering above my head while someone just beyond my blurred vision mercifully coaxes ice chips through my pitifully parched lips.

Once I regain full senses, it embarrasses me to think that all eyes have centered on me as I slept, shook, and drooled my way out of unconsciousness. Then it occurs to me that the angel with ice is none other than my heavenly hubby, and his look of relief and love is enough to break the spell and get me moving into my street clothes and out the door.

With the invention of outpatient surgery, an oxymoron was born. On one hand, the thought of not having to endure hospital food, its sleepless nights, endless noise, and bedpans is priceless. On the other, it has created the illusion that because you can mutilate your body, remove its vital organs, stitch it back up, and send you home all in one day; you get lulled into thinking that what just happened was not a big deal. The after-surgery care becomes more of a list of suggestions that we read and tuck away for future use in the event that something hurts more or longer than we expected. I came home from surgery number two with similar thoughts, and because I felt such relief about shedding my plastic prison, any pain I experienced was relative. That lasted for three days.

Women are repeatedly accused of taking things personally.
I cannot see any other honest way of taking them.
- Marya Mannes -

I've always had a severe sensitivity to surgical tape and Band-Aids that are left on too long, so it didn't surprise me that my bandage was beginning to hurt beyond the usual itch expected. They'd sent me home with several sheets of gauze that blanketed my chest just over the implant incisions, with rolls of white surgical tape that covered the entire area and attached to my skin like a bra that had no straps or hooks to tie it down. The tape wound its way around the upper half of my body, causing it to chafe the skin all the way around my neck, under my arms, and across my back and stomach. A spot just under my right arm toward the backside was the worst and began to ooze some sort of mystery fluid on day four. I called the doctor's office with my symptoms and left a message with his nurse, clueless to their significance and still blissfully unaware that all wasn't well.

Nearly all confidence in my doctor had disappeared weeks ago, too far into the reconstruction to turn back but far enough in to create a paperwork nightmare for Mr. Rowe. This particular plastic surgeon came highly recommended by my breast doctor and turned up on my list of insurance providers, though I came to find out too late from a very old and obsolete list. He assured us that it was a minor glitch, and that he was in the process of recertification.

Not a week passed by without a visit to the insurance coordinator's office, but that soon ceased when we got the message not to bother them anymore because, according to the doctor, he had it covered. That was easy for him to say – he wasn't the one with a vulnerable credit rating and a half-finished set of new breasts.

By the time I began to question his charming bedside manner and tastefully decorated waiting rooms, we were well past the first surgery and into weeks of saline injections that made my eyes water. I'd signed my name on all the dotted lines *before* discovering that our insurance deemed us 100% *un*covered and liable for all the back-due notices accumulating on our desk. I just couldn't seem to reconcile a decision to start all over with another surgeon who'd be working with someone else's handiwork. It resembled much too closely, our cabin's incompetent plumbing disaster that left us with the ruination of too many floorboards to count. What if making a change midstream left my chest the same way…or even worse…what if his replacement and the cabin contractor turned out to be relations.

With this kind of history and a constant flow of fluid dripping out the edges of my taped up skin, I called their office for the third time since blowing me off for the first two hadn't deterred me. They behaved as Ginger does when caught with her paw in the treat jar…ignore the source that's holding the mirror to your face of guilt and look the other way. They knew they shouldn't have started cutting before the papers were final, but what does a little fine print matter when there are plenty of others lining up for your masterful transformation. I trusted them to do the right thing, forgetting that the almighty dollar is what decorated their office in the first place.

Upon reaching the scheduled follow-up after surgery the next week, large sections of tape had loosened and been reapplied to relieve the painful discomfort of moistened adhesive against tender skin. That allowed for momentary relief but opened up the containment of smells best left to the operating room. All of my begging to get in sooner had fallen on deaf ears because of course, the "experts" knew better than the frantic woman on the other end of the line did. I tried, in vain, to express my concern that something smelled spoiled, despite the fact that

I had no fever and the drips had run dry. They assured me that I was overreacting – famous last words.

We arrived with time to spare for our appointment and ate our picnic lunch in the shade of a parking lot tree with the windows rolled down for ambience. Other than the peculiar smell and sight of the bulky bandage beneath my shirt, I probably appeared close to normal as we walked off our food in a leisurely stroll along the promenade of medical office parks. Anxious to shed my noxious covering and thrilled at the prospect that I would soon see the promise of what would stare back at me in each morning's mirror, we entered the doctor's office the minute they reopened their doors and settled in for our long-awaited fate.

The doctor began peeling when I dispensed with our usual small talk, saying instead that all I wanted in the entire world was to rid myself of this disgusting bandage. I ignored the sound of ripping flesh and only winced slightly as he gathered the bundle and prepared to unveil his handiwork. Without the benefit of the bandage's buffer, the smell of rotten eggs was overpowering, and the doctor nearly fainted as he pulled away the last bit of tape.

From my vantage point atop the examination table, I saw rust-colored gauze that wreaked of impending doom. I threw out a nervous comment about it looking quite the mess and focused on Mr. Rowe instead. His face turned eight shades of gray with a mixture of shock and horror, while the room turned very still as the doctor struggled for composure and something to say. If he hadn't been sitting already, I think he might've tumbled to the floor.

This man was an expert in his field, fresh out of medical school and riding high on a wave of prosperity. His skills had catapulted him into the city's network of preferred providers in a lucrative business of turning ugly ducklings like me into beautiful swans. Judging by his reaction, I don't think he knew the meaning of failure, but just now it was staring him in the face. My right breast had burst open from the weight of the implant, opening my body with a ragged tear that invited the immediate spread of infection throughout the area. I suspect that it exploded on the day that rivers of fluid started streaming down my side, when I first brought it to his attention. I often wonder if he might've been able to save his work if he'd only taken the time to listen. Oh well, it was too late now and yelling at him wouldn't change a thing except my blood pressure.

The nurse must've pinched him or something, as she took the bloodied bandages from his paralyzed hands, since he finally emitted a strangled cough and informed me that I'd better plan on emergency surgery that very day. N-o-o-o-o! This couldn't be happening. I was supposed to be admiring my new bumps in all their glory, choosing the final design for the perfect tattoo, and making plans for all the things we hadn't been able to do since the *last* surgery…barely seven days ago.

Mr. Rowe and I stared at each other for several minutes and tried to make sense of the horrible news, while the doctor left to secure a late afternoon operating slot. I didn't know what to say but remember feeling like I should've been able to fix it somehow, or at least smooth over the shock and turn off the prickling of my raw nerves. You'd think that the gaping hole on my chest would throb from losing its life source but all the blood was pumping to my head instead, threatening to explode and leave me feeling worse than I already did. Just about the time you think you're having your worst day, the devil blasts out of nowhere to remind you that he's only getting started.

I'd been given the choice of scraping infection from the right side and leaving the left implant as it was, but when I was told that they'd never be able to match in size again, I opted for another clean sweep. This was just too much to swallow, and I didn't think I could manage another assault on my tortured skin – especially while living as a one-breasted wannabe. Hadn't I been through this scenario before and decided that I'd rather be safe than sorry? Well, now I'd rather be safe anywhere but on my way to the hospital, but sorry or not, here I was, heading that way again.

Worry is largely a matter of thinking about things at the wrong time.
- Sarah Young -

By the time in our lives when Mr. Rowe and I met, we were both well acquainted with the realm of sickness and fear of walking alone in the aftermath of spousal disease. We specifically looked for new partners full of life and well-being in a selfish attempt to cheat an early death. Ha! The joke was on us. Our lives were full of baggage that circled on an endless loop at some airport carousel in the sky, waiting for us to claim them once something caught us with our guard down. Here we were again checking another claim tag from an unzipped bag that just had its contents strewn about the floor.

Once hospital admissions stumbled upon the information that someone had actually packed and eaten their wholesome lunch from home, they informed the oddball (that would be me) that regulations required a full six-hour wait for digestion before attempting surgery, so I'd better plan on settling in for a very long wait. Trussed with tape and an armful of plastic wristbands, I wasn't going anywhere for fear I'd set off the security alarm and bring the candy stripers running. Torn between the comfort of his support and dashing home to pack an emergency bag while relieving Ginger's fears for food and lodging, I sent a reluctant Mr. Rowe homeward bound and braced for the wait and a long solo haul.

They moved me from chair to chair until finally scoring a rollaway cart in their corridor of accelerated waiting where they began the task of trying to find a vein. Déjà vu, only this time it included added complications of deep regret, heart-hurting disappointment, and a massive dose of fear. My prayers were short and to the point. Help me. Please. I knew He could hear me but I couldn't shake the feeling of being alone, which was crazy when I thought about lying in the middle of all this crowded chaos. My only connection to the outside world lay in the phone on the wall that allowed local calls only. We lived in the middle of nowhere, so *all* of my memorized numbers would be long distance – save one.

I dialed my daughter in the city and tried to prepare a sane message to leave on her machine. Unfortunately, when I heard the beep and started talking, the emotion from the day caught in my throat, and the tears I'd held back for so long fell out in a frantic plea for something I couldn't seem to put into words. I belatedly realized what I'd done and hung up the phone like it was on fire. My disjointed babble would provide no clues explaining my distress, and she'd have no way to know where to find me. I could now add regret to my long list of feelings crowding the space where my brain used to be, but I couldn't summon the nerve to call back.

I'd just spent several hours in a room full of strangers, holding my breath from sitting amidst all the closet smokers, and trying not to lose my head from constant shaking side-to-side as I tried to make sense of the senseless. I could only hope that she'd forgive me, allowing that having breasts explode after months of painfully making way for their existence might create temporary insanity in even the most stable of minds.

The Good Lord takes away and gives back tenfold. Just about the time I was gearing up for meltdown squared, the curtain gave way to a lifesaving grace. Mr. Rowe had exceeded safe and sound speed limits and accomplished the impossible in record time. Ginger was well on her way to spoiling in veterinary arms, and a bulging care bag now lay at my feet. It's a wonder that he was able to think clearly enough to keep our needs straight, but at that point, who cared. Ginger would've enjoyed my prayer shawl just as much as I would her foam bed, but I was truly grateful for my own toothbrush and the absence of hair. The truth was, one glimpse of his beautiful smile coming through that cubicle curtain and I really didn't need another thing.

**If you can't be a good example
you'll just have to be a terrible warning.
- Anonymous -**

Life isn't fair. If it were, we'd all be in trouble. Even so, it seems grossly lopsided that Mr. Rowe would be expected to endure endless hours in frigid, smelly waiting rooms, wondering if this would be the time when the doctor would come bearing bad news or whether I'd even wake to see another day. Waiting through three surgeries in four months was a lot to ask of anyone, but I never even had to ask. His love is my perpetual can of WD-40 and duct tape, all rolled into one.

Blessed with the prayers from one well-placed message that traveled multiple phone trees and mysterious internet connections throughout the world, I found myself, once again, in the hands of several recovery room nurses and the ice chip man. My delayed surgery had placed me in an unlikely post-op room on the maternity ward, for which we experienced more delays as the previous occupants made several flustered trips to their car in numerous attempts to retrieve all their pink flowers and baby sundries. I celebrated their joyous journey with newborn in tow but couldn't avoid the hollow emptiness that settled in their wake.

I wasn't looking forward to spending the night in the company of exhausted mothers who would wake on schedule to feed their hungry bundles and ten-count their awesome fingers and toes while watching a schedule of pre-dawn infomercials. Mr. Rowe was sure to toss and turn on the wretched concrete sofa that someone had jammed in beside me; so his prospects for the night didn't look any better. Attempts to sleep were futile as I couldn't ignore the mourned loss of my mammaries *or* the lights in the hall and ultimately heaved the hours away into bedpans that filled with my body's rebellion against the best toxic concoctions that medicine had to offer. I'm thankful for escaping the horrors of spreading infection, but the decision to feed overzealous antibiotics directly into my poor collapsed veins bordered on the absurd.

Here I was in the middle of misery with too much time on my hands to think, desperately wracking my brain for things to distract me that offered more diversion than the endless loop of TV nonsense on the wall. For some reason, it had me remembering my brother in the middle of the three of us kids. He was the valedictorian of the family and always seemed to be collecting knowledge in the most unusual ways. I have to say that the season he required regional soil samples for his science project probably tops the list, not because he would ultimately win first prize for his entry or even that his theories were rather brilliant. It has all to do with my Mom's penchant for picnics and a foot of snow.

Of course, the timing of the annual science fair shouldn't be held to blame since nobody forced my brother to retrieve the impossible from frozen samples of earth. Nevertheless, the whole family was required to participate anyway, regardless of subzero weather and having to use the same soil sample shovel to clear the table before eating.

As far as my Mom is concerned, any day is a good day for a picnic. As soon as my brother's task was complete, there we were, pulling cold meat sandwiches and frozen baked beans from the basket and hoping to be the first with our cup beneath the thermos of hot chocolate. It was so cold that the forks actually stuck to our tongues – who'd have thought they weren't kidding in "A Christmas Story" when that kid's tongue sticks to the flagpole? Returning to clicking through mindless TV wasteland brought me to the conclusion that I sure could use a diversion like winter picnics right about now.

Morning brought a beautiful day of sunshine and a wheelchair for my early dismissal as another new mother required my room, and the discharge papers revealed my doctor's signed declaration that deemed me fit as a fiddle. Incredible as it seemed, they believed him...even as they wheeled me around pools of my own vomit on the way out the door. I don't know if the orderly was holding his breath from the stench or just didn't know what to say, but he steered me down three floors and several corridors without a word, no doubt catching a whiff and an unavoidable glance of the overflowing pan on his hasty retreat from the curb.

Mr. Rowe hurled a few choice words under his breath at the

back of the shrinking coward and tenderly folded me into the car. Ready or not, we were off for home, hoping for patches of smooth, open highway and a tummy that could outwait the distance. I would soon discover the folly of holding my breath over potholes and wisely switched to hyperventilation instead.

I shut my eyes in order to see.
- Paul Gauguin -

Ginger and Mr. Rowe possessed all the compassion and empathy that I always seemed to lack. Add in a daily dose of humble pie that Ginger was always quick to deliver (accompanied by plenty of eye rolls and sighs) and you get the gist of my rehabilitation. I've always been short of empathy when listening to others who fail to see the option of moving forward out of excruciatingly painful situations, which I've been in myself, so I understand their desire to hold my feet to the fire whenever I slide down the slippery slope of self-pity.

Ginger endured more than her share of situations over the years, especially when you include having to deal with mine. Her own initial seizure occurred on her first Independence Day during a rousing introduction to homegrown fireworks. The "men" of the family thought it would be great fun to include her in the undercover operation of setting off rows of misguided missiles and colorful stars between nightly rounds of the local police and occasional inspection by our worried next-door neighbors. I would've been content to watch from inside the air-conditioned windows but images of burned fur and scorched grass kept me close – at the end of her leash and one hand ready on the knob of the door.

The evening began quite harmlessly with an occasional pop or fizzle from rogue firecrackers, but as the show intensified,

265

Ginger's wariness unfolded into her own show of frenzy. While undue stress causes me to bite the skin around my fingers, she barks at an ear-piercing pitch and whirls in circles until her leash winds impossibly tight around whatever's closest – which usually turns out to be me. About the time that the cherry bombs began to burst, her panting tongue hung low to the pavement and she was dragging both of us in a beeline to the backdoor. She never made it inside, collapsing forthwith while managing to shake all over as her body stretched taught with all fours reaching toward me in a pitiful plea. Her eyes were as round as the saucers in mine, focused in a wild stare as her mouth frothed and sweat began to pool at my knees.

The vet always asks, after the fact, how long these seizures last. Really...like I took the time to consult my watch as I stroked the soaked fur of my best friend and wondered if she might be dying. What probably only lasted minutes seemed like days, and I haven't enjoyed patriotic firepower ever since. It took days more for Ginger to emerge from a quiet stupor, gently coaxing her out of her nerves and back into life, as we knew it. The chances were good that this kind of episode could happen again, if not protected from undue stimulation. Well unfortunately, there was slim to none chance that *that* would happen in a three-kid hyper household with a penchant for bling, bang, and boom.

Slim to none and six months later found us at the end of seizure number two. It came near midnight on the evening of our annual Twelfth Day of Christmas bash...the one when my husband always insisted we invite everyone he knew and serve that particular season's leftover cookies and punch. Being the social introvert that I am, I dreaded the event, especially since I would no longer have further excuse to delay dismantling of my copious decorations, and I'd have to clean the house that I had just cleaned upon their departure.

Ginger did a good job of hiding and avoiding some of the more tedious toddlers who insisted on pulling the tail that wasn't there, and by night's end she was more than ready for mommy to make it to bed. She parked herself near the vanity, willing me to hurry through my bath, staring with one eye open and a meaningful look that sent waves of guilt across the floor. I was just in the process of my final rinse, when she suddenly leapt to her feet and dashed toward the tub.

My first thought was that she meant to take a flying leap into the suds. Instead, she fell into an awkward heap as if she'd run into a force field that zapped the spark clean out of her writhing body. I grabbed a towel and dripped my way to her side, dreading what surely seemed the only logical conclusion for her behavior.

This seizure was a doozy and probably lasted as long as it felt. Every one of her tortured breaths was my breath. Every spasm traveled through both bodies as though we were one. The vet prescribed a mild sedative (for Ginger) and advised us to both relax, regroup, and think about ways to slow the stress to a minimum. The medicine turned my previously attentive companion into a zombie that didn't even have enough energy to pout.

The miracles of modern science would keep the seizures at bay but weren't worth the price of seeing my frisky friend turn into a sedated couch potato. After hours of hashing it over, Ginger and I agreed that God-given gifts like our friendship shouldn't be shared under the influence of anything but faith. We pitched the pills and decided that taking one day at a time *together* was worth any bump or bruise along the way.

**Joy is what happens to us
when we allow ourselves to recognize
how good things really are.
- Marianne Williamson -**

What's good for the goose is good for the gander, or so my annoyingly accurate canine companion reminded me. As my days of recuperation endlessly churned on without mental improvement, it was clear that my choices were numbered. I could either spend the rest of my life avoiding the disgusted stares of my exhausted caregiving committee of two or adopt the philosophy of faith that had worked so well all these years for Ginger. It was time to accept what was never coming back, what my reality was now, and whatever it was that I wanted to become. Getting a new life had the potential for excitement, and it was high time that I dredged the dusty catacombs of my memory for inspiration.

The threat of creditors banging down our door mysteriously disappeared with the emergency surgery that removed the remains of my chest. It was as though the last six months of our lives never happened, and I was determined to erase all bitter regret with the same eraser. My brain contains no storehouse of original thought, but God is full of ideas and placed a few beauties in the forefront of mine.

The yellow pages had me thumbing through the wonderful world of prosthetics and psychological experts that promised to heal and put this Humpty Dumpty back together again. It was a perfect combination – one to reshape the outside and the other to revive my soul within. I would combine my daughter's offer to shop until we dropped, discard my wardrobe of three sizes too big, and organize the new "me" by color and coordination. With the help of the original Potter, I would reshape my lump of clay through lessons learned the hard way in an ongoing series that I hoped would last a lifetime.

The "Bra Lady" walked tall and lovely into my life of disorder, teaching me all there was to know about the wonders of a science that really would create the illusion of putting me back together again. Faux breasts come in all shapes, weights, and sizes to match what you used to have, or in my case now, whatever I wanted. The pair I chose came complete with nipples (though I couldn't for the life of me figure out why) and filled an engineering miracle of spandex and straps that managed to keep the heavy lovelies from sliding too far south or ending up under one arm or the other. If I didn't plan to wear plunging necklines or strapless gowns, no one would ever suspect that they came removable for storage or that their sheer weight could be used as lethal weapons if the need should ever arise. They were hot, heavy, and uncomfortable, but oddly provided a welcomed illusion that filled my blouse with curves and my self-esteem with floundering courage.

Now all I needed was the will to wear them in public and the confidence to go along with the courage. Enter Dr. Pike. She was like having Mr. Rogers and Albert Einstein rolled into one, with a calm and loving approach to asking all the hard questions, and her brilliant connect-the-dots mind making sense of each heart-wrenching session. I discovered a lot about myself, not the least of which is that everything about me connects in a significant way, despite how insignificant I keep trying to make it. Choices that I made years ago thread their way through the knots and tangles that bind me today, but they don't have to strangle me in the process. The key is realizing that I can wear the threads any way I choose.

That's where my daughter proved invaluable. Prior to our

planned spending sprees, she suggested that I begin watching "What Not To Wear" on one of those obscure cable channels that I'd never even heard of or paid attention to before. I never realized that so many fashion do's and don'ts existed and that all of the latter resided in my walk-in closet. Who knew that pointy-toed shoes make you look taller, black really doesn't shed pounds, and that white (hold on to your seats, all you ladies over the age of 50…) can be worn after Labor Day? The mini-skirts from my youth are evidently frowned upon for those of us who are well over 35, and colors don't have to match as long as they "go." I'm not sure where they're meant to "go," but I wanted to be there, so I watched season after season of re-runs that Mr. Rowe painstakingly recorded and slowly began to correct the error of my frumpy ways. I might never walk the runways of the chic and shallow, but now I touted an empty pocketbook and plenty of style – and the nerve to go with it.

CHAPTER 13

LOVE IS NOT IRRITABLE OR RESENTFUL

Love one another and you will be happy.
It is as simple and as difficult as that.

- Michael Leunig -

My parents belonged to a dance club for as long as I can remember. One Saturday night each month, they would don their best dress, suit, and tie, and head for the local golf club for an evening of music that put a twinkle in their eyes and produced soft hums of the latest tune and a new shuffle in their steps for weeks to come. Their date in December was the best. Mom would tuck me into bed, dressed in her V-neck red velvet sheath with rhinestone necklace and eardrops to match, always leaving me with a kiss on my cheek that smelled of expensive perfume and a promise for the next morning's report of who wore what and when they'd be going again.

On nights like those, my brother in the middle, unfortunately, became the logical choice for my supervised care. Too young to have plans of his own but much too old to be tucked in himself, he was resigned to watching his little sister and making the best of it. He even adapted with grace to the inevitability of me finally being able to stay awake until we both heard the Star Spangled Banner signing off and fell asleep to the Indian test pattern.

He always tuned in to one of our three available channels (decades before the onslaught of cable and reasonably clear pictures) with a night of "Mannix" and an enormous bowl of popcorn. I think the extra salt and butter probably got *him*

271

through each episode, but for me, the thought of sharing the night with Mike Connors and his hip new secretary paled in comparison to the reality of spending hours on the same couch with a wise older brother who never complained.

It may have meant nothing more to him than a few bucks in his wallet or maybe a night off from washing dishes for a family of five. No matter. To a little girl with expensive perfume on her cheek, it meant the world. A few hours of undivided attention and unfettered swipes at the Jiffy Pop…now *that's* love.

**A friend is someone who knows all about you
but loves you anyway.**
- Anonymous -

I sometimes wish for the simplicity of those Saturday nights and the freedom to allow myself a kinder view of loving my own body. I threw away the scales long ago, realizing that God's idea of what makes me beautiful does *not* necessarily coincide with science and some scale manufacturer's idea of the perfect weight. I've spent way too much time fretting over half an ounce here or there and the dreaded "plateau" of which anyone who's ever dieted is well aware. It's the moment of decision when you cease to lose quickly all the water weight that's accumulated from too many pieces of chocolate cake and day after depressing day of climbing on the scale produces nary a downward turn of the needle. The euphoria of quickly shedding liquid pounds suddenly turns into a masochistic game that's impossible to win, so you quit playing and pick up the fork for more. Hence supporting my theory why I believe scales and the devil are one in the same.

It took years to overcome my addiction to the neat circle of numbers that whirled to the right in a rising battle of the bulge, but "Oh, happy day!" when I finally threw that nasty piece of bondage into the trash and began to rely on the easy zip of my jeans for more accurate readings. One would think that I could – and would – apply the same principle to looking in the mirror, but I'm still working on that. Making peace with the image that stares back at me each morning seems harder to deal with, somehow, than any of the body issues I've dealt with before. Enter Ginger...

Her hump, that doctors assured me was something that could grow without concern, had now sprouted to massive proportions despite their best guess and my anxiety at each of Ginger's yearly exams. Our friendship had grown right along with it to the point that I really didn't give it a thought until strangers inadvertently blurted out their sympathy for her deformity or my cruelty for not correcting the obvious. "It" was always explained with regurgitated words the doctors had delivered to me, and since Ginger didn't seem to mind my reticence for biopsies or invasive surgeries, we politely ignored her hump like an unwanted pimple on the end of a teenager's nose.

Her physical appearance never hindered her ability to leap the creek or arrive at the food bowl first, and since she dismissed it so easily, so did I. Her prone profile more closely resembled that of a princess on a very large pea instead of the slim and svelte queen that she imagined, but oddly enough, its peculiarity never entered our minds. We both figured it served to put her in a better position for petting, so it never became an issue.

The point is, she never bothered to look in magic mirrors to measure her worth by what she saw or longed to see again. I loved every morsel – hump and all, and any portrait I paint in my mind highlights her expressive face with silken ears and a set of warm, furry paws…never even including the extra bulge. I knew it was there – I just didn't "see" it.

If I had to guess, I think she'd probably say the same about me, though with much more color commentary. I'm not so sure about the drawing… but the fact that I no longer had breasts meant nothing to her. She wasn't bothered by my lack any more than I considered her excess. If eyes are windows to the soul, maybe she just blinked more than usual and used her night-ray vision to cut through the nonsense and see what really mattered. I could learn a thing or two from this less-than-perfect animal. The more that love grows unconditional, the blinder sight becomes, turning our hearts into the same cameras by which God really sees.

Sooner or later
we all quote our mothers.
- Bern Williams -

Ginger would succumb to the smell of Saturday night popcorn with the best of us, but perfected the science of ignoring anything else she deemed irrelevant. With the absence of breasts, keeping my balance within tight spaces now hindered my ability to maneuver our tiny kitchen without fear of falling and necessitated the new rule of no dogs allowed during food prep or dishwashing. This was hard on both of us since she had years of unrestricted access to unlearn, and I couldn't seem to get the hang of not having to step over the furry bundle that had always been under foot.

Not having her there was like trying to decipher an elusive ingredient to Grandma's spaghetti sauce recipe. I knew something important was missing but just like being without the benefit of Grandma, divulging her secret prior to passing on, I found myself in the kitchen alone having to make it work without either one.

The galley shared an opening with our dining room on one end and the living room on the other. Ginger took my Mom's old saying about "never being cornered in a round house, Nelly" to heart and used the openings to prove her point about irrelevant rules. A million times, I'd remind her to stay out of the kitchen. A million times, she'd leave by way of one door and peak around the corner of the other, waiting until my back was turned to make her way to the very spot from which she'd just been evicted.

I'm not sure that her vocabulary even included the word "no," and she'd play that game every meal until she tired of hearing me fake exasperation. She knew all along that I didn't like the new rule any more than she did and despite her fondness for being obstinate, I think her real motive was probably meant to distract from the reason for the change in the first place.

It is only possible to live happily-ever-after on a day-to-day basis.
- Margaret Bonnano -

Picture this. You're careening down a hill, dead-set on returning home before curfew and having to explain the swimming suit that's soaking through your clothes. An extra set of laps and a game of chicken had kept you in the pool, blissfully unaware of the time and the lengthening shadows. As the lifeguard blew his whistle to clear the water for the night, you glance at the clock and audibly gasp at the thought of extra kitchen duty for the next 40 days. You hastily grab your towel and manage to drag your t-shirt and shorts over the dripping swimsuit while unchaining your bike from the rack near the road. Just as you round the bend with home in view, your bare foot slips from the pedal and time stands still. Your big toe now bleeds skinless, and you're sucking air in a valiant attempt to make it into the house and all the way up the stairs without bawling like a baby. We're all one breath away from change – and we never see it coming.

Getting from one week to the next is always more palatable with the thought that each set of seven days will begin with a Sunday. That morning's routine at our house is much like the mad dash down the hill on my shiny blue Schwinn and consists of several predictable patterns that are accomplished in due haste so as not to disappoint God if I appear in church without a clean mind, body, and pair of underwear.

I've tried getting up earlier to avoid the rush, but habits and the comfort of knowing exactly how many minutes it takes to dry and straighten my hair, grab the only pressed dress in the closet, and ease into the pew just before the organ begins to play is too comfortable to mess with. Once I've finally reached the day on which I'm supposed to rest, my mind is set on making it happen even though the means by which that's accomplished belies the purpose intended. I was making good time on the morning of one such day, out of the shower and on my way to step two, when one crucial moment stole the joy out of my next breath and changed everything.

When my kids were little, they followed me everywhere. So much so, that one day I announced in exasperation that I felt like Mary and her three little lambs. The statement impressed my daughter so much that she's called me by that name ever since. Even her friends are unaware that it's a loving *nom de guerre*, and not a disrespectful use of her mother's first name. Ginger became the fourth lamb by proxy, and seemed duty-bound to carry on tradition long after the children had deserted my side.

No desertion for Ginger on that particular Sunday as she lay in strategic position to afford the best opportunity to follow my whereabouts without moving an inch. She knew my routine better than I did, anticipating moments to stretch in avoidance of shower drips or errant hairspray without expending more energy than necessary. I took the inconvenience of careful footing and extra steps in stride, accepting without question that wherever I was, she'd always be there too. There's comfort in mundane expectations, so it never occurred to me to expect otherwise. I guess that's why the next several breaths were taken away with such surprise.

I caught uncharacteristic movement out of the corner of my eye and felt the first inkling that change was seeping in like the steam from my shower that was slowly escaping from the crack beneath its door. Ginger was on the move, and I hadn't even gotten to the point in my pattern where she usually rewarded me with a raised eyebrow and whole body sigh for interrupting her sleep with the startling whirr of the blow dryer or clatter of dropping my comb for the umpteenth time.

She began staggering toward me in a hauntingly familiar gait that took me full circle in the blink of an eye. Her first seizure would mirror her last, but unfortunately, this one intensified and lengthened to horrific proportions in a devastating blow to mind and body – for both of us. Half clad in pantyhose and a towel, I fell to my knees as she collapsed at my feet, wrapping myself around her rigid body in a feeble attempt to ward off the pain. Science claims that animals in the throes of seizure feel no pain and cannot recollect the event with any clarity. If that's true, then why I wonder, does she always seek me out, arrest my attention, and not surrender to her paralyzed paws until she's satisfied that I'm aware of impending doom and drop everything to nurse her through? Humph…so much for science.

Wave after wave of tremors moved through her body, starting at her glassy eyes and shooting out each rigid limb until the floor was soaked with her sweat and my pitiful tears. A puddle of bubbles stretched from the gape of her frothing mouth, all the way around each ear in a weirdly shaped halo that suggested a much gentler depiction of what we were actually living through. Her panting escalated to the point where I thought she'd just finally run out of air, but the agony kept on and on, until I desperately shouted, "Lord, have mercy!"...and He did.

Ginger went perfectly still as surreal calmness settled within the room. Here we go again, I thought, making each breath more dramatic than the last, but realizing how much each one counts. I was witnessing a real-life answer to the provocative question of, "What would Jesus do?" and trembled at the thought that He noticed, He heard...He cared enough about my practically perfect pooch and me to intervene. Of all the billions of people on the planet who clamor for attention, He chose that exact moment to respond to *me* with an act so swift and supernatural that I'd have no doubt about His miraculous power and all-consuming love.

You'd think that I'd be used to this by now. A miracle happens to me at least once per day, when I wake to see another sunrise and thank Him for whatever awaits once I push back the covers and set my feet on the floor. Thank you, thank you, and hallelujah! Ginger would be walking beside me for at least one more day.

**A daughter may outgrow your lap,
but she will never outgrow your heart.**
- Anonymous -

My enthusiastic optimism was short-lived. Once Ginger blinked her way out of her stupor, she hoisted her spent body onto shaky legs and proceeded to coat me with the spray from several vigorous shakes. A few tentative steps took her headlong into the wall, and then had her searching in erratic circles, attempting to find the door. I called her name to soothingly reassure her that everything would be all right, but she couldn't stand still long enough to pay me any mind. When I reached out to stroke her and she flinched away – that's when I knew something was drastically wrong.

My Honey Dog didn't even know me, and like a meth baby who can't stand to be cuddled, my wild child seemed bent on getting as far from me as she could. After a decade and more of trailing my every footstep, now her focus was primal, self-preserving, and all about personal space. She didn't seem to be able to remember much of anything, let alone recognize the end of my nose, and even clapping at each ear produced no response. She was a familiar stranger in her own home. This wasn't good.

Beside myself with unfamiliar rejection, I watched in dismay as the object of my affection presently hid under the bed with her own nose turned to the back of the wall. I knew she'd never choose this chilling dismissal on purpose, but my brain couldn't bypass the hurt in my heart long enough to accept the possibility of this logical conclusion. I've seen my share of rejection, but never had it been so abruptly presented by someone so irrevocably joined at my hip.

This was even worse than the time I spent at my first stay-awake-all-night slumber party, actually staying awake all night because I was petrified of what the other girls would do to me if I fell asleep. How quickly the tide turned at an innocent celebration of a "friend's" 9th birthday, when one ugly thought morphed into the dare that changed everything, leaving me with the knowledge of how the bruised apple feels when it's culled from the cream of the crop and never makes it into the prized pie.

We all arrived with sleeping bags, our favorite pair of pj's, and presents that charmed our hostess with the most candles for the day. We were an odd assortment of short and tall with glasses or braces or both, giggling at each other's corny jokes and taking turns at the turntable of 45's. How was I to know that a plot was brewing, and I was "it?" Birthday girl's mom finally sent us to the basement after her third rebuke for us to "please quiet down," and I met my fate at the bottom of the stairs.

The sleeping bags that we'd lined up earlier, strewn over the floor with all sides touching in the shape of a giant square, now lay with a conspicuous empty space in the middle, looking more like the uncompromising fortification someone meant it to be. The missing bag was mine – its signature homemade colors crumpled in a lonely heap in the corner, thrown from the rest with mysterious intent. Muffled giggles, many finger-pointing and whispered slurs flung across the room with sufficient volume to spear their target, until I finally gave up acting as if I cared, unzipped my bag, and crawled in for a long, lonely night.

It hurt – a lot – to be the brunt of a cruel joke that I didn't even understand. One minute you're having fun, and the next you're in the middle of a confusing conspiracy that's being doled out at your own expense. Go figure. I spent the rest of my waking hours in a conversation with myself about whether I should call my parents to come get me, demand to know what this was all about, or spend the rest of 3rd grade living within the zippered shelter of my bag of many colors.

Little girls (and let's be honest – some who never grow up) are a fickle lot, and by the time the sun was beginning to peek through the glass, the group who'd just spent hours insulting or ignoring me had finally fallen asleep through the night and awoken with apparent amnesia. They greeted the morning and me with smiles in their big fat yawns, chatting with ease about next week's science test and a litter of new baby kittens.

I silently removed the invisible toothpicks that had kept my own eyelids from falling and blessed the inclination of my parents for always wanting to be first in the pick-up line. Hypocrisy is a tough lesson to learn at any age, but at the tender age of nine, I found the backseat of our Ford looking mighty good and escaped the pack of now-friendly pretenders with a request to press the gas and fly home. Without explanations or apologies for such an insufferable night, I guess they did me a favor. I would never again feel guilty about sending regrets for occasions where two or more could gather against me.

Rejection is a lot like revenge. To dwell on either only hurts the one who thinks they've been the "hurt-ee." Ginger meant far more to me than any of those ill-mannered girls whom I can't even remember, and I knew she didn't possess a malicious bone in her body. We had history that transcended any lapse of memory, and our unconditional love went both ways. I would practice patience, and remember that even if she couldn't remember me, hope springs eternal and my sleeping bag always has room for one more.

Dogs can see movement up to 985 yards away.
That's the length of more than nine football fields.
- The Daily Extra Fun Fact -

It was official. My poor puppy was well on her way to being blind as a bat and deaf out of the one good ear she had left. I could sympathize. Forty years of wearing contacts and I'd recently been told that I'd finally outgrown my prescription and would need to wear glasses for the rest of my days. Reconciling the value of sight over vanity, I still grapple with the hassle of fumbling through the change of regular glasses for sunshades while carrying an oversized purse and three grocery bags from the car. I went through three hairstyles trying to accommodate the rims of plastic that now adorn my face before finally giving up and whacking it all off. Trying to hide the inevitability of age is like saying that Ginger's hump is merely the result of a mosquito bite. Denial is a convenient scapegoat but doesn't change the facts.

This massive seizure was changing our lives in ways I'd never dreamed of. Ginger could no longer hear my reprimands (as if she ever paid attention anyway) or even come running when I called from the backdoor with treats in both hands. Through an exhaustive process of elimination, I accidently discovered that a short – and very shrill – whistle delivered with a quick twist of the lips was the one sound and pitch that her diminished ears could still hear. At certain times of the day my summons were hard to discern from all the other birds in the neighborhood, but she quickly figured out that the red blur standing against the gray blur of the house was me and not a large flock of cardinals gathering for their afternoon siesta.

Old habits cling like plastic wrap. They gave us both a sense of comfort when all the other maladies were wreaking havoc on our simple, ordered lives. Ginger still had her sense of smell, and used it to best advantage on the days when I served a lunch of tuna. She couldn't hear me open the can but knew it was coming just the same. I can't explain the mystery of how she smelled the mere *idea* of having tuna, but she always appeared at my feet before the fish even hit the bowl.

She knew if she waited long enough and applied just the right touch of pity to her pathetic (and admittedly adorable) face, that I'd fill my own slices of bread to less than brimming and leave the rest for her to lick out of the bowl. I confess to buying tuna in bulk and always opening more than required for suggested servings for two. After all, I concluded, life was too short not to hear the satisfied tinkle of dog tags against the side of my bowl in pursuit of this one, simple pleasure.

**But may the God of all grace,
who called us to His eternal glory by Christ Jesus,
after you have suffered a while,
perfect, establish, strengthen, and settle you.
- 1Peter 5:10 -**

God keeps me on my toes with constant tweaks to the well-oiled machine of my life. It makes for an interesting ride. Ginger and I had fallen into complacent routines of walking, eating, and sleeping after months of rehabilitation and reconciliation to our new circumstances with daily reminders that each day was probably as good as it was going to get. As my breast surgeon likes to say at each uneventful check-up, "Boring is good." Unfortunately, for the rest of my family, "boring" and my life never seem to exist simultaneously.

In order to avoid this conundrum, perhaps I should stay out of the shower for it is there where I always seem to hear from

God. One minute I was lathering up and relishing the thought that nothing crucial was on the calendar for the next thirty days. In the space of the next, the spray was peppering my body with hot water when I heard the distinct directive to "SELL." "Sell what?" I asked myself, as I looked around the bathroom to see if Mr. Rowe was jerking my chain or if Ginger had suddenly acquired a decidedly masculine voice.

After satisfying my curiosity that no one was about, I turned my attention back to the water and heard the clear command again. "Sell *THE HOUSE.*" Well, now I was beginning to get a little nervous, for I knew where this was coming from and that eventually I'd be knee-deep in packing paper and moving boxes to God only knew where – literally. Poor Mr. Rowe... he sure wouldn't be expecting this one. Ginger, on the other hand, always seems to know God's plans before I do and would probably be packing her crate before the break of dawn.

It took several weeks for the shock to diminish, but Mr. Rowe finally reconciled his manifest of misgivings and threw his support into the holy ring that I was certain we were to follow. I had no doubts about the overall concept of obedience but have to admit that worldly logic told me this was insane.

I loved our little cottage on the hill, perfectly placed along the side of the highway that easily connected us to doctors in one direction and mountainous pleasures in the other. We had no debts or steps and plenty of familiar paths that Ginger had meticulously memorized for sightless search and smell. We had cleaning down to an hour flat and a new box of 2,000 address labels sitting on the kitchen counter. Life was good and nobody was complaining.

Everything about this venture belied conventional wisdom and the safety of the material world. Financial planning and common sense always fall easily against my faith in my Father's plans. I had it in writing…His ways are not our ways, and I was counting on someday learning what on Earth He was thinking. I had a feeling that I'd no longer be on that particular planet by the time I found out.

As I've mentioned before, this perfect little house stood in the middle of a newly constructed neighborhood that now mostly languished in foreclosure. On the afternoon that we invited a realtor to expedite this unlikely endeavor, he did his best not to laugh at our expectation to sell. I asked for his professional opinion on what it would take to sell quickly, and only through divine will was I able to accept his ridiculously low figure without fainting. It was tens of thousands less than what we'd paid (not counting the tens of thousands we'd added later) but in his opinion, if we wanted to sell anytime soon, that was the piddly price the bank would allow people to pay.

Well, if this was what we were supposed to do, there was no point in procrastination. He pounded the sign into the front flowerbed, put a ream of colorful advertisements in the waterproof box to its side, and left to place our home on the multiple listings that blasted the web with news of our faith-driven folly. The house was clean and ready to show as I settled into the mindset of watching streams of strangers file through our belongings until the right person walked through the door. This could take weeks, or months – or even years to accomplish. Huge sighs and a heavy heart took me outside to sweep the sidewalk and fill my mind with something other than despair.

If I hadn't been so immersed in my own musings, I might've noticed the car at the end of the driveway and not ventured outside to dust the walk in the first place. One of the occupants called me over with a wave of the flier they held in one hand and asked if they could see it now, as they pointed with the other. *What* did they want to see now? I didn't know these people and had no idea what they were talking about. The one behind the wheel handed me her business card as my face turned eight shades of red when it finally dawned on me that they were here to see *the house*. Ohhh…this was not what I was expecting. God was certainly ready once I was willing.

One hour after placing our ad on MLS, we had an offer at full asking price. Thirty days later, we would close the deal. The movers were scheduled, the boxes were packed, and only one thing remained. A tiny detail, really. I rather wanted to know where, exactly, we would next be resting our weary little heads.

> **The longer you wait for your prayers to be answered**
> **the closer you are to a breakthrough.**
> **- Sarah Young -**

Time was of the essence and it seemed reasonable to believe that we'd encounter a vast inventory of homes from which to choose. For years we'd ridden the Harley past dozens of three bedroom, two-bath ranches on two acres or less that would easily fit the bill. Unfortunately and much to our dismay, none of those were for sale and the ones that came remotely close to our desires fell into a sorry lot of foreclosures that now housed rodents and were breeding grounds for mold and major repairs.

Our realtor's car was equipped with GPS (and some sort of mystery smell that we never could identify) every time we entered the "show zone." Directed by the voice of a woman with a thick British accent, we roamed the woods and every back road within a 30-mile radius – on every day that he'd take us until freezing rain and our impending eviction at closing drove us home and into the realm of rentals. Reality soon settled over our mood of miraculous expectations as we resorted to the classifieds in a frantic search for temporary lodgings.

Here we were, homeowners since the age of majority, filling out background checks and questionnaires designed to humble those without down payments or the ability to pass credit rating criteria. We had the blessing of having more than enough in our savings to afford multiples of the rental properties to which we applied, but here we were, groveling at the property owners' feet for an early move-in date and creative short-term lease.

Ginger thought I'd lost my mind, and on the nights that we returned empty-handed, I'd retreat to the privacy of the back porch and agree with her at the wrench of each woeful sob. My knees began to show signs of permanent indentation from throwing myself to the floor in total submission. I didn't understand how we could enjoy such smooth sailing for the sale of our home and not have the perfect place to move into. I knew that I'd heard His message correctly. I was certain of its direction. I just couldn't see through the tears for the answers waiting on the other side.

The lesson was becoming all too clear. Trust and obey. Years of working hard and doing pretty much whatever I wanted had made me a spoiled American wife with expectations of grandeur that only a family and home with the white picket fence would satisfy. Somewhere along the way, I became too entrenched in my own ability to make things happen. I've always been a patient person, but this was more than simply waiting ten people back while a cashier changed the ribbon on her register and then placed an "out to lunch" sign that sent you into the next long, waiting line without having your head explode with a string of words that were better left unsaid.

They say that good things come to those who wait. Some

days I think I'm still waiting, but we eventually found interim housing that provided a roof over our heads and sufficient heat to keep the pipes from freezing during one of the harshest winters the South has ever known. Like it or not, the holiday season would occur within the foreign walls of borrowed room and board, missing most of all the usual trimmings but climaxing with a wonderful Christmas Eve surprise.

Months of endurance had finally netted a gift that fell short of Christ's coming but surely filled our stockings with delight. Our most recent offer to buy would be accepted by the end of the year, and we'd finally be owners of more than renter's insurance again. Our pleasure was fleeting as reports of more ice and snow on the very day that we scheduled to close, were threatening our new deal. In desperation, I took a pick and shovel to the ice at the bottom of the rental's driveway on the night before just to ensure our departure early the next morning. Three inches of deep frozen water were no match for my burning desire to cradle the deed to our own four walls in my loving arms again.

Monsoons had nearly thwarted the last closing on our beloved little cottage a scant two months prior, as a weather pattern of biblical proportions began to make me wonder if this was *not* what we were supposed to be doing. Ginger was a nervous wreck at the first sight of a suitcase – let alone what it takes to move a whole household, so she opted out and safely tucked away at Brother Bailey's home during all this cataclysmic weather and multiple moves. Otherwise, she'd certainly be suspect number one for throwing our earth's tilt off its axis. Suspect number two would have to be me.

**Insanity is doing the same thing over and over again,
but expecting different results.**
- Albert Einstein -

I am nothing, if not predictable. Ginger had endured five moves in twice as many years, with enough wall removal, paint fumes, and general contractor disputes to outpace any cat with nine lives. It came as no surprise to her that I would once again turn everything inside out and upside down in the continuing saga of remodeling disasters, taking her and Mr. Rowe hostage on my next endeavor to change our world.

I'm not sure why I can't stand to leave things be. This "new" house didn't leak, passed inspection for power and light and had provided a comfortable home for three previous families who'd lived blissfully unaware that it lacked character or updated charm. When my visions of sugarplums began to include resurfaced cabinets and new doors too, I could sense my loved ones' call for retreat long before they wisely chose to watch my latest debacle from afar. Six weeks and just about everything inside replaced later, we finally moved in.

Then it was time to work on the outside. Perhaps I should've warned them in advance, but love covers a multitude of sins – including my brainy ideas for a new screened porch, fenced-in garden, and the total re-sodding of the lawn. My insanity would finally rest after the removal of a dozen trees (to allow proper sunlight for the garden), the installation of gutter guards (for the leaves of the trees left standing), and replacement of all but half a dozen bushes. Obviously, I was planning for the possibility that this would be the last house we'd ever own – which is ludicrous given my track record, I know.

When my first father-in-law, the war hero, finally returned home from four years of battle in the skies, he vowed never to set foot on an airplane again. The birth of his firstborn son's first child would see him eat those words and arrive on our doorstep one month after our bundle of joy's birth. A year after that, he would board the plane again and travel halfway across the nation to help blow out the candles for her first birthday. This was obviously a momentous occasion, and I had prepared accordingly.

In an attempt to impress my in-laws and assure photo-ops of a lifetime, I was making a carrot cake from scratch with cream cheese icing and extra sugar flowers on top. I already knew this was a favorite with the birthday girl and began baking immediately after she finally lay sleeping on the eve of her celebration. I managed to grate the carrots without shredding my knuckles into the bowl, placed the rest of the yummy ingredients into previously prepared pans, and set the timer to await the delicious aroma of success. For once in my short tenure as new daughter-in-law on the block, I was confident that my efforts would match the reward.

All these years later, you'd think that I would've learned. The cake that so perfectly slid into the oven blew-up just the same when I neglected to notice that I'd added baking powder to the flour that already had that powerful ingredient in it. Boom! One minute you're making small talk about the latest miraculous feat that your wonder baby has performed, and the next, you're cleaning an oven at midnight and re-grating carrots for cake number two.

Just like my dreams of culinary perfection, the unrealistic attempts for creating the perfect home have traveled a very expensive and imaginary path that never quite meets expectations. I always seem to be cleaning up the messes of my own doing, hoping that next time I'll work smarter, or harder, or at least approach with caution and a bit more wisdom. The good news is that, knowing me, there will surely be another chance for a wiser "next time."

CHAPTER 14

LOVE NEVER FAILS

Animals are such agreeable friends.
They ask no questions, they pass no criticisms.
- George Eliot -

As I sit to write and peer through the front window of this house we now call home, I take in the beauty of the flowers that bloom just beyond my reach. The hummingbirds visit the black and blue salvia that weave a ring around the silver gazing ball and dance among the carpet roses in their perpetual dance of survival. Ginger likes to lay to the side of one favorite azalea, especially now that it's spring, when the peach-colored blossoms attract the bumblebees that put her to sleep with their buzzing. She lays there whenever I'm weeding, not because she welcomes the scratchy bed of pine straw or swath of scorching sun that inches its way around the side of the house, but simply because she enjoys the pleasure of my company as much as I do hers.

I learned this lesson of pleasant company as a small child during one memorable summer spent in the care of my Grandma as she made the journey each day between her house and mine to fix our meals and make sure my brothers didn't tease me to death or get into too much trouble of their own. I remember many hours entertaining myself with Barbie and Ken and countless others spent quietly with crayons and scissors that created the endless flow of refrigerator art that graced the front of our big white box for each night of my working parents' perusal.

Grandma cooked and cleaned between bouts of refereeing and still managed to make time for one very special day just for me. It was a perfectly planned tea party under the canopy of two old oaks, complete with real spearmint tea in a tiny china pot and petite sandwich squares – minus their crusts of course – on the tray in the middle. She even interrupted her busy day to sit and partake in the grand celebration with knees to her chin and aproned body spilling to either side of my doll's chair as she poured for the miniature crowd who sat staring in silent admiration. What a wonderful day.

At the time, I took it for granted that people – and pets – would want to spend their days (or nights on end) with just me. It's easy to forget that we all have a choice and that it matters how we spend our time and who we spend it with. The fact that I was the recipient of pieces of their precious lives humbles me. Every memory is another chance to pay it forward since I'm no longer able to pay it back.

Some wise soul once wrote about the importance of the "dash" on every person's tombstone. It's what happens between the time we're born and when we die. John tells us at the very end of his gospel that there were many other things that Jesus did that he didn't mention but supposed that even the world itself could not contain the books that would be written if he had. Likewise, it serves as quite a testimony to Ginger that so many aspects of my life have been shaped by her presence and how much I would've missed if I'd never given in to reason and accepted God's gift as the blessing she was meant to be.

Oh, the colors I'd miss in the dawn of each sunrise or the dazzling display of starlit nights when the moon casts its rays on the path to Ginger's open-air respite. Without her, who would fill the yawns of silence or greet me at the door when no one else answers? Who would be my constant shadow and heal all my broken hearts? Who would play without notice or keep all those wayward squirrels at bay? Who would turn belly up at the drop of a hat or come running through the darkness whenever they hear me call their name? Considering such a busy schedule, it really is amazing she's decided to stick around so long and hasn't slept even more than she does.

Barking serves a vital biological purpose:
If a dog does not release a certain number of barks per day,
they will back up, and the dog will explode.
(Whenever you hear an unexplained loud noise in the distance,
it's probably a dog exploding.)
- Dave Barry -

To be honest, I think Ginger's had her equal share of me and all the times I've catered to *her* whims and fancies. There's nothing that reminds me more clearly of this than at Christmas. Starting from the time my children were born, Santa Claus was always at the heart of family festivities. Even though they're well past the age of majority now, my brood still gathers each Christmas Eve to recreate carefully crafted childhood memories. Their father took the holiday quite seriously, shopping year round as surrogate Santa in an attempt to leave a legacy of love in dozens of boxes full of boxes filled with gifts for anonymous (and born of his loins) good girls and boys.

It was a given in our neck of the woods that Santa would always leave a perfectly placed stack of gifts for each member of the family – including whomever happened to be visiting that year – and me. Our live-in "Santa" truly believed in the power of dreams and spent a lifetime belying the notion that at some arbitrary point in every young person's life they must be informed of the truth that Santa only exists in the minds of those who believe that he does.

Over all those years, I think the gift that evokes the most emotion from me is a marvelous toy train that I lovingly rearrange each season in a new design of tracks around my decorated tree. It's the crowning glory to the bottom, what the star is to the top. It initially began as a set of four, complete with engine, tender, passenger car, and caboose. The set includes animation, lights, and sound as Santa waves from atop the engine and alternates greetings on a push-button controller with, "Ho-Ho-Ho...Merry Christmas!" and "All...Aboard!" proclaimed in a wonderful voice that booms with holiday cheer and a smile you just know he has to be beaming.

Each year following, without fail, another couple of cars would appear from "Santa," until now I have so many in the treasured set that it's mandatory that I run it *very* slowly around the track for fear of watching it career off its rounded curves. Every color of the rainbow decorates the cars for the bakery, toyshop, woodshop, ice rink, and rocking chair of Mrs. Claus. The lights blink on and off in red, green, and yellow as lifelike elves bake cookies, pack toy soldiers into Santa's pack, chop wood, and even twirl on a pond of simulated ice.

As much as I enjoyed its sights and sounds, it always kept poor Ginger during her puppyhood at a safe distance from family fun until the cute little cars would come to a silent stop and all was quiet again. She honed her barking skills on that train and never failed to remember its irritation every single year it made its debut out of the closet. They both arrived in our home about the same time, so maybe she figured it was worthy competition. Whatever her reasons, she nearly drove us crazy with her simultaneous barking each time we flipped the switch.

This should never have come as any surprise. Ginger has always positioned herself as the center of attention, barking and jumping at anything that moves – especially thriving on out-shouting new people and things. No wonder the Christmas train evoked such a rousing response. Her bark could pierce steel and was the impetus for more than one family headache. She wasn't happy until she had everyone herded and stationary, so a constantly moving object that never seemed to get anywhere – and never stopped – would certainly have puzzled her logical brain. Forever at odds with a sane solution, it's little wonder she continued to bark at the top of her lungs. The question of sanity should really lie on the rest of us, as each year we'd continue to hold out hope that she'd finally make nice and ignore it…maybe when pigs fly.

You are lucky when you are loved by someone in this lifetime.
You are really lucky when you are loved so much by that someone
that once they are gone…you still feel like they are here with you.
- Trisha Yearwood –

Thankfully, puppies eventually turn into dogs and in Ginger's case finally grow into their ears and lose the sharp edge of irritating barking. Over the years, she's mellowed to a dull shine with a bite that disappeared long ago with the need for food from the blender. Her seasons of life began to change more rapidly with the appearance of gray hair, but she still seemed more than willing to rally on my account each looming spring.

Springtime in Georgia is lovely if you can survive the storms. Tornadoes, flash floods, and even the occasional hurricane make life interesting but truly don't compare to the barrage of emotion that seems to befall me every time the calendar hits March-April-May. It's hard not to pray for an early summer, when each year seems to bring a cycle of mind-numbing chaos that changes everything.

I lost my breasts and three of the most influential men I've ever known to the months of April and May. The irony of it all is never more clear as I marvel at the blooming redbuds that were planted as sticks just months ago or watch in fascination as a neighbor's summer newborn takes his first giant baby step at the same time that fall's planting of bulbs is erupting into spring's profusion of daffodil wonder. God's reminder of new birth grows side-by-side with nature's remnants of last year's womb and recaptures a hope for the future that seems impossible with the passing of so much I hold dear.

Beginning with Eden, the whole idea of gardens has always fascinated and soothed my soul with the magic of dirt and water. Add a little sunshine and even the worst of gardeners like me can watch something grow. I've never had a green thumb and don't have houseplants for a reason, but outdoors is different and seems to level the playing field for the most challenged among us. Ginger has always endorsed my efforts, though sometimes I wish she wouldn't dig quite so deeply among my prized roses or devour my organic mulch as if it were a special of the day.

She willingly lays for hours in the sole occupation of watching me work and has even acquired the habit of listening as I drone on about flowers, veggies, and weeds, rather than expend energy on things she wishes she could still do but no longer can. Occasionally glancing up to admire a passing lizard or acknowledge my awe at the latest bloom on the blueberry bush, she always knows when the last spade returns to its shelf in the shed, and it's time for us to finally be moving on. Even though she no longer does anything except be there, no better "helper" there ever was, and I find myself taking her presence for granted instead of facing the inevitability of her warranty's expiration.

Without even knowing, Ginger would leave me a special gift on her last day as guardian of the garden gate and anything pertaining to the great outdoors. The morning began as usual, with the two of us making our way within the fenced perimeter that held the deer at bay and allowed my feeble attempts at city farming to thrive as much as possible amongst the weeds and recent influx of slimy slugs that swayed upon the leaves of my bushy beans.

The plan of the day meant to tackle the weeds and put some semblance of order into the neat little rows that make up my little plot of paradise. Ginger's role was simple. She was supposed to lay quietly at the foot of the rows and wait until the sun drove us both back inside. At least that's what *I* thought, until I happened to glance over my shoulder and saw her chasing butterflies from one neatly hoed row to the next, leaving a trail of divots that marked her frolic with undisguised glee.

The fact that she was still even *able* to move that quickly came as quite a surprise. Either aliens had abducted my furry friend and replaced her with this athletic imposter, or I'd somehow become so absorbed in the daily drama of her geriatric decline that I failed to see the possibility of small wonders. For some strange reason, the situation brought to mind my odd and extremely eccentric art teacher in high school, who once came into class and asked each of us to take a good look at our surroundings and write down one thing that appeared out of place.

Surely, she was joking. Her classroom was full of kids desperately looking for ways to display their individuality and artistic natures and had the hair, makeup, and wild wardrobes to prove it. After all, this *was* the 1970's and most of us had scads of flower power muumuus and peace sign T's that we'd raided from our hippie parent's closets. She assured us the answer she sought had nothing to do with us and to look carefully for something staring more closely in our faces.

We spent our guesses for naught and ended up clueless by the end of the day. Our teacher stood still and tall as the bell rang for dismissal, giving us a smirk while pointing a finger at each ear. The answer really was staring us in the face. She'd worn two completely different – and horrendously gaudy – earrings throughout the entire day without anyone noticing. It seemed to me that something so obvious should've stuck out like a sore thumb, but because I assumed the answer would appear from more elaborate powers of deduction, I failed to see the simplicity of humble observation. Ginger's brief romp through the garden was no less subtle, but I sure was glad I didn't miss it.

A friend is one who knows you
and loves you just the same.
- Elbert Hubbard -

Sensing our time together was fleeting, I made myself a promise not to miss another thing. More sitting, more petting, more talking (if that were possible) as we spent our last days together, and I felt her slipping further away. Ginger's last breath would take away mine on a mellow day in March, leaving me solo (and so low) with my thoughts and talking to the clouds. Within the puffy balls of cotton, there emerged the shapes of my favorite flower and several animals besides. One rounded clump reminded me of Ginger's nemesis – that nasty growth that had blossomed and ballooned out the side of her hip, which slowly transformed into wavy strands that eventually disappeared into the great expanse of blue. I could imagine the same thing happening to Ginger as her body became whole, new in heaven, and smiled at the thought with genuine pleasure as the hollow place in my empty heart now registered one memory fuller. I don't know if all dogs really do go to heaven, but I like to think that she could be sitting at the feet of Jesus as they both await my arrival.

People who say they live with no regrets are to be envied – or at the very least, given a wide berth and healthy dose of skepticism. My own list reaches embarrassingly epic proportions but considering my desire for living out loud, I suppose my margin for error is greater than most. I'm particularly sorry for all the times I frustrated Ginger when her constant nose-bumping didn't produce the attention she desired, and I left her for something that always seemed so much more important at the time. Likewise, I'm guilty of hiding my hands on more than one occasion, tucking them under a leg or burrowing into deep pockets to avoid the hazards of her wet caress.

With Ginger's passing, I suddenly found myself living the consequences of "Be careful what you wish for," and long for such devoted pestering. She'll never bump me again and just the thought of it has me misty-eyed. I never understood how much her continuous pestering fed my soul and starving need for tactile contact. She knew how much I needed to be touched, reaching deeply with an occasional claw when her nose just wasn't enough. What a smart dog.

Life is never what it seems when we're always looking forward. Ginger concentrated on one moment at a time and only within her designated sphere of importance. There was a reason God saddled her with me – poor thing – and sometimes I was so caught up in begrudging her even the smallest of pleasures that I missed the point that she was just doing her job. All the licks and barking, all the jumping and wags, even the bumps and teasing were gentle reminders about what's important. One look could melt my heart. Persistent bumping molded it into the shape it needed to be. I may no longer feel her nose on my hand but her touch on my heart makes it beat strongly just the same.

Infinite goodness has wide arms.

- Dante -

I learned about The Dog Whisperer too late to reap the benefits of his wisdom and wonder now how Ginger managed to survive and thrive so long in such a dysfunctional household. Years of clinging to *my* side alone would explain her occasional barking frenzies as well as that nervous tick in her big brown eyes. It defies all logic why she eagerly followed me anywhere I wanted to go and hopped through whatever door I ever opened. Even attaching me to her leash had always been more of an example to other dogs than any need she had to announce that a "master" led her anywhere. We both knew who wore the pants – or doggie diapers – in this family.

All the times she pranced, stared, and circled like a vulture discerning its prey, I thought I'd never miss being the object of her obsession. It's funny how perspective changed once I lost what I thought I didn't want, and I mourn even those mornings when I awoke to find my dog using her "depends" for a pillow instead of the carpet protection for which it was intended. I still haven't figured out how Ginger ever managed to unbutton those panties in the first place.

The bittersweet truth is we're all one breath away from change. God gives each of us a finite amount of air while we muddle through life and try to make sense of it all. Heavy doses of physical and emotional pain have taught me to eke out as much air as possible from each breath, much like cutting the food on my plate into as many pieces as possible to make the portions appear larger. In His infinite wisdom, He saw fit to bless me with an incredible secret weapon named Ginger. After fourteen years of thinking that she needed *me*, I admit to a permanent lump in my throat, and the understanding that *I* was the one who had really needed *her*.

Some cause happiness wherever they go.
- Oscar Wilde -

It took years to realize that Ginger's brand of "continual coming," mentioned in Luke's gospel about the parable of the persistent widow, was just her way of wearing me down until she had my undivided attention. Every time she pinned her ears back, growled in a low staccato, and stared me down, it was never (and I'm giving her a huge benefit of the doubt here) in retaliation. Even when I didn't give in each time she barked at the treat drawer, heap on praise for unrolling the toilet paper, or fail to share the people food she thought I was fixing just for her, she still met me at the door and chose *my* lap at the end of the day. I truly believe she just wanted me to know, the only way she thought I'd notice, that she loved me.

The fact that she acted more like a spoiled teenager, with the wisdom of a soul much older, was entirely my fault. From the moment I realized I was granted exclusive rights to her responsibility, I chose to treat her as the friend I'd always wanted and avoided all warnings about blurred role consequences to the contrary. Aside from eating from a bowl on the floor and her preference for outdoor plumbing, we shared everything else that two best friends would.

My apologies go out to anyone I ever belittled or shook my head at over extravagant signs of affection they may have shown their "human" dogs. This was, of course, before I ever had one myself. I understand now. I get it. You were the blessed ones who realized from the beginning what a precious gift lay sleeping at your feet or ceaselessly pestered you for constant affection. I still don't understand why anyone would utter "baby talk" to a distinguished dog several decades their senior in canine math but confess to moving over in bed on several occasions to provide more room and cutting the juicy corner off a perfectly good steak before eating it myself in order to assure leftovers for my friend.

Ginger's trail of footprints still guides me in the garden, though time and nature's daily stamp of approval wear down the deepness of their tracks. They serve as comforting reminders that even though she's gone, her mark on my life will never be forgotten. Blessings flow from all directions and often come from streams of unexpected sources. Ginger's frolic through my carefully cultivated row of beans was a gift for the future. It was a tender reminder that love reveals itself in sometimes very exasperating ways. My exasperation turns into a smile (and sometimes a tear or two) whenever I happen upon her paw prints, as I touch the indentations of earth that now connect me with my fading friend. How marvelous that God left me a trail of helpful reminders to follow every day.

If you have one true friend,
you have more than your share.
- Thomas Fuller -

Out of all the senses, I think feeling the touch of all that surrounds me is what I would miss most if I suddenly went numb or lost limbs – or even my mind. Nowadays the first memory that floods me during random thoughts about Ginger is always the same. I feel the warm softness of her paws, then a liquid kiss from her sandpaper tongue, followed by an overwhelming sense of comfort that wraps me in a heartwarming blanket from the brush of her silken fur as our heads meet somewhere in the middle.

In all the years that she and Bailey both tried (and failed) to shower me with wet, sloppy kisses, I never succumbed to that measure of sugar on my lips. I just couldn't shake the feeling that it'd be like kissing the sister I never had – yuck on both counts. Nevertheless, during those last moments when we were together, I found myself heaping love to *her* forehead and never thought twice about the strands of hair sticking to my lipstick or the taste of old fur that was bound to haunt me forever.

On the afternoon that Ginger and I said goodbye, Mr. Rowe and I opened the door to a very empty house. It hit me like a ton of bricks that I would never come home to her again, and I cried. No flowery words – just "I cried." It made me think about "Jesus wept" in a completely different way. I have a plaque that encourages me to "Live for moments you can't put into words." I hope days like that aren't the ones they're talking about.

As much as my loving husband enjoys the rare moments that I cease talking and the house is quiet, he reacted in the only way he knew to help me and took to clearing the house of anything remotely reminding me of Ginger. Like a human vacuum, he cleared the cage, food bowl, leashes, and treat jar simultaneously from sight and whisked them away for a quick trip to Goodwill. Ginger's well-worn blanket – undeniably scented from too many nights without doggie depends – was slipped into the trash when I wasn't looking. Except for a few hairs on the sofa and one of Ginger's long-forgotten tennis balls under my chair, no sign existed that we were anything but empty nesters again. I felt as though I had some sort of lethal condition, one that left me with time on my hands and only the sound of my shallow breathing between every tortured breath.

It was a long, lonely night without the constant sighs and peculiar noises I'd become accustomed to hearing from beneath the bed, but somewhere between watching the moon cross over the outline of muted trees and discerning the first of dawn's early light, I made a decision of momentous proportions. Digging deep into the bin that held yesterday's leftovers and Ginger's smelly discarded blanket, I pulled the latter to safety with a deep breath and plans to put it through the wash cycle immediately.

If I removed my glasses and squinted just so, the blanket's white snowflakes looked *almost* like paw prints and when no one was watching, I could hug and stroke the bundled softness as if my friend was actually still there beside me. Even with the scent of soap from its recent wash and rinse, I could swear I still smelled her. She may have been taken from my sight and sound, but she'd never be removed from my memory or heart. An endless game of give and take had now expired with her passing, but everything that I touch – from the blanket she wore like royalty to the petals of her favorite fallen rose – still feels like Ginger...and I remember her love.

There are so many ways that people touch one another with their love. My Mom belongs to a lovely group of women at her church who comprise their small but mighty prayer shawl ministry. On occasion, I've had the privilege of sitting in on their Tuesday morning get-togethers, and marvel at their nonchalance for the powerful contribution they weave with just a bit of yarn, needles of various sizes and dog-eared patterns that make the rounds several times over amongst the small sisterhood who regularly attend.

Their creations run the gamut from celebration of newborn babes to the warmth and encouragement of those suffering through illness. I have the dubious pleasure of having received two such shawls for multiple hospital stays and endless rounds of painful tests. I cherish the love and prayers found wrapped within their folds and search each time I wear them for their tiny metal crosses, bow-tied and double knotted to one corner, always ready and waiting to hold and caress during times of stress. Countless rubbing wore the sheen clean off my crosses long ago and simply serve as a reminder that once the glitter is gone, what matters is still there. In times of need, no matter what ails me, I remember that I'm holding everything I need in the palm of my hand…and that someone much greater than I holds me in His.

God bless the thoughtful anonymous soul who continuously provides my kennel with an unlimited supply of hand-knit blankets for those who ultimately endure a final farewell with their furry or feathered loved ones. Just as my Mom's mission covers people with unassuming grace, this kindred spirit bundles the rest of God's creatures with loving care. My heart still warms at the thought of the rainbow of color that wrapped my precious Ginger in tranquil safety as we spent costly moments together and whispered our last goodbyes.

Friends are kisses blown to us by angels.
- Anonymous -

I definitely believe in angels. They've followed me all the days of my life, sometimes choosing to show themselves in ways that I belatedly realize and treasure. I named my first angel "Harvey," a glimpse of *something* that I'd catch out the corner of my eye during a time in my life when I really needed a friend. Halfway between leaving the safety of home and embarking upon making my own with another, he followed me daily in a silent battle against evil and protected this clueless female living single in a city full of sin. Even after marriage and children, he'd pop up now and then to remind me of his presence and to reassure me that I was never alone.

Anyone acquainted with black and white movies will surely remember Harvey, the giant white rabbit that befriended Jimmy Stewart and unfortunately remained invisible to all but him until the story's final credits start to roll. I've always felt myself a kindred spirit with both characters – feeling invisible to the world and speaking a language that few can understand. The name Harvey seemed only fitting for an elusive angelic figure that only appeared to me.

A few days after Ginger's passing, strange things began to occur. I chalk them up to supernatural phenomenon of equal measure and consider them glorious blessings. Prized pictures started falling off the walls and a TV that sat silent as we left one morning suddenly found itself on and playing loudly upon our return that afternoon. Mr. Rowe always did say that Ginger slept her days away after watching late show comedians by night. A wind chime that hung above her favorite perch on the porch suddenly fell to the floor without a scratch. No wind to move it, no broken cords. My "Harvey's Angel" seemed alive and well in other dimensions. It's just too weird to believe otherwise.

307

Time is a companion that goes with us on a journey.
It reminds us to cherish each moment,
because it will never come again.
- Jean-Luc Picard -

By the time fourteen years had its way with our lives; Ginger's list of well-worn names became legendary. It seems odd after having so much trouble naming her in the first place that so many labels would apply. She became my Ginger Dog, G-Dog, Sister, and Sweetie… Goofball, Nutcase, Big Dog, Little Dog, Honey Dog…and just plain Ginger. Perhaps it came from too many times people couldn't get my one and only name right that I had such fun in creating several for her.

In my penchant for words and names, quite a collection had grown consisting of newspaper clippings, cartoons, and famous quotes from various infamous sources. My goal has always been to utilize them in brilliant creative endeavors, preferably before my kids could trash them with the remains of my moldy estate or the fire marshal caught wind of my paper habit and lit a match to my musings. I knew that one day I'd know just how to use several dog-themed clips from a day-to-day calendar consisting of old "Far Side" cartoons, finally finding the perfect time to let go and let God inspire me to put it all together in a tribute to my friend.

My favorite photo of Ginger actually graces the cover of this very book. Taken at the height of her glory when health and happiness reigned supreme in our little cabin in the wooded mountains, it embodies a rich testimony to a life well lived. That same photo and several hilarious cartoons wrap around its visual focus in a collage that includes a tongue-in-cheek ode to canine cologne, elaborate definitions of what dogs *really* call themselves, and an apt depiction of dog's obsessions with peculiar body parts scratched in equally peculiar places.

The day I picked up this masterpiece from the framers, I cried a sea of non-salty tears that left a counter full of compassionate dog-owning customers weeping in my wake. Tears of love are never salty; for God knows that moisture weeping from the heart is something that's never wasted, so He preserves those moments for fond contemplation and saves the salt for later.

With a lifetime of memories safely tucked beneath my arm, I never looked back and took the long way home to laugh and linger with Ginger's memories all by myself...and to remember that love never fails.

Don't cry because it's over; smile because it happened.
- Dr. Seuss –

CPSIA information can be obtained at www.ICGtesting.com
Printed in the USA
LVOW12s0815100216

474460LV00004B/6/P